RHI..

HUNT

A novel by Nick Higgins

Boys will be boys

Girls will be vengeful

To my wife, Lyn,

Not only have you had to suffer me over the years, which must be difficult, you've also had to cope with chronic M.E. for the last seventeen years. I don't know how you've managed.

Thanks for everything.

P.S. Tea's in the oven; I'm off for a quick pint.

To Kate and Tom,

Thanks for your support and sometimes brutal feedback on my first foray into the literary world. The scars have nearly healed and the head-doctors say I can go near sharp objects soon.

To everyone else who has given me their advice, expertise and assistance during the writing of this novel, I thank you all.

Rhino Hunt

Chapter One

Alcohol: it comes in many forms, and most of it is bloody lovely, but it's basically a mind-altering drug that can change your character, actions and perceptions of everyone and everything around you. Unfortunately, the massive amount I'd drunk over the last few hours had changed my state of mind to such an extent that I was convinced my girlfriend would love a call from me at stupid o'clock in the morning.

As a result, I found myself leaning against the outside wall of the newest trendy disco pub in town. It throbbed slightly as the bass boomed out on the dance floor, two feet the other side of the battered and weather-beaten Victorian bricks.

I was staring at the screen of my mobile phone in the pissing rain. As the raindrops hit the phone and rolled down the plastic screen they looked like little magnifying glasses running over the illuminated numbers. The little blobs of water seemed to pixelate and change colour at the edges as gravity took its hold on them.

For a second, I thought I'd been drugged. Rohypnol was quite common around the pubs and clubs; especially late on at night when most people didn't have a clue, nor did they care what they were drinking. If it was a liquid derived from grape, grain or anything that produced alcohol during fermentation, then it went down their throats as quickly as possible and in most cases, the quicker the better.

I focused on the letters and numbers and decided that I was only drunk and wouldn't wake up in the morning in a pokey little hotel room with an arse like a wizard's sleeve.

Finally I found the name I was looking for: Sarah, the current love of my life. I really liked Sarah. She was attractive, had a good job, her parents were loaded and she was amazing in the bedroom. She was also amazing in the kitchen, the front room, the bathroom and once on the top deck of the number 48 bus. I still regret not buying a return ticket.

I was starting to have trouble with my mobile. Why do they make these buttons so bloody small? It was ringing. I could just hear the ringtone above the throbbing beat of the music. D.J. Manny was spinning his grooves, trying his best to instil a bit of enthusiasm amongst the drunk, drugged and desperate. D.J. Manny, my arse! His full, self-appointed and deluded title was Manny Fagnet. Nothing could be further from the truth with this sallow-faced, spotty, drug-addled troglodyte. I went to school with him; his real name was Dean Smith. I still remember him picking his nose at the back of the class and flicking it at the girls. These days, the only thing that goes up his nose is the smell of his mum's cooking and a couple of grams of cocaine a day.

Other people around me had come out of the club to make their well-intentioned, but fatal call; they were fuelled up on cheap lager and shots, wandering around in circles or moving backwards and forwards while they talked on their mobiles. Why can't people stand still when they're on a mobile phone? It seems impossible to stay in one position, especially in public. Clubbers were wandering around, looking at the floor, kicking at the odd bit of shite they encountered while they clamped their phones to the side of their heads.

The ringtone suddenly stopped and I was taken away from my alcoholic musing about the effects of microwaves on the brain.

'Hello,' said the gorgeous female voice; I imagined her in her silk nightdress with a pair of red satin knickers on. That was it; all reason went out of the window and despite the whole composition I'd planned and all my preparation for the coming conversation, all I could think about was hot, sweaty sex.

'I'm coming round to your place and when I get there I'm going to rip your knickers off, throw you on to the bed and shag the living daylights out of you. What do you think of that?'

I was pleased with myself. I didn't think I'd sounded drunk and I'd moved away from the club so the music wasn't as loud. You don't want to give the wrong impression do you? I'd been a bit blunt but I knew she would be gagging for it; at least that was what I'd persuaded myself.

No reply. As the seconds slipped by, I felt initially intrigued. This quickly changed to unease, then rapidly to a sickly feeling in the pit of my stomach. There was the slightest clearing of a throat at the other end of the phone.

'How very interesting, young man; I suppose I should feel flattered but I think you would do better speaking to my daughter, preferably on her mobile phone in the morning. Goodnight.'

I'd suffered from Fat Finger Syndrome. Oh fuck, what had I done? Well, that was pretty obvious now; I'd dialled Sarah's house phone and not her mobile. The bloody raindrops had done a better job of screwing up my focus than the E.U. lager lake I'd drunk. I didn't think that Sarah's mum was the type to readily accept that her daughter was getting biffed by a pissed-up estate agent with very few prospects in life, and the possessor of a stupid name.

The rain suddenly seemed to be getting heavier, or it might just have been my mood. Looking around, I could see a few others still on their phones. From what I could see, it just confirmed how stupid we all were. Ringing at this time of night and in this state was definitely not going to win any Brownie points. God, I felt miserable.

The munter closest to me was on her phone, slagging off her boyfriend because a friend had apparently just told her that he was shagging one of her mates on the side. The dyed-blonde hair and fake tan had taken a bashing from the rain. She was stamping her Ugg boots through the puddles and calling him all the names that she could muster from her apparently very limited vocabulary. As she stamped her feet, her boobs started to bounce up and down at an increasingly alarming rate. By this time, I was fascinated to see the emerging tattoo of a dolphin gradually appearing on her left boob over the edge of her bra. As she stamped and ranted, so the dolphin was making its break for freedom and then, in one magic moment, he was over the side, free and unfettered. It wasn't for long, though, as she quickly scooped it up in her free hand and he was back in his 36 Double D hammock for the night.

The rant was mostly monosyllabic stuff but there were the odd words with two syllables - such as fuckin' and shaggin' - hurled down the phone. It seemed that Chantelle was going to 'get it'. From what I'd heard, I thought she already had!

Sod this, I needed a drink and some consolation from my mates; they'd tell me it wasn't as bad as I'd first thought.

'You did what, you stupid twat?'

That wasn't the response what I'd hoped for. The three of them stood swaying in front of me and then the laughs started to come; little girlie giggles at first, then coughs into a hand desperately trying to cover a face that knew it shouldn't show any signs of finding the situation funny. Finally, well bollocks to it, this is bloody hilarious; there were belly laughs from the three of them at my expense. They were spilling beer all over the place, and I thought that they would either split their sides or piss their pants. At that point I realised that if I wanted sympathy, the only place I'd find it was in the dictionary somewhere between shit and syphilis!

The laughing only stopped when they realised they were spilling their beer all over the floor. Beer took precedence over a mate's misfortunes, especially at the prices they charged in this place.

I looked for a moment at my mates, all swaying about like they had just taken a right uppercut from Mike Tyson.

We made a strange bunch. Together since junior school, we'd progressed through secondary remaining the best of mates despite being totally different people. Perhaps it was these fundamental differences that had drawn us so closely together.

As for me, I came from a totally dysfunctional family. I'd brought up by my mum, after my dad had done a runner just after the birth of my sister. Life had been a struggle for all of us, but especially for me, as I was the eldest. Still, it had made me worldly-wise as some would say and I now had a cushy little job as an estate agent.

The one thing I couldn't put behind me was my name: Richard Head. I often wondered if my dad was Johnny Cash. I was Richie to my mates, but Dick to people who wanted to wind me up. If they did, I would inevitably get them back, no matter how long it took. Revenge is a dish best served cold, as the French first said.

Victor. He is probably the nicest guy you could ever meet and perhaps the most different out of the four of us. As kids we did all the normal stuff. We played football, a bottle of cider down the bottom of the fields and, of course, chasing the girls around the estate. We were all gobsmacked when, about two years ago on one of our regular benders, Vic calmly announced over a pint that he was gay. None of us had suspected a thing. Vic had been there with the best of us, pulling the girls after a night on the town, but thinking back we realised that he'd never had a steady girlfriend. Between gulps of beer he just said that he'd never really fancied girls. On a night away at a conference he'd found himself in a colleague's room who, as it turned out, was gay. He'd had a lot to drink and to cut a long story short, Vic discovered that he could play a mean tune on the blue vein flute.

Vic's decision to drive on the other side of the road had no effect on our friendship. If anything, it strengthened the bond between the four of us. We felt that we had to look after our mate a bit more; not that Vic needed it. Like a lot of gay blokes, Vic looked after himself very well and he was as fit as a butcher's dog. As he said, 'The fitter you look, the better the guys you pick up'. The only time I really saw him kick off due to comments about his sexuality was a few months back when one of our old enemies from the local private school made a comment to Vic in a taxi queue.

'I hear you're a crafty butcher now.' The bloke was with his mate and a couple of very low voltage mingers.

'What do you mean by that?' asked Vic, his tone very flat and strangely lacking in emotion.

'It means that I've heard that you like your meat delivered around the back, gay-boy.'

You could hear the sharp intake of breath from some of the people in the queue, especially those who knew Vic. Despite the odds, this bloke was about to discover a whole world of pain and the funny thing was that he didn't know it yet. Vic just left the queue very calmly and walked up to the group, facing his accuser. The bloke looked pretty pleased with himself at first, but then he saw the look in Vic's eyes.

Vic faced him front on and said, 'I suppose I'll have to go down on my knees and give you what for.' With that, well, that's exactly what he did.

He dropped out of the bloke's line of sight so he was on one knee in front of him. In one swift movement, a short right punch crunched into the bloke's wedding tackle, practically ripping it away from the tendons and blood vessels attaching it to his groin. There was a stunned silence amongst the onlookers. It had been so quick, so efficient and downright brutal. The only sounds were the increasing screams from the homophobic eunuch rolling about on the floor. Nobody has ever taken the piss out of Vic since, not to his face anyway.

Bloody hell, I needed a drink.

'After ripping the piss out of me, I reckon I deserve a drink. I'll have a pint of whatever doesn't taste like cat's piss.'

'You might be struggling there, Richie, but I have it on very good authority that the French cat piss harvest was one of the best in recent years. I would recommend the Cat's Piss Nouveau; a cheeky little number with hints of ginger tom, a bit tabby on the palette with overtones of fur-ball and a recently-licked arsehole.'

'You always were a smart-arse, Devon. Just get me a pint of wife beater, pretty please!'

Devon wandered off towards the heaving bar.

'I'll give him a hand,' said Martin as he brushed past Vic and myself, catching up with Devon after a couple of body swerves around various couples shouting into each other's ears, trying to be heard above Manny's very loud music.

Devon and Martin could have been brothers. They were both about six foot two tall, very athletic, but not overly big, with that smooth movement of people who are very fit and confident. The main thing that set them apart from each other was that Martin was white and Devon was as black as coal; the other thing that set them apart was politics. Martin, or Martin Bormann for his full name, was to the right of Enoch Powell when it came to immigration and what he saw as the dilution of the Englishness of our country. We never got to the bottom of his name and whether he was named after the Nazi hard liner, but certainly some of his views were straight out of *Mein Kampf.*

Devon on the other hand, was second generation Afro-Caribbean. He was very proud of the fact that his grandmother and grandfather had been some of the very first black immigrants to arrive in the UK from Jamaica, on the MV Empire Windrush, back on the 22nd of June 1948. He could see the benefits of immigration and the two would often have some friendly banter over the subject, normally after a few pints.

Although he was now twenty three, Devon was still trying to make it as a professional footballer. He'd had trials before with a few clubs but, just when it looked like he'd make it, he would get crocked and it would all go for a ball of chalk. He reckoned he had one chance left and it looked like it might be at Arsenal in a few months' time. We all wished him the best for his future in football but, in the meantime, he was doing okay in the Fire Service. Martin, meanwhile, was well into his rugby. He didn't play as much as he once did due to his job as a local copper, but he still played for the local police side in the week and sometimes on a weekend, depending on his shifts.

So, in a nutshell, these were my three mates and we were out on one of our all-too-regular piss-ups around town.

At the age of twenty three, we were all starting to feel a bit old for the disco scene. The girls, especially, had started to look very young and I was sure that quite a few in here were jailbait. None of us were in a hurry to end up on the Sexual Offenders' Register for shagging a little stunner.

I could picture the naïve parents that had watched their little darling go off to bed at nine o'clock to watch telly. Sat in their front rooms watching celebrity wannabes make tits of themselves, they had no idea that the apple of their eye was slipping out of her bedroom window with half of Boots' cosmetic counter plastered on her face, a bra that made her tits look like they were defying gravity and a skirt so short that you could almost see what she'd had for breakfast; she would be heading to the disco for a night of fags, shots and Christ knows what else.

Martin had nearly come to grief with one of these little lovelies a few weeks ago. She had come on to him in a city centre pub, while he was out meeting a builder mate about a possible job on his house. She'd bumped into him at the bar, probably deliberately, and before you could say 'my cock rules my cranium', he was giving her a lift home by way of a secluded lane at the back of her house.

The next thing Martin knew was Lolita's irate dad pulling up alongside in his car, looking for his underage, overdue daughter. Luckily for Martin, dad was in a small sports car and couldn't see into his own car. So a quick flash of his warrant card sent him on his way. He dropped the girl off a couple of streets away, after administering a severe bollocking to her and setting her straight on her underage antics. She could have ruined his life.

It was a sobering experience for Martin and one which we all took on-board, even Vic. He'd heard enough 'small boy' jokes not to be caught out like that.

The night was drawing to a close and our back teeth were floating. None of us was in a fit enough state to pull a good looking girl, so there was only one option left to salvage the evening.

'Rhino Hunt?' said Devon, as his eyes scanned the dance floor.

The first of the slow records had come on. Some of the nicer-looking girls had grabbed their handbags and were scurrying away from the dance-floor to the relative safety of the bar. They knew what was coming. Other small groups of girls, many with the femininity of a 1970's Eastern Bloc shot-putter, were making their way in the opposite direction and hanging around the edges with a *vacant* sign around their necks. This was their best chance of the night to grab a bloke. Any bloke, it didn't matter.

The blokes, on the other hand, were like a pack of wolves. They were the hunters; the girls were their prey. It may be the alcohol, but it's almost primeval to watch. The girls were in small groups, flashing glances towards the circling pack of blokes. The slightest show of weakness or eye contact and one of the hunting males would dash in, pick off a helpless victim, and drag her off to the dance floor. A natural history presenter would be in his element:

'Welcome to the primitive, and often hostile, Disco Lands. Inhabited for only a few hours a day by both the male and the female of the species, Homo sapiens, or if the male gets very lucky, Homo erectus. The only vegetation found here is the plant Cannabis Sativa; despite this, it is a very wet environment. Fluids are regularly brought in from Belgium and Denmark and are then often drunk as cold as possible. The female wears little in the way of covering, apart from on

the face where she has copious amounts of war paint. This is apparently to cover up numerous spots and blemishes and is used to attract a mate. The male on the other hand, rarely wears makeup; if he does, he can be turned upon and attacked, both verbally and physically, by other members of the pack. The male often has markings on his arms called tattoos. These can range from the names of their tribal elders to the names of a team of violent males who are known to attack each other on a Saturday afternoon. Both sides of the species can be very violent, especially later in the evening, when they have drunk large amounts of their fermented grain.

As you join us, various small groups of males are roaming around the edges of a barren area known as the dance floor. Some females are bunching together for protection as males are using posts, tables and other larger groups of males for cover while they creep up on an unsuspecting female.

Look there, off to the right, one female has been distracted by taking too big a drink from her fluid container. She has become detached from her small group and is now alone and extremely vulnerable to attack from the predatory males. See there, two males are approaching her from different directions. The tall spotty male has laid claim to her by placing his arm around her waist. The other male's shoulders have slumped in a show of defeat and he is now heading back to the watering hole.

On the dance floor, the mating ritual is about to begin. The male has placed his arms around the female's waist, but she has both hands bent in front of her, with her hands on his chest in a defensive posture. The male then begins to swivel his lower abdomen and legs from side- to-side whilst attempting to force his right leg between the female's legs. The female's defence to this hostile move is to slam her legs shut with the force of a crocodile's jaws. The male,

15

unperturbed by this overt showing of rejection, continues to move from side to side. He then tries another angle of attack; he tries to talk his victim into submission. After about one minute he can be observed slowly introducing his leg, in particular his upper thigh, which he rubs vigorously against the female's reproductive organs. It is thought by some scientists that a verbal form of attack is the most efficient when phrases such as 'Another Bacardi 'n' Coke then?' or 'Fancy a kebab on the way home?' can be used.

The mating ritual is nearly over. The climax will invariably take place away from the Disco Lands, often against a bin around the back of the local kebab house. Sometimes names, even contact details, are exchanged as a result of mating, but come the following week it is thought they could pass in the street and not recognise each other.

Join us next week when we follow the female and her new baby in their new one bedroom council flat. We see their first journey out together to the Benefit Office, and follow her daily search for cigarettes and another mate. Goodnight.'

Our objective was slightly different and had a completely different end game. I'm not sure how Rhino Hunt came about; we'd been doing it for a few years, but none of us could actually remember the first time we'd done it or who had originally suggested the idea. Rhino Hunt had become an alternative to standing around wishing you had talked to the gorgeous girl you thought was eyeing you up, but you didn't have the confidence, or enough alcohol, to follow it up.

Basically, the idea was to pick up the largest and least attractive girl at the disco. Chatting to them was not enough. The least you had to do was smooch with them on the dance floor. Anything else you did, or could get away with, all contributed to the overall winner, who was either judged upon that night or at a later date down the pub.

The main rule was you had to appear sincere and in no way show any signs of disrespecting them or that they were part of a game. 'Munters have feelings as well', as my mother often said. She didn't really; I just made that up to stop any feelings of guilt I might have for what we were about to do.

'Ah shit, do we have to? I really don't feel in the mood. Besides, what am I going to do with a big fat munter? I don't even fancy fat blokes. It's like trying to shag a big pink hairy bean-bag or being smothered by the world's biggest blancmange!' Victor was not impressed.

I must admit that I wasn't feeling in the mood either. After my run in with Sarah, or her mum to be precise, I just wanted to go home and crash into bed. The idea of chasing calorifically-challenged munters around a disco dance floor in this state, at this time of night, was bordering on the downright dangerous.

Vic and I started to slide away from the action, leaving the other two lads eyeing up the biggest pair of low voltage slappers I'd seen in all my life. They weren't the kind of girls you could easily miss; they left a lasting impression on you for all the wrong reasons.

Martin had initially choked on his beer when he'd seen them emerge from the shadows. In fact, I think they were causing the shadows; there was a partial eclipse of the disco ball. After coughing and wiping his mouth with the back of his hand, he got his composure back.

'Dev, will you look at that?'

He didn't need to point because quite a few lads were looking in their direction, along with a few girls. You could see the smirks in the girls' eyes - 'How can you let yourself get into that state?', or 'Here come the fat slags.'

Whatever they were thinking, none of them were giving them eye contact or getting in their way. These lassies were not to be pissed off or you could easily end up looking up at your dentist's nasal hair for a very long time the following day.

The lads' reactions were completely different. A few were just completely gobsmacked by their sheer in-your-face 'look at me - if you don't like what you see, then fuck off!'

One or two were trying to hide behind pillars or their mates; you could tell that they were more than a bit embarrassed. It's odds on that these lads had sampled the delights of their ample tattooed flesh on a previous occasion and didn't want to be recognised by the pair or have the piss ripped out of them by their mates.

By far the majority of the lads around the floor had another look in their eyes. This was very out of focus; the eyes opened wide, and then closed tight shut, with the head moving backwards and forwards, trying to coordinate their brain and body. That's not easy after ten pints. This was followed by a deep breath and an attempt to try and stand upright and stop swaying. It was too much for one lad; he just fell over. Those that did manage it all reached the same conclusion - they would certainly be in for a shag if they could pick up one of these!

'Bloody hell mate! If we can bag off with those two, we'll win for sure.' Devon sounded a bit more excited and enthusiastic than he should have done.

'Are you completely sure about this, mate? This might be a step too far for our reputations to take.' Martin was having an attack of conscience when he got a good look at the pair, as they pushed their way to the side of the dance floor.

'I mean, there's a fair few yeast infections flying around in those crevices, and if she turns around too quick, those bingo wings will split your lip if you're not careful.'

'What the hell is a bingo wing?' Devon asked, not taking his eyes off the pair.

'It's the big floppy bit of skin and fat under your upper arm. See, the one on the right has got one of those barbed wire tattoos around her right one but it's been stretched so far it looks like a blue Curly Wurly. Must have been like trying to tattoo a jelly.'

'Look mate, you've got longer arms than me so you'll have to take the really big one. There's no way I'll be able to dance with that. It's like the Michelin Man in a charity shop dress.'

It was Devon's time to get a conscience.

'That's not a dress mate. See how she's stood nice and straight? It's a bloody bell tent, only she's forgotten to take the centre pole out before she put it on.'

Martin took a glance at Dev.

'A faint heart never fucked a pig, so it's now or never. I'm not saying that they're pigs, or that we do anymore than dance with them, but if we don't move now we've lost the Rhino Hunt for tonight.'

A quick look between them, a quick slurp of beer for a large dose of courage, and they were down the steps and heading for the two visions of lumpiness.

There was no way I was going to win tonight, not with Devon and Martin picking up those two. Victor was talking to someone at the bar but I couldn't be sure if it was a man or woman; it was sort of asexual. Was it a 'tache or a gash? I didn't have a clue. I caught Vic's eye and motioned that I was going up to the chill-out bar. I really had had enough.

It was a lot lighter in the chill-out bar and the music was nowhere near as loud. There were a few people hovering around but in the main it was quite quiet. I decided to have a soft drink as I didn't think I could, or should, have any more alcohol. The adverts and recent publicity about binge drinking amongst the young was starting to focus my mind a little on the long-term effects I might be inflicting upon my body.

My mantra had always been: 'My liver is evil - it must be punished.' However, now I was beginning to realise that I wasn't immortal and that I was actually damaging myself. It was just that asking for an 'orange juice and lemonade' didn't have the same manly ring to it as a 'double Jack Daniels and coke'.

I didn't know anyone around the bar so I asked for a softie in the deepest manly voice I could manage.

Glancing around the room, there were the usual suspects, but I was drawn to a girl sitting alone on a sofa next to the bar. She was a fairly big girl, slightly overweight, with a baggy red dress on. Her black hair seemed to be a bit too shiny but what did I know about the latest in women's hair technology?

At first sight, she didn't seem that attractive but the more I looked at her the more I became drawn to her. I soon changed my mind. She was attractive but there was something else, something not quite right with her overall demeanour, as if a vital spark was absent. However, it was her eyes that had got me. Captivated was too strong a word for this time of night, and especially after copious amounts of alcohol, but they were the most amazing eyes I had ever seen. I continued to gaze to confirm my initial 'diagnosis'. They were large blue eyes, slightly dewy, like those of a young puppy. It almost looked like she was on the verge of crying or was under a bit of stress. She appeared quite vulnerable but there was strength in her eyes that I couldn't quite place.

I continued to stare, then suddenly realised that she was speaking to me. A quick scrunch of the eyes and a deep breath and I picked up what she was saying.

'Can I help you?' Her voice was slightly reedy, almost too small for her body.

'I'm sorry, I didn't mean to stare but it's your eyes.' It just came out without any delay or thought to what I was saying.

'What? What's the bloody matter with them?' It was an angry response, as though she was expecting something to be wrong. She started to look around, looking for some support, but she was on her own.

'No, nothing's wrong; far from it. I was just thinking that they were the most amazing eyes I've ever had the pleasure of looking into.'

'Well, staring could be construed as letching, especially with your mouth wide open and your flies undone.' Her tone was not as hard but she still had her hackles up.

Christ, my flies were undone! I looked down immediately, expecting the worst, but I was zipped up tighter than a camel's arse in a sand storm. I glanced back at her and there was the slightest smile on her face.

'I had that coming I suppose. My name's Richard. Can I get you a drink?'

I was still stood next to the bar. A very pissed-off Russian barmaid had been waiting for me to finish my very poor introductions. She could wait a little longer as there was no one else at the bar.

'Nicola.' It came out short, sharp and confident. 'I'll have a glass of water, thank you.'

'Nothing in it?'

I was slightly pleased that I hadn't been stung for a very expensive nightcap and that she appeared to be warming to me a little. I wasn't interested in the Rhino Hunt with this girl, she just looked like a very interesting person to talk with.

'No, just ice and a slice of lemon, please.'

The Russian girl had made one up almost before I turned around to her. I chucked a tenner on the bar and she whacked the shrapnel change down into the palm of my hand. I smiled sarcastically at her as I turned my back.

'I'm sorry to hassle you this late in the night, but do you mind if I join you for a minute?'

It was a bit of a weak request but it was bloody late and I needed to sit down. She thought about it for a second, giving me a quick appraisal as I got a bit closer to her.

'OK, but not for too long though. My friends will be back soon and they may give you a bit of a hard time.'

'Why is that?' I was genuinely intrigued as I fancied myself as a bit of a catch; a down-market Brad Pitt, in a very dark light.

'It's just that they can be a bit protective. They're really good friends and I suppose they've got my best interests at heart.'

Before I could jump in with the obvious comeback, she changed the subject.

'Here on your own, or are you with someone?'

I let it go as she obviously didn't want me to follow up her comments about her friends. There was an almost immediate regret that she had raised the subject.

'There are three of my mates somewhere in the club enjoying an intellectually stimulating night, just like me.'

I was trying not to sound as if I was a threat to her or her friends. She'd seemed to mellow a bit and was sipping at her water.

'I'm sorry I was staring earlier. I was just thinking about an Annie Lennox song when I was looking at you.' She glanced down, losing eye contact, slightly embarrassed.

'Are you thinking of *Cold* on the *Diva album*?'

'Bloody hell, you know your music, don't you? There a line in that song which, if I can remember it, goes......?'

'"*I want to swim in the pools of your eyes.*' It's one of my favourite songs as it happens.'

I was really beginning to warm to this girl. Within five minutes, she'd taken the piss out of me, impressed me with her knowledge and choice of music and intrigued me more than any girl I had ever met. I felt as if I had known her for ages but, in fact, all I knew was her name and that she had feisty friends.

'It was exactly that. The line from that song just jumped into my head and I kept running the line over and over.'

'Well that's a bit Tom Jones; I do it all the time. Use song titles or artists to describe things.'

'A bit Tom Jones? What do you mean?' I was getting a bit discombobulated.

'*It's not unusual.*'

I could see she was enjoying toying with me and, to be honest, I was enjoying it myself. It felt so different chatting to a girl on a boy's night out and not wondering if I was going to get a quick knee-trembler out the back.

'You know, Tom Jones.' She'd eventually got it into my thick head but it'd taken a while – which wasn't unusual.

We chatted for another few minutes until the lights came on to finish the night's excesses.

The bouncers were mingling with the drinkers and kissers, urging them to drink up and move to the exit. We stood up from the sofa in unison.

'Well I guess that's it for tonight. Thanks for listening for the last I-don't-know-how-long. I've really enjoyed it. I suppose you're off home with your mates?'

Nicola glanced at me sideways, trying to work out if there was a bit more to what I'd just asked. I quickly jumped in, remembering how defensive she'd been at first.

'I'm grabbing a taxi with my three mates so I'm afraid I'm not in a position to offer you a lift home, or any of your friends.'

She seemed to relax a bit. Perhaps I wasn't a Saturday night trophy hunter after all. A word was forming on her lips when four girls appeared through the door and headed towards us. It was a Girls Aloud moment - '*Here come the girls*'.

'You okay, Nic?'

'Who's this joker then?'

They split up just before us. Two went to Nicola's side and two peeled off and stood directly in front of me. They were very protective indeed. I actually felt a bit intimidated with these four girls almost snarling at me.

'Girls, it's okay. This is Richard. We've been chatting for a little while and things are cool. You don't need to give him a hard time...please!'

She looked at them in turn and the talons were withdrawn, a little.

'You sure Nic? I've seen this one around before. He's bad news.'

As she spat out her vitriol I vaguely recognised her face. Maybe it was from a long distant disco or possibly from school; I couldn't remember.

Just as the girls were calming down I caught a glimpse of Victor, probably looking for me. He saw me with the five girls and smiled; then he saw the looks on their faces as he wandered over. The smile was fading all the time as he got closer and I think he had the idea of saving me. Before he got to us the other two lads wandered in, minus their conquests. All three of the lads were heading for us and I could see things would probably get a bit ugly, so I headed away from the girls, stopping the lads before they reached us.

'Thanks again for the chat, Nicola. I felt a bit like Chris De Burgh.'

She looked at me for a minute then broke into a great big smile. Her friends looked at the two of us and weren't sure what had passed between us. It was like our little secret.

'We'd better make tracks before all the taxis get taken. Maybe see you around sometime?'

Her friends started to huddle around her like mother elephants around a young calf. Again, they were very protective; I couldn't work out why. She glanced up and half smiled.

'I'll look out for you. I owe you a drink.'

With that, she was surrounded.

Both sets of friends had had enough of us. The girls were getting each other organised and my mates were starting to think about kebabs with a gallon of chilli sauce. It was another little ritual that had developed over the years; a trip to the local kebab house after a night on the lash. The Kebab Palace was only just down the road. We were regular visitors on Saturday nights and had become friendly with Spiros and his wife, Angelina, over the years. Mind you, it was hard to tell them apart. Spiros had the biggest man boobs you have ever seen, almost matching his Missus, whilst she had nearly as good a moustache as her husband.

As we filed out of the club, the bouncers were starting to get a bit more verbal and a bit physical with one or two lads who, like most very drunk blokes, think they can take on the world. These guys were easy pickings for a sober bouncer. The bouncers you had to watch were those who were out to impress; mates or girls, it didn't matter. If you wound one of these guys up and couldn't defend yourself properly, then you were in big trouble. Luckily we knew the guys and to have a copper with us was an added bonus. Even the most stupid doorman wouldn't have a go at Martin. We nodded at them as we left.

'Kebab it is then,' shouted Devon as we hit the fresh air. It had stopped raining and everything felt fresh and cool after the sweat and smells of the disco. Everyone was spilling out on to the pavements and heading their various ways. Some were with their mates, some alone and quite a few with a new partner on their arm. They all had to watch where they were treading though. There were various pavement omelettes scattered in the immediate vicinity and most walkers were making their way through as if they were in an Afghan minefield.

'Just a minute mate, I'll catch you up. There's something I have to do.'

I needed a pen and paper. The only paper I had was a five pound note. No pen. I was next to a girl who was sparking up a cigarette.

'Excuse me love, but have you got a pen?'

She looked at me for a minute, trying to decide whether I was 'chatting her up' or taking the piss. As she handed one over I was tempted to say 'Not that type of pen; a farmyard pen because I reckon you've escaped for the night!' No, I wasn't that heartless and she wasn't that much of a pig. In fact, she wasn't a pig at all. Another time, another place, who knows? But not tonight; I had another girl on my mind.

'I won't be a minute.'

I started scribbling on the fiver and gave the pen back with to her with a big smile. 'Manners cost nothing my boy', my granddad always said.

A quick look over the thinning crowd and I spotted what I was looking for; very shiny black hair. It looked even shinier out here for some reason. Surrounded by her mates she looked taller than I had imagined; tall but with a slight stoop. A couple of quick body swerves through the crowd and I was nearly at her side, without her Secret Service entourage spotting me. All that was missing were their shades. I was clocked five feet from my goal.

'What the fuck do you want? Go and play with your mates on the swings or better still, in the traffic.'

I still couldn't remember where I knew this girl from but it was becoming ever more apparent that she didn't like me one little bit. I must have seriously pissed her off in a previous life.

'Is this personal or do you just hate all men?'

It was a genuine question but I couldn't be arsed to get into a slanging match with her, especially not in front of Nicola.

'Nicola, I've got the five pounds I borrowed off you.'

With that I held my hand out and pushed it towards her. All credit to her; she took it without question and put it in her bag. I hoped she wouldn't spend it on the taxi because I'd written my mobile number on it and a 'please ring'.

I turned away from Nicola to catch up with the lads but I ended up facing Little Miss Attitude again.

'You've got something on your chin, love.' She immediately started to brush at it with the back of her hand.

'No not that one, the other one.'

That was it. I thought she was going to fly at me but just before she had finished hissing 'bastard', I was away into the crowd and legging it after the other three who were on their way to Mrs Spiros' moustache.

I caught up with them just short of the kebab shop. I thought they had stopped to wait for me but they were looking down the road towards the shop from a small alleyway. All they were missing were the AK47s and a quick blast of fire from down the street. They were definitely ducking in and out of cover.

'What's up guys? It's not like you lot to skulk in the shadows.'

It made them jump, especially Martin and Devon. Vic had a funny grin on his face and he seemed to be enjoying himself.

'These stupid fuckers have got themselves mixed up with some scary birds; the two from the Disco. Turns out they're after a good night and won't take 'no' for an answer. Seems like both hubbies are inside for a while sewing mailbags and their lovely wives are missing their masculine charms. These two have been chosen to fulfil the carnal desires of our oestrogen and vodka-fuelled gangsters' molls.'

'For fuck's sake shut up. If they come out, they'll see us.'

Devon looked and sounded a bit scared. The only time I'd seen him scared like that was when we put deep heat in the crotch of his pants after football a few years ago and convinced him he'd got a dose.

'I've got it so far, but why are you hiding down a dark alley? I can't see anyone.'

I wanted my kebab and a fast black home.

'They're in the Palace. Must have used up a lot of energy chasing us down the street.'

Martin then went on to explain that he and Devon had asked the two munters for a dance and were dragged on to the dance floor. What had started as a bit-of-a-laugh soon turned into being something a lot more serious. The predators were now the prey and they were being hunted by bigger and more dangerous hunters. A bit amorous at first, the conversation rapidly turned to 'come back to my place and I'll show you a good time'. When the lads said 'No' they started to get the threats. 'Come back or I'll tell my hubby you slapped me about a bit and he'll break your legs', etc. etc. After agreeing to see them after the disco, they slipped away but they were seen by the girls outside.

I couldn't imagine those two chasing Martin and Devon anywhere but here they were, hiding in an alley, facing the prospect of a couple of 'crims' breaking their legs because they wouldn't shag their wives.

I could see the funny side of it but I really didn't want to get involved.

'Look guys, I sympathise with your predicament but I'm going for a Spiros surprise.'

I looked at Vic who took the hint.

'I'll join you. It wouldn't look good for me getting arrested in a back alley with two blokes, would it? Although I suppose I'm more used to a bit of back-alley boogie than you lot. It wouldn't look good for you either Mart.'

'Fuck it, I'll take my chances. I'd rather face the Magistrate or my superintendent than those two in there.'

Martin looked at Devon for a bit of support as the two of us left them in the alley.

'I'm alright in dark alleys man; no fucker can see me!' Humour in the face of adversity; typical Dev.

It was only about fifty yards to the Palace. A faint drizzle began to fill the air. The road was busy with taxis and cars taking people home after a night on the town. A few heads and arms were hanging out of the back windows, either getting air or trying not to ruin the inside of the car. A souped-up *Saxo* had a new textured paint job over the rear wheel arch. It looked a proper vomit-comet as it roared by. No kebab for him then; or maybe he'd just had one.

There was a small queue. The visions of lumpiness were showing how they'd acquired their fuller figures; what they had in their trays most normal people would have to eat with a shovel: pickles, pitta bread, meat, onions, peppers, chillies, buckets of chilli sauce, and a bit of salad. Their five-a-day probably related to kebabs and not the scant amount of greenery on display.

They turned from the counter as we walked in, with their laden trays in front of them, and looked at us. You could see the quandary. Shag – kebab, shag – kebab, shag - kebab? They both looked down at their food, took a handful in unison, stuffing it into their mouths. Ever seen a hippo yawn? I don't think it could compete with these two. Both of us gave a sigh of relief but in the backs of our minds we both knew that two sex-hungry girls had just passed us over for a tray of reconstituted meat and chilli sauce. I was sure my ego would recover.

The girls walked out of the shop talking to each other with mouthfuls of kebab. By the time they had reached the door they were wearing most of it. There was a pool of fat, chilli sauce and salad collecting in their cleavage.

'Usual please, Spiros, and the same for Vic.'

Spiros started to carve chunks of meat off what looked like an elephant's lower leg. I'm not even sure what kind of meat it was but it was almost compulsory after a night like the one we'd had. Despite my worries about its origins, I was looking forward to a bellyful of kebab and then home. The voice from behind me changed all that in a split second. I didn't need to turn around to see who it was; I'd recognise that stupid, upper- class affected accent even if I was running from a burning building; Tim Sharples. This was a prize twat if ever you've met one but this boy had a violent and sadistic streak that set him apart from your usual run-of-the-mill twats.

We first ran into Sharples at comprehensive school. He was in the same year as us but at the public school down the road. Over the next few years we played football, rugby and sometimes cricket against him and his gang of stuck-up, arrogant mates. More often than not we'd beat them fairly and squarely but, over the years, Sharples developed a penchant for deliberately hurting people. It wasn't punching and kicking in front of the referee. No, his was a cynical approach that put a number of our mates in hospital with various strains and breaks. He was very good at it.

It all started in the second year when we played them at rugby. We had a lad called Mark Wall, whose family was short of a bob or two at the time so he couldn't afford a pair of boots. What Mark decided to do was use his walking-boots for the game. Unfortunately, especially for Sharples, Mark decided to give himself a bit more traction by putting inch-and-a-half nails all around the outside of the soles. No one noticed this until he ran into a ruck, at the bottom of which was Sharples. In a contest between about thirty sharpened

31

steel spikes and someone's face there was only going to be one winner. I can still remember the screams to this day. The referee stopped the game and pulled the players apart. Sharples was left on the floor with his hands covering what looked to be a pork jigsaw. His face recovered over the years but it left him with a burning hatred of our school and the four of us in particular.

'Well, well, well; if it isn't Dick Head and one of his three Mustbequeers.'

He knew how to wind me up. Carrying a name around like Richard Head, or Dick as Sharples called me, carried with it a bit of mental scarring. I could cope with that. The physical scarring that he had, albeit slight, is not something I'm sure I could handle.

I knew we were in trouble by the tone of his voice. He would have at least three or four mates with him; too many of them for the two of us. He was confident and cocky which meant he thought he could kick the shit out of us with not a lot of comeback. Fuck it, if I'm going down I'm going down fighting.

I took my kebab from Spiros, who looked at me anxiously. He didn't want any trouble in his place; it was bad for business and also his insurance premiums. I gave him a little wink as I grabbed hold of the big plastic squeezy chilli sauce bottle. If one of his mates came at me as I turned around, he was going to get both eyes full of chilli.

'Never been a gambler, have you Ena?'

I'd turned around to find four of them. They were all very drunk but, consequently, spoiling for a fight they knew they could win quite easily. They were in the same mould as Sharples; nasty little fuckers who wouldn't face you one-to-one. They were like a pack of hyenas; race in for a sly dig and leg it back to the pack for protection.

bead of nervous sweat was dangling off Mrs Spiros' moustache. Despite this, I could have kissed her, but at that moment I guess I was no different than the two munters; a greasy kebab was more important than any exchange of bodily fluids.

'Another two for the Lone Ranger and Tonto please, Spiros.'

'Hey that's racist, man; I could sue your ass for that.'

I knew that Devon was joking. He was always laid back about his colour. He never referred to himself as being black; he was chromatically-challenged, as he put it.

'How do you know you're not the Lone Ranger, Dev?' We all had a little laugh, more out of nerves and adrenaline rush than anything else.

Another two kebabs appeared over the counter.

'My treat lads', I said as I paid for the four. We wandered outside, half expecting a few bricks to come flying our way, but nothing happened. I'd put a bit too much of the hot chilli sauce on mine and my mouth had suddenly lost all feeling. It felt like I had blisters on my tongue and my teeth were melting. When I finally got my voice back, I started to ask Martin and Dev about the girls from the Rhino Hunt. They were genuinely worried about what they had got themselves into. Martin thought he knew one of the husbands and he was not good news.

'Bit of a nutter if it's the bloke I'm thinking about. No respect for anyone or anything, especially other people's property.'

'Well, you've got something in common there then - going after the poor bloke's property while he's fighting off the advances of every stroller of the Bourneville Boulevard in the nick.'

Vic had finally found his voice and wasn't holding back.

'I don't think I'd make advances like that to this bloke. He'd snap it off and use it to stir his tea!' Martin seemed a bit concerned; time to lighten the mood a little.

'Listen guys, I'm off. I've had enough excitement for one day. Give you a ring in the week and don't you two worry about Cinderella's sisters. I bet they won't remember a thing tomorrow. Either that or they'll be found drowned in a pool of chilli sauce on the way home.'

With that, I was off down the road followed by shouts of 'be careful', muffled by mouthfuls of food. I would have to be careful; I didn't want to run into Ena and his mates.

It was only about twenty minutes to get home but I decided to take the back streets, just in case. I needed the walk to get a bit of perspective on the night. It had stopped raining and it was quite pleasant being completely alone and immersed in your own thoughts. It's not very often you're completely alone, so to speak. Even in your own room, the telly's often on or your ears are getting bashed by your *iPod*. You're being bombarded by noise while your brain is in neutral.

Firstly there was Sarah. I would have to see the Doctor to have my foot surgically removed from my mouth. What was I thinking about, telling her mum I was going to rip her knickers off? That was the problem; I wasn't thinking at the time. My cock and balls sat on my shoulder whispering into my ear that she would be gagging for it. To be honest, I didn't think the relationship would get over this one. I would have to play it by ear the next time we spoke and that was a call I was not looking forward to making.

Then there was Nicola. She wasn't a stunner. She didn't have the best figure in the world and she didn't offer it on a plate. But there was something about her. I'd connected with her like no other girl I'd met before and to tell the truth, I wanted some more of it. There was also a curiosity about her; as if she wasn't telling you everything. Maybe she was a man? I quickly got rid of that thought. Vic sometimes dressed up in women's clothes and was very convincing but I reckoned I could tell a trannie from the real thing. Just look at the Adam's apple. There was no way I was going to end up with a handful of meat and two veg. No, there were a few pieces of the jigsaw missing, just like Sharples' face.

Despite all of that, I was pretty sure she wouldn't ring anyway. She didn't seem the type to get into a relationship after meeting a guy for a few minutes and then having his number on the back of a five pound note. Maybe the guilt of having my money might get her to ring? That was for tomorrow. It was time for bed. Well nearly; there was one more thing I had to do tonight. And in some ways it gave me more of a buzz than the entire night out.

We lived in a 1930's semi, in a quiet road, in a nice part of the city. It seemed alright on the face of it but the problem we had was our neighbour, Rodney Pratt; Pratt by name, Pratt by nature. Shame really, because his wife was actually very nice. Why on earth she married a total tosspot like him, I don't know.

Mum and Dad had moved to the house just after I was born. Apparently Pratt had been nice as pie, then but when Dad left, after my little sister came along, he completely changed. He had a thing about single mothers and thought it was Mum's fault that Dad had left. As I grew up he started having a go at me: 'Don't kick the ball on to my garden; you're damaging my flowers!' All sorts of shit like that. Anyway, as I grew up I started to deliberately wind him up in any way I could. As a result, we hated each other's guts and I still wound him up whenever I could. I've never forgiven him for giving Mum a hard time. Just when she, and us kids needed some support he turned into an arsehole. His wife, Maureen, or Mo as I called her, did what she could behind his back, but if he caught her he'd give her a stern lecture that he didn't want her mixing with 'the likes of us'.

Pratt had two loves in his life; unfortunately neither of them was his wife. Shame, because she'd been a bit of a looker in her time. She didn't quite qualify for a GILF - Grannies I'd Like to Fuck - but time wasn't on her side.

His first love was a car. It was a red *E-type Jaguar* which he kept in his garage under a cotton cover so the dust wouldn't get on it. Every Sunday morning, he would bring it out and give it a wash and a once over. I often thought he should be doing that to his Missus. He let her drive it on occasions if he thought she might impress some friends. Other than that, it didn't go far.

His other love was his garden; there was a lawn and ornaments out the front, and another lawn with an allotment at the back. There wasn't a blade of grass out of place or a bit of mould on his lettuce leaves. It was a slug-free zone; I think they were too frightened to go in as it meant certain death. His only little indulgence was a tortoise which he called Fang. Fang the fuckin' tortoise! I didn't know if he had a sense of humour or if he claimed tax back on it as a guard tortoise. After all, he was an accountant at the Council, which probably explains a great deal.

After a big night out on the town I often jumped over the wall into Pratt's back garden and rearrange things just to mess with his head - like moving all the gnomes around his small fishpond. He'd come out and scratch his head and put them back as he wanted them. He always looked over at our house when he was fixing stuff, because he thought it was me but couldn't be sure.

The most spectacular joke I played on him was also my most complex. His front lawn was a lush light green carpet. It was his pride and joy that he often remarked upon to the other neighbours. Last spring, I went to the local garden centre and asked for a big bag of the darkest green grass seed they had. The guy who sold it to me was a bit quizzical at first but I said it was to provide a dappled effect on my lawn. That wasn't entirely a lie; it just wasn't going to be on my lawn. Over a three week period I set my alarm for 03.00 and crept out the house with a small bag of seed and a mesh template. I then laid the mesh out on Pratt's front lawn and sprinkled the seed over; making sure it all went down under the current growth.

As it was spring, it didn't take that long to seed and shoot. Close up, the design was difficult to make out but the further away you were you could make out the dark green outline of the biggest cock and balls you've ever seen. Pratt hadn't noticed it whilst he was cutting his grass. It took the wife of the local councillor who lived across the road to point it out to him and to raise her concerns with him in the strongest possible terms. He was lowering the tone of the neighbourhood. It just wouldn't do, you know!

When Pratt went over the road and saw his lawn from a distance, he was apoplectic. My mum saw him jumping up and down and went out for a look. It didn't help when she burst out laughing; she later said that it was a very impressive bit of manhood. He spent all day digging up his lawn in an absolute rage. He was digging up his pride and joy and what was worse for him (and better for me) was that the local hierarchy thought he was a pervert. He always suspected it was me but he couldn't prove it.

So it was over the back wall and on to his back lawn. I'd had a bad night and Pratt had really upset my mum earlier in the week about the state of our front garden, so I decided to go a bit over the top. After the beer and chilli kebab, my insides were doing somersaults. I could imagine his reaction when he got up in the morning to see a fresh delivery in the middle of the back lawn.

'Row, row, row your boat, gently down the stream, belts off, trousers down, isn't life a scream!'

And that was it; the deed had been done. I had probably gone a bit too far this time but in my drunken state I could easily justify it. I quickly looked around to see the end result but in the gloom I couldn't make out my deposit. Ah well, it must be a combination of the gloom and my burned-out retinas from the disco lights, and I wasn't exactly going to go down on my hands and knees to look for it.

A quick hop over the back wall and I was in through the back door and into the kitchen. Mum and little sis were in bed by the sound of it. All the lights were out as well. I grabbed a quick shower and off to bed. I'd treat myself to a lie-in and maybe read the paper in bed with a cup of tea. Luxury!

However, as with most of the best laid plans, they don't always come to fruition.

Chapter Two

I couldn't remember the last time I'd woken up on a Sunday morning and not felt bloody awful. This one was no exception. My mouth felt like the bottom of a parrot's cage and my guts were doing back-flips and the odd triple salco. The only difference from usual was the commotion coming from Pratt's house, or his back garden to be precise. I looked at my clock; it was eight o'clock for Christ's sake! It was the middle of the night as far as I was concerned. I took a large swig of water and turned over and went back to sleep. I could hear the muffled rantings of the old git through the double glazing as I drifted off to sleep with visions of him giving his wife a bollocking for wearing a short skirt on the Sabbath, or because there was a skin on his porridge.

Mum would bring me a cup of tea at eleven so I wouldn't waste the entire day in an alcohol induced lie-in. As I got older, I appreciated her even more. She was my conscience, confidante and emotional crutch when I really needed to talk to someone. Take last night; you confide in your mates and they end up kicking you in the emotional crutch because you've fucked up beyond all belief. A mum will listen, assess and judge, although not necessarily in your favour! Well, at least mine would. She was not averse to sitting me down and giving me a bit of wisdom, or a bollocking, depending on how you looked at it. They were subtle bollockings, to try and get me back on the straight and narrow. After all, she wanted the best for Sis and me and didn't want to see us ending up like her; scraping and struggling every day of the year to pay the bills and put food on the table. Still, it was a bit easier now I was contributing financially to the family income. It would be a lot better if I didn't waste a large percentage of my money on punishing my internal organs and put it towards bread, milk and the electric bill. However, despite my hangover, I was enjoying life. It's not a dress rehearsal, so make the most of it.

Eleven o'clock came around all too quickly. Mum always knocked on my door before coming in. She'd only needed to see my embarrassment and red face a couple of times when I was a young teenager to give me an advanced warning before entering; to be caught with a copy of a bash mag, open on the bed, at the latest full length spread of a girl with pneumatic tits, desperately trying to pull up my trousers, is not a sight for a mother to see. It caused embarrassment and guilt for both parties, and what seemed like a nine-month pregnant pause. I was twenty three and she still knocked.

'Here's a cup of tea for you, lazybones.' Despite everything, mum had never lost that cheery optimism that I found so amazing, bearing in mind all the crap that had been thrown at her.

'Did you get up to anything in Mr Pratt's garden when you got home this morning, Richard?'

It was a bit matter of fact rather than inquisitive. She couldn't give a monkey's toss about any problems Pratt had after all the grief he'd given her.

I'd heard him ranting about something earlier but I couldn't for the life of me remember anything about coming home. It was a bit too early. I needed a cup of tea to get the brain into gear.

'No, Mum, I'm pretty sure I was a good boy. Besides you'd be the first to know if I'd done anything to upset old Mr Pratt features.'

'Well just to give you warning, he's on the warpath.' She looked me in the eyes for a second. I could tell that she didn't believe me for one moment. There was a hint of a knowing smile on her face as she got up from the side of my bed and left the room.

Tea, a shower and some breakfast, then perhaps I could try and focus on what had happened last night.

It was the shower which finally brought everything flooding back; the phone call to Sarah, the all-too-brief encounter with Nicola and her 'friends', Ena and his mates in the kebab house and lastly, the quick deposit in Pratt's back garden. It was this that I couldn't quite get my head around; there was something wrong and I didn't know what.

I could smell breakfast, or more likely lunch, wafting up the stairs; there were voices too. That meant that Mum and Sis were chatting in the kitchen. I wasn't that hungry but I knew a bit of food would help the Sunday morning hangover.

'Morning, ladies.' They were both at the kitchen table tucking into bacon sandwiches. Sis was the first to offer me Sunday morning words of wisdom.

'God, I can smell you from here, dog breath. You stink of beer and garlic. I suppose it was another wild night on the town with your mates?'

It wasn't an accusation, more a statement of fact based on a few years of observation.

'You could say that, Sis. A few lost brain cells, a few memories and quite a few lost quids. C'est la vie. What about you? What did you get up to that would enhance the family's reputation for debauchery?'

I could tell she'd been out last night. She looked a bit rough around the edges and her voice was a touch on the raspy side. I knew she smoked and I'd tried to talk her out of it but all her mates smoked and after a few drinks she just went along with them.

'Just around and about with the usual crowd; a few drinks, a chat and I was home way before you. Dirty stop-out.'

It was a bit guarded, but then I was her brother, and there is no way she would let me know what she got up to in her private life; no way, unless she was in big trouble. Thankfully that hadn't happened yet.

'Here's your bacon sandwich and a cup of real coffee to clear your head, and maybe get rid of that odour that seems to be leaching out of your pores. Beer I can stand, Lord knows I had enough of it with your father,' she hesitated for a moment, realising what she'd said. I thought she was going to spit on the floor at suddenly remembering him.

'But it's that bloody garlic; it stinks. I think you need a bit of fresh air after your sandwich. Do me a favour and get the washing in for me. Oh, and watch out for Mr Pratt. I'm off to work for twelve. After you've done the washing could you tidy up around the kitchen and sort out anything else that needs doing?'

With that, she was off to change into her supermarket clothes and dash off for her shift. She'd worked at the supermarket for a few years doing all sorts of jobs in the store. Sometimes she acted up to supervisor but she preferred it on the tills. It gave her a chance to chat to people but she also liked to 'people watch' as she put it. She would 'check out' people's shopping and try to work out what they did for a job, if they had one, were they married, and just generally try to work people out. Analyse the daily or weekly shop, then the same for the customer and try to build a picture of their life, or lack of it. 'Till psychology,' as she liked to call it; it sounded better than just being nosey. After a while I started to get into it myself. I'd wander around the supermarket following various people or families, and try to work them out, together with a bit of shopping for Mum as I went. I'd

44

look at their shop, listen to their conversations and study their body language.

The more I got into it the more I've become a bit disillusioned with society in general. I'm not that old but I can remember when a day out with the family was to the park, cinema or even the beach, if you were lucky. The more I've stared at family groups, the more it's become evident to me that a day-trip out for a large number families is to the local supermarket. The kids look at the shiny things and hassle their mum and dad at the checkout for even more sweets than they already have in the trolley. Looking at some of the trolley-loads, I can't believe that a family can eat and drink the whole pile of crap they've collected - a trolley devoid of any fresh fruit, vegetables, fish or meat. It's mostly frozen ready-meals, crisps, biscuits, fizzy pop and sweets of various garish colours. I've got a theory that it's not really their shopping. I reckon it's a game called E Number Bingo. When they get home, I reckon they check off the E numbers on the stuff they've bought against their bingo card, and the first one to get an E number line gets an apple. Sadly, looking at dad's builder's bum and mum's arse - the size of a small country - I don't think that this is the case.

The other thing that winds me up is the kids' names. I would pick a family and try to find out the names of the children, and more often than not I wasn't disappointed in my theory. I now call them Scrabble Kids. When they're born, I think one of their parents puts their hand in the Scrabble bag and pulls out a handful of letters, throws them on the floor and whatever it spells, then that's their name. When a parent calls out a kid's name down the aisle I've often thought, 'How the hell do you spell that, let alone pronounce it?'

It's the kids I feel sorry for. They'll go for the rest of their lives with everyone they meet asking them, 'I'm sorry, could you spell that for me please?'

What's the matter with normal names? I can't imagine Jesus meeting his apostles and having the same problem.

'Ah, there you are, Matthew. Welcome, John, Mark and David. And how are you, er, what was your name again? And how do you spell that?'

I think we should have a Names Minister. When a child is born, the prospective name is submitted and vetted by the Minister's staff. If it's a stupid name then a suitable one will be allocated by the Ministry, and that's that. Over the child's life, he or she will be saved all the time-wasting and conjecture over a jumble of vowels and consonants.

And with the family-bonding trip over, it's off to the nearby burger shack for a sumptuous meal of saturated fats, carbohydrates and fizzy suspended sugar; yum yum. 'Do you want heart disease with that, or go large on the diabetes?'

Sis had finished her brunch and had headed off to her room to do what seventeen year-old girls do. Frankly I didn't have a bloody clue. It probably involved *Facebook*, *Twitter*, *iPods* or texts; probably all at the same time. It was time to get back to the real world and start doing a bit of work for mum.

I wandered outside to the back of the house to get the washing. It wasn't a bad day; a bit breezy, but sunny; a perfect drying day! I winced that I had come to that conclusion. I shouldn't be having thoughts like that. If I told anyone I'd be outed as a house-proud domestic skivvy. The ignominy amongst my friends; I wouldn't be able to bear it.

The various bits of clothing were getting folded and piled into the basket when I heard footsteps behind me in Pratt's garden. I didn't want to turn around in case it was him.

'Good Morning, Richard. Nice to see a young man a bit domesticated.'

It was Mrs Pratt. Even though she didn't mean it, her statement sounded like young men in general were a wild species which, unless captured and trained, couldn't or wouldn't do anything around the house.

'Don't tell anyone, Mrs P. It'll ruin my reputation around town.'

I liked Mrs Pratt. We often had a chat over the garden fence, especially when her husband was out. In fact she was quite winky; a bit too old for me, but not quite GILF. She was attractive for her age, still had a great body, when she wasn't wearing frumpy clothes, and had a sexy voice which sounded like she'd just had a spoonful of honey. And she was always just that little bit suggestive. There was always a little innuendo combined with a little lick of her lips as she said it. To be honest, I wouldn't trust myself if I met her out on one of our Saturday benders, especially late at night, but in retrospect there was no way I was going to plough the same furrow as Mr Pratt.

'Oh, your secret is safe with me, Richard. I can just see you in a little frilly skirt and a feather duster in your hand.'

Her hand went up to her chest and on to her neck as she spoke.

'I was just thinking the same thing about you, Mrs P.'

With that, there was a loud crash and a string of curses from her upstairs' back bedroom.

'Mr P seems to be in a bad mood today. What's the matter with him? He seems a bit grumpier than normal, if that's possible.'

Her expression changed a bit at the mention of her husband, or was it something else?

'He had a bit of a surprise this morning, when he went out into the garden. It seems that somebody decided to have a number two and it was all a bit messy.' She looked at me questioningly.

'Do you know anything Richard?'

I tried to look and sound all innocent and shocked.

'You mean someone crapped in your front garden?'

I hoped that the mention of the front garden might deflect some of the suspicion she, and most likely Mr Pratt, had of me.

'No, no, it was in the back garden. Rodney is beside himself, he's furious. He's already rung the police to get them around to investigate. He wants forensics and DNA tests; the whole business.'

Bloody hell, I had to think fast.

'Could it have been a badger or a fox or something?' Yeah that would do. A wild animal would often leave a little calling card on peoples' lawns in the middle of the night.

'I don't think so Richard. I don't think that badgers eat sweet corn, tomatoes and carrots. Besides, I don't think they would be able to poo on the poor thing.'

Poor thing? What was she on about?

'I thought you said the poo was on the grass?'

I was getting a bit lost now. I could remember crapping on the lawn but, that was my little head-worm, I didn't see anything when I'd turned around.

'No, it wasn't poo on the grass. Someone got into the back garden and pooed on poor Fang.'

I didn't engage my brain before I spoke.

'Someone shat on your tortoise?'

It sounded more of a statement than a question; or more like an admission. I thought back to this morning. I hadn't seen my dump; I must have missed Fang on the lawn and it was bombs away; straight on top of the poor bugger's shell. No wonder I didn't see anything. The poor little sod would have scampered off as quickly as he could. It can't be nice having a great pile of crap suddenly falling from the sky on to your house. Poor old Fang.

'Yes, and Rodney is furious. He thinks it might be you, Richard; I do hope it wasn't, because the police are coming round tomorrow.'

I could see the local newspapers - the posh one, '*Man pleads guilty to animal cruelty after DNA test*' and the local rag, '*Tortoise Turd Trauma*'. This was all getting a bit out of hand for my liking.

'I can assure you Mrs P that I wouldn't for one minute do anything like that to Fang. If there's anything I can do to help, just ask. If I hear of anything, I'll let you know.'

My head was spinning by now. I knew I'd gone a bit too far with this one but didn't think it would escalate to this extent. Time for a bit of damage limitation,

'I didn't hear anything last night but I'll ask Mum. By the way, you can't get DNA from poo after the first couple of hours. Apparently, the acids and enzymes in it break down the DNA complex, making a match impossible. It would also be contaminated in the early stages by the sloughing from the shell exterior where it has been attacked by digestive fluids. And did you know that the only part of the human body that hasn't any DNA profile is in fact earwax?'

All complete bollocks, apart from the earwax bit, but I hoped she'd pass some of that on to Mr P. With that, he came out of the back door. His face went crimson when he saw me talking to his wife; for a second I thought the end of his nose was going to burst,

'Maureen, get in the house at once. I don't want you talking to that boy after what he's done.'

'Hold on there, Mr Pratt.' I emphasised his surname when I could. It always got to him and this time was no exception.

'What about the premise in English Law which holds that a person is innocent until proven guilty? You seem to be judge and jury and have already made your mind up that I'm guilty. Look, I'm very sorry about Fang and will help in any way I can, so just put your petty little crusade against me and my family aside for once and maybe we'll get somewhere.'

He was crimson again. He always thought of me as a snotty-nosed thick little shit, so on the odd occasion I spoke to him and showed that I had a formal education, and had not spent my teenage years up the park on drink and drugs, it upset him even more. He turned his back on me and was pushing his wife in through the back door. I could hear him muttering that he knew it was me and that the police would sort me out tomorrow.

That gave me a little idea. Perhaps a call to Martin this afternoon could be in my favour. After all, he was one of the local coppers for this area. This wasn't the only call I'd have to make this afternoon. I needed to call Sarah to see how things were.

With the washing gathered, I spent the next thirty minutes tidying around the house so mum wouldn't come home to a mess. Hopefully she'd come back with some marked-down food from the supermarket and we wouldn't have to cook for tea.

It was nearly one o'clock. There was a deep growl of an engine from next door. It was Pratt's Sunday ritual. He always cleaned his *E-type Jag* on a Sunday. Despite my loathing for the old sod, you had to admire his choice of car and wife. He hadn't done badly with either although, from what I could see, the car was much higher maintenance than the wife.

I decided to call Martin; he'd be up by now. I rang him on his mobile and explained what I'd done. Once again, I would only find sympathy between shit and syphilis. He was working a day shift tomorrow and there was a good chance he would pick up Pratt's complaint. It was his time to play mentor to one of the new recruits. If he picked it up he said he would do what he could, but he emphasised it would be within reason; there was no way he would risk his neck just because I was stupid enough to crap on a runaway tortoise.

Right, that was one awkward phone call out of the way, now on to another. I wasn't sure what I should say to Sarah. Should I joke that I told her mother I was going to rip her knickers off and shag her silly or just go down on both knees and beg for forgiveness? I'd let her dictate the response; I'll just ring up, listen to her reaction and go from there.

She answered her mobile after a couple of rings. I was just about to speak when she launched into me.

'Of all the stupid bloody things I've ever come across, this takes the biscuit. Of all the stupid people I've met, you're up there at the top of the tree; the stupid, grinning, drunken fairy. Why did you ring me at that time of the morning?'

I was tempted to butt in and say I hadn't rung her, I'd rung her mum, but somehow I knew it wouldn't go down well. That was a bit of an understatement. Just grin and bear it and see if Hurricane Sarah blows itself out.

'Don't even bother answering that one. You were pissed and thought you could pop around for a quickie. I thought you had a higher regard for me than that. Am I just a piece of arse that you think you can ring up and biff whenever you get the urge? My mother is mortified. Firstly, from the phone call; I think it went something like 'chuck you on the bed, rip your clothes off and shag you.' That's about it, isn't it?'

She wasn't waiting for an answer. She was in full flow now. I was gauging her reaction as I'd planned but I hadn't expected it to be quite as cut-and-dried as to our future. It wasn't looking like Sarah was going to be the future Mrs Head.

'Secondly, she's amazed that I could have got mixed up with a pisshead waster like you. Not her words, just my inference. And frankly, after last night, I'm amazed as well. You're a loser Richard, and so are those mates of yours. It's about time you grew up and started to take life seriously. I can see now that you didn't take our relationship seriously.'

She paused for a breath. Hurricane Sarah was getting its second wind. In my mind's eye, I could see the corrugated roofs being ripped off and the yachts and fishing boats being washed up onto the pavements down her road.

'We're finished. I've been thinking about it for a while and last night finally persuaded me to do something about it. You've upset me and you've upset my mother and I don't want to see you again; ever.'

She had finally finished. I realised that I hadn't actually said a single word so far. I could hear her catching her breath down the phone. I bet her heart rate was racing away and her face was as red as a smacked arse.

'Well aren't you going to say anything?'

There wasn't a great deal to say really. She'd dumped me and it was clear she wasn't in the mood for mediation. Bollocks to it; I might as well go down in a blaze of masculine bravado.

'I suppose one last spine-shattering fuck's completely out of the question then?'

The scream from down the phone was so loud that I had to take the phone from my ear. The phone went as dead as our relationship. Ah well, it was good while it lasted.

I needed to get out of the house, clear my head a bit, and try to cheer myself up. I didn't like getting dumped, even though on this occasion I had it coming. It somehow hurt the male pride. It should be the man who dumps the girl - not the other way around. It was a bloke thing, I suppose.

I decided to walk across the park and visit Devon and his mum and dad, Mr and Mrs Ambrose. I still don't know why they called their lad Devon. Devon Ambrose; it sounded like a tin of custard to me.

'Sis, I'm going out for a bit. I won't be long.' No answer. I knew she was in her room because I could hear her moving about.

'Liz, I'm going round to Devon's, ok?' Still no answer. Ah well, best not to pry into a hormonal teenager's bedroom.

The walk across the park normally took about fifteen minutes but today I stretched it out a bit. It was a lovely afternoon. The parkies were gathering up the nets and flags from the morning's football matches. I used to come and watch the games a while back but there's only a certain amount you can take of watching mostly-overweight blokes trying to run off their Saturday night hangovers, often puking up in the centre circle after a bit of exertion.

A few young families were wandering the paths with some of the kids trying to master their first bikes, with more than the odd fall and crash, which most dads were filming for 'You've Been Framed'.

A few benches were occupied by teenage couples, probably on one of their first dates. They must be very young; otherwise they'd be in the pub. I started to think about Sarah, but quickly put that to the back of my mind; spilt milk and all that.

I thought instead of Nicola. I bet she wouldn't ring. Her mates would have dealt the poison about me and after that she'd spend my fiver. Perhaps someone else would ring my mobile number if they saw it on the note? No, that only happens in films and it doesn't often have a happy ending.

After about thirty minutes, I was in Devon's road; it was a long Victorian terrace. The houses looked fairly small from the outside but inside they were quite substantial. Devon and his family had lived here for quite a few years now. Typically for West Indians' houses, there were always splashes of vivid colours everywhere and Devon's was no exception. It was even called Montego Bay.

As I got closer, I could see a small family group working its way up the street. Male and female, in their mid-thirties, formally dressed, but a bit grey and drab. The two children were in their Sunday best with their hair sporting a severe parting in the middle. I knew who they were. Very few people would be out dressed like that on a Sunday apart from the God Botherers. We often got them knocking at our door. I used to ask them where they lived so I could come around later and spread the word of atheism when they were having their tea. It didn't do any good; they just kept on trying to indoctrinate you into their way of thinking and beliefs despite the sarcasm and lack of interest.

We all arrived at the Ambrose's front door at the same time. They looked at me for a moment as if trying to work out if I was ripe for conversion. I didn't want to get into any discussions with them, so I took the initiative.

54

'Good afternoon, I take it you're spreading the word of the Lord around this neighbourhood?'

The adults started to nod. I jumped in before they could speak.

'Well, Mr Ambrose is very interested in religious teachings and he has often talked about finding a new path. I was just about to go in and have a talk with him. Give me a minute and I'll send him out. He would just love to talk to you. There is one problem though, I'm afraid Mr Ambrose is very deaf indeed. If you want him to hear you then you'll have to shout at the top of your voices. Now, if you'll excuse me, I'll pop inside and tell him you're here.'

With that I was up the small path, a quick knock at the door and announced myself to the Ambroses.

'Come in, Richard. Have you had any dinner? If you haven't, there's plenty to go around.' Mrs Ambrose was famed for her cooking. We used to raid Devon's lunch box at school, if you'll pardon the expression, because his food was always a lot nicer than ours and a damn sight more interesting.

'What brings you around here, lad?' Mr Ambrose had a bit of a West Indian lilt, despite being born here.

'Just popped over to see Devon and steal one of Mrs Ambrose's delicious cakes. Oh, by the way Mr Ambrose, there's some people outside that need your help. I think they're lost and need directions. I don't know this area too well, so do you think you could help them out?'

'No problem son, always happy to be of help.' He was quickly up and out of his chair and on his way to the front door.

'One problem Mr Ambrose, they all appear to be very deaf. I had to shout at the top of my voice to make myself heard and understood.'

Mr Ambrose stopped for a moment and nodded to me. He was still quite a striking figure with his salt and pepper hair and big barrelled chest. I could just see him with a cricket bat in his hand or steaming in on his run-up, ball in hand, about to knock a batsman's head off. He was already filling his lungs for the benefit of the deaf family on the street.

'Hello mate, I didn't expect to see you today. I thought you'd be sat at home with your tail between your legs after trying to chat up your girlfriend's mother.'

Devon had come in from the garden. A mug of tea steamed in his hand.

'Fancy one?' He raised his mug slightly as he asked.

'Yep, I'd love one, and by the way it's ex-girlfriend. We split up this afternoon.' I tried to sound a bit matter-of-fact.

'She dumped you, more like. Still, plenty more fish in the sea. And I don't mean girls with cold scaly skin, bulging eyes and thick pale lips, like your usual girlfriends.'

Before I could salvage a bit of my pride, the shouting started out the front.

'My young friend says that you're lost and need some direction.'

It was at the top of Mr Ambrose's voice. I swear the front windows shook slightly. To their credit, the God Botherers stood their ground.

'No sir, we do not need direction, we already know what path lies before us. The Lord has shown us the way.'

The father was shouting at the top of his voice. I imagined there would be about two feet between them. Little drops of spit were flying out of his mouth due to the effort he was putting in to it.

Mr Ambrose wiped some spit off his cheek.

'The Lord, hey? Personally I use my Sat Nav!'

I quickly explained to Devon what I'd done and apologised for stitching up his Dad but said I couldn't resist it. We went to the front door to see what was happening; as we arrived at the door we could see that a number of the neighbours had come out to investigate the shouting. The father of the group was starting to go red in the face. You couldn't tell with Devon's dad, but he was in full voice.

'Don't you think that it's you who could be lost sir? Don't you think that a change in your direction may bring you some extra fulfilment in life?'

The whole family were nodding now. The shouting and adrenalin were starting to have an effect.

By now, a large number of neighbours were out in the street looking and listening to the shouting match. A few had started to snigger. Devon and I were trying not to laugh but weren't having much luck.

'Me? Bloody lost? But I live here! How the hell would I be lost?'

Mr Ambrose looking around and was beginning to become aware of the gathering crowd along the road. His suspicions were starting to become aroused. He continued to shout at the family, but not with the ferocity of a few moments before.

'I thought you were the ones who were lost! Just who are you?'

The father dipped into his bag and produced a small pamphlet.

'We're spreading the word of our God and would like you to have this book on our teachings.' His outstretched hand held the book towards a now agitated and angry man who was beginning to realise what was going on.

'Are any of you deaf?'

The family looked at each other with a puzzled expression on all their faces. Shouting again, the father replied,

'No, none of us. Why do you ask?'

'Because I'm not bloody deaf either! Why are we shouting at each other?'

Mr Ambrose knew the answer and by now, so did most of the street. Devon and I were crying with laughter along with the immediate neighbours. I gathered my breath and glanced towards the small group at the gate; they were all looking at me but it was Devon's dad's expression which took the smile off my face and the laughter from my belly. I was in deep doo-doo. I had made a fool of the guy in his own home and in front of his neighbours and if looks could kill, I was six feet under already.

'Devon, is your back door open?' I was starting to inch back towards my escape route.

'Yeah, why ask?'

'Because I've got this distinct feeling that your dad's going to rip my limbs off and beat me to death with the soggy ends.'

I spun on my heels into the hall and ran for the back door. I could hear the shouts behind me which didn't sound too good. Shame, because I was looking forward to tea with the Ambroses. It dawned on me that this was the second time in two days that I'd come very close to having my face reconstructed, as I jumped over the wall at the bottom of the

58

garden and into the road. The shouts, or West Indian death threats, receded as I ran down towards the park. I would have to stay out of Dev's dad's way for a few days but he'd calm down after a while and hopefully see the funny side of it - hopefully.

The walk across the park was uneventful. Nobody jumped out at me from behind the bushes and beat me to death, because I had reduced his standing in the local community to one of a completely gullible idiot. A few people were still about but, in the main, most had headed off home for a well-earned Sunday roast.

I toyed with the idea of popping in to the local boozer for a quick pint and catch the football but I was still feeling a bit fragile from last night and was still worried about what I was doing to my insides. Turning them into pâté, most likely. I'd be better off heading home to see what Mum has brought from the supermarket or rustle up some comfort food like beans on toast. Soft toasted bread with loads of butter, a bit of black pepper in the beans, topped off with some grated mature cheddar and popped under the grill. I was dribbling down the front of my shirt.

My mobile went off in my pocket. It wasn't a number I recognised. Christ, had Devon given his dad my number so he could tell me how he was going to slowly torture me before feeding me to the piggies? Sometimes I wished I didn't have such a vivid imagination.

'Hello, who's that?' I didn't want to give my name. If the worst came to the worst, I could always put on a funny voice and deny it's me.

'It's Nicola, I was wondering if you wanted your five pounds back?'

Bloody hell, who needed Sarah anyway? I suddenly got this weird feeling in the pit of my stomach; in my bollocks really. It felt like a goldfish swimming around my scrotum. This girl really did strange things to me.

'I'd given up hope that you might ring. To be honest I thought I'd been in too much of a state last night, or earlier this morning, to make enough of an impression on you. Or was it just the five pounds bribe I gave you?'

'Gave me? I thought you might want it back or you could spend it on a phone call to me. At today's rates a young girl on the phone would cost between one pound and one pound fifty a minute, depending on the subject. Unfortunately for you, I just want to talk about last night, so you might get a bit of discount.'

I'd rung one of those phone lines and stupidly expected to be talking to the girl in the photo. Not a chance. After about a minute, or a couple of quid's worth, I had this vision of a late middle-aged granny sitting in her front room talking to me whilst she had the sound turned down on '*Eastenders*'. Never again.

'I hope I didn't get you in trouble with your friends; they seemed very protective. Actually, I really enjoyed our chat once I'd got myself together. Do you honestly talk in song titles?'

'Most of the time; especially when I'm out on the town. You know, the bright lights and music.' She sounded a lot brighter than she had last night. After all, it was late when we met.

'What are you up to this afternoon?'

'Bright lights and music; this isn't a test, is it? If it is, I don't know the song. I'm having a *Blur* afternoon if you want to know.' It was her turn to work it out.

'That's easy. You're in the park, *'Parklife'*. You're not sat on a bench, with a bottle in a brown paper bag, ogling the girl joggers, are you?'

She was pretty sharp, this one, asking more questions and not saying a great deal about herself.

'Neither. If the truth be told I'm escaping from an irate six foot two West Indian father who, at this present moment, would like to use my wedding tackle as a paperweight.'

I went on to explain about Devon's dad and the 'deaf' God Botherers. She seemed genuinely amused. We talked as I walked slowly across the park. Despite a few questions about her house, job and boyfriends, I got absolutely nothing from her. She side-stepped every question with one of her own. I was beginning to think she might be a politician or, even worse, a solicitor.

After about ten minutes or so, she knew everything about me and my family, where I lived, my mum and sister, my work as an estate agent and an awful lot about my friends, although I was a bit guarded there. I even told her about Sarah but said we'd split last night and not today. I got the impression that she might not like me trying to chat her up when I was technically still going out with someone.

'Anyway, about this fiver you've got. I don't think I've had five pounds worth of girlie talk, so how about converting it into a glass or two of wine followed by an Italian? I know this great little restaurant near the centre. Would you be up for that?'

The reply came a lot quicker than I'd expected,

'You know what, I'd love to, but I won't be able to stay out very late and I won't be drinking. I'm off the alcohol for a little while.' She sounded genuinely interested.

We arranged a time and a place to meet for the coming Wednesday. We could have a couple of drinks in our local pub and then on for a bite to eat in the Italian.

'You know what, I'd love to as well but I'll be drinking; not much though because I want to remember all of Wednesday night and not little bits like Saturday. One last thing: will you be on your own or will you be chaperoned by your security guards?'

She gave a little chuckle,

'I'll be on my own. Sorry about them, but they mean well. Listen, I've got to go. See you Wednesday.' With that she was gone. I saved her number in my contacts and wanted to ring her back, but that would just look far too desperate.

I was soon across the park and walking up our road. Pratt was out cutting his front lawn. The cock and balls had long gone under new grass and it was again a pristine green carpet. I'd have to think of another trick and look out for is a camera or CCTV. It wouldn't be long before he invested in one if I kept on bursting his idyllic little bubble.

'Hi Mr Pratt.'

He didn't really speak; it was a sort of cross between a grunt and a burp. Either way he couldn't bring himself to acknowledge me properly. He would be running through his prosecution case for the morning. I really did hope that it would be Martin that turned up and not some tight-arsed jobs-worth with no common sense - academically gifted, but with no common sense or life skills; they were the dangerous ones. It was either black or white, guilty or not guilty. I'd have to wait until tomorrow to find out.

'Hi honey, I'm home!' I liked winding up the females in the house. At this age, I couldn't see myself saying it to my wife, in my own house, any time soon. I was an estate agent and knew that the housing market wasn't geared up to young people who wasted all their money on drink and girls. If only they had a beer savings-card; the more you drank the more you saved. Wishful thinking.

'Hi Richard, Devon's been on the phone. He said you were engaged earlier so he told me all about this afternoon. I wouldn't go anywhere near Charlie Ambrose for the next few days, if I were you. He sounds almost as upset as Mr Pratt. They might even get together and start up a local vigilante group and run you out of town.'

She was half-joking but you could pick up on the concern in her voice.

'Mum, I admit I was guilty of a practical joke on Charlie Ambrose but, in my defence, a lot of people in his road tested out their incontinence pads. It was a hoot, but not for Charlie as it turned out. As for Mr Pratt, I had nothing to do with that. Must have been someone or something else. The guy's just got a downer on me and the family. Anyway, what delights have you salvaged from the reduced section down the market?'

Again, I knew she didn't believe me but she let it pass.

'Ok, but just be careful. One of these days you're going to get yourself in real trouble with one of these practical jokes. The last thing you want is a criminal record, no matter how small. You'd lose your job and where would you be then?'

She was right as always. I needed to be a bit careful, especially around Pratt.

'What's for dinner anyway? I'm starving.' My hangover had worn off and after a bit of fresh air, I was ready to eat some food.

'Steak and kidney pie, mash, and green beans with onion gravy,' she said with some relish.

'And all for the price of a bag of crisps!' This was added with some pride. A hearty meal for just a few pence. I was like Pavlov's dog by now. I was salivating at the mention of some of my favourite nosh.

Mum and I ate in the kitchen whilst Sis took hers to her room. We had a brief chat but both of us were tired. I did the washing up and we both headed off for a well-earned sleep. It had been an interesting couple of days to say the least and I was a bit anxious about tomorrow; so much so that I was thinking about ringing work with a short term domestic-emergency excuse just so I could hang around and see what happened with Pratt and the police.

A quick flip through the TV channels and, as suspected, there was sod-all on. I was fed up with reality this and celebrity that. The reality shows were full of talentless wannabes and as for the celebrities, I'd never even heard of any of them. Time for bed.

Chapter Three

Monday morning came around all too quickly. I'd slept fairly well, but I had this nagging feeling about Pratt and his interview with the police. There was no doubt that he would finger me for the crap on Fang. I was hoping that Martin would turn up. After breakfast, I hung around the front room, looking at my watch every other minute, and peering out of the window at the sound of every car driving down the road. I was turning into a proper curtain twitcher.

I could see how some people get addicted to what was going on in their road. As people come and go, your mind becomes filled with all sorts of scenarios.

The husband of the girl down the road went off to work, then about ten minutes later, a car drew up and this young lad jumped out. Thirty seconds later, bedroom curtains were being drawn. That one was pretty easy. Perhaps I should change my career to blackmailer but, on second thoughts, it wouldn't look good on my passport application.

It was getting on towards nine and I'd have to think about ringing Carol at work to say I'd be late. I'd just say that my mum wasn't well or that I needed to meet the gasman. Carol would be okay as we didn't have any viewings until this afternoon. She was pretty laid back, although the Regional Manager was getting on her case about the lack of sales through the office. It wasn't our fault, because the market was pretty crap. One or two agents in the area were doing okay; what they were doing was just plain illegal, but they were getting sales and we weren't.

A car pulled up outside. I was at the window in a flash, being careful not to move the curtains. It was a police car with a rather official-looking Martin in the passenger seat. I bet he thought he was like the Guv'nor in *The Sweeney*. Martin got out and looked around; I'd half expected him to stay in the seat whilst the young lad who was driving ran around and opened the door for him. He had that air about him today. It was an 'I'm in fuckin' charge' sort of look. The PC with him looked like he should still be at school. His uniform didn't fit him very well and he didn't have that air of confidence that probably comes from having a couple of collars, as Martin puts it.

As they headed up the path to Pratt's house, I called Carol to say something had come up and I would be a bit late. By the time I got round to the side of the house, out of sight of the Pratt's, Martin was at the front door. I'd found from a previous eavesdropping that I could move from bush to bush up the side of our house and hear, and sometimes see, what was going on in the front and back rooms of next door. It was Mr Pratt that answered the door.

'Mr Pratt, Rodney Pratt?' I cringed as Martin emphasised the surname as I always did.

'Yes, do come in officers.' He was in full obsequious mode. I'd changed my position to get a better view. Martin flashed his warrant card.

'I'm Constable Bormann from the local police station, Sir. I'm responding to your complaint from yesterday morning. Sorry we couldn't respond earlier, but we had a lot of cases to finish from a rather hectic Saturday. Some serious cases needed our immediate attention. I'm sure you appreciate that, Sir?'

Nice one Martin. Your complaint had to wait because we had some real work to do. Thing is, I didn't know if it was true.

'This is my colleague, Constable Carter.'

With that, they went into the house and on through to the kitchen, which was good for me because I could both hear and see most of what was about to unfold.

'Would you like some tea, officers? I've just boiled the kettle.' Maureen was already in the kitchen. From what I could see of her, she looked as if she'd made a bit of an effort; full makeup, a rather short skirt and a bit too much cleavage for nine o'clock on a Monday morning.

'Yes please, Mrs Pratt; that would be very nice.' I could see that she had Martin's attention. Even from this distance, I could see him checking her out, completely ignoring her husband.

'Oh, please call me Maureen.' She didn't have to spell it out that she hated her surname.

'And how do you take it?' As she said it, her little rosebud-like tongue was running sensuously across her lips. Christ, the two of them were flirting. If Martin says hot and strong, I'll burst out laughing.

'Milk, no sugar, thank you….. Maureen.' Just a little bit of hesitation and the use of her forename. Things were getting a bit informal between these two already. Mind you, I wasn't surprised, because Martin would shag a barber's floor if he had the chance.

Mr Pratt cleared his throat, clearly annoyed at his wife's interference.

'I'm very glad you came officers; this has been going on for far too long and it's about time things came to a stop.'

Martin and his colleague had sat down and were getting their notebooks out.

'Steve, you won't need your book for this one; I'll do all the questioning and notes, if that's okay?'

It was a rhetorical question; Martin was making it plain that he was dealing with this. The young officer just nodded and put his notebook away.

'I'm sorry, Mr Pratt; we've got a report to say that sometime on Saturday night into Sunday morning, your tortoise, Fang, got covered in excrement. I've checked the records and this is the only complaint of this type you've logged, so how can this have been going on for a long time?'

Before he could reply, Maureen was in front of Martin with his tea.

'Here's your tea, officer.' She stopped a little distance away from the low table in front of him. This had the effect of making her bend at the waist as she put the tea down. For one moment I thought her bangers would swing out of her bra and knock his tea over, but the bra and blouse held under the pressure and averted an accident.

'Thank you very much,' replied Martin, not taking his eyes off the ample amount of flesh being flashed in front of him.

'It's been going on for ages. It's that wretched boy from next door, Richard Head. He's trouble, and he's been making our lives hell. This incident with Fang is just one in a long line of crimes he's committed against my property and I've had enough of it. I want him arrested for what he's done.' Pratt was getting it off his chest. All the spite he'd saved up over the years was starting to come out. The good thing was that he was losing it slightly and was coming across as a bit vindictive.

'That's a bit strong Mr Pratt. You are accusing someone of criminal actions against your property and are demanding an arrest. I take it from the strength of your accusations that you must have substantial evidence to back them up?'

It was said in a very matter of fact way, but Martin had put him directly on the spot with his first question.

Pratt was taken aback by this. I'm sure he had in his mind that the police would listen to his story in full then march around to my house and I would be bundled into the back of the police car in handcuffs. After all, he was an accountant for the council; a very important man in the neighbourhood, if not the entire town.

'Evidence? Just ask any of the neighbours and they will all say that he's a bad one and that he's responsible for everything bad that goes on around here. Take that obscene shape on my lawn; a big penis, don't you know. The vicar's wife doesn't speak to me anymore. It's outrageous that he's getting away with these unspeakable actions.'

Martin was making notes now.

'A big penis you say; on your lawn. Just how big was this penis?'

'It was huge. About fifteen feet long with, well, dangly bits underneath.' He'd blushed at the mention of the dangly bits.

'That is a very big penis Mr Pratt. Did you recognise it?'

'I beg your pardon? Recognise it; I'm not sure I know what you mean.' Pratt was beginning to lose it big time. His composure and confidence of earlier were beginning to wear very thin.

'It's just that sometimes these garden graffiti artists model their art on famous people's anatomy so it could be the bits and pieces of an actor, a sportsman or even Michelangelo's David.'

'No, of course I didn't recognise it. Anyway, who are these garden artists? I've never heard of them.'

So far, not much about Fang, the main reason Pratt had called the police out. Martin was drawing him away, confusing him and putting some doubt in his mind. Besides that, Pratt was definitely not comfortable talking about cocks.

'I'm very surprised that a man of your standing and obvious knowledge hasn't heard of this new phenomenon. A group of youngsters have moved away from using spray paint on any surface they can find and have started using gardens as their new canvas. It obviously takes longer and doesn't have quite the same impact but they believe they are putting something back into society, and nature. They often use flowers in borders. This is the first I've heard of grass art. In a way, Mr Pratt, you should feel honoured. These people only pick upon the finest gardens in my experience.'

Martin glanced sideways at his partner. He could feel the stare. The look on Carter's face was, 'What the bloody hell are you on about?' The look on Martin's was 'Shut the fuck up and speak when you're spoken to.'

'Oh I see. Now you come to mention it, I have heard of these fellows. And of course, if they were to pick on a garden in this area they would naturally pick on mine as it is by far the best.'

Pratt was almost purring with satisfaction. It was confirmed. His garden had been chosen as the best in the area for the outline of one of the biggest cock and balls outside of the carvings on the rolling chalk downs of southern England.

'Anyway, away from large penises for the moment,' I couldn't believe that he'd looked at Maureen as he said it. 'I have to come back to the evidence. What evidence do you have that Richard Head is the perpetrator of this alleged crime?'

'As I said, everyone knows it's him. He must have jumped over the back wall and done it. As for evidence, I

70

have the poo in a bag.' Pratt looked satisfied with himself. In his mind, this was the clincher to have me convicted.

'If possible, I'd like to see your evidence for myself. Just to confirm, when do you think this incident occurred?' Martin was writing in his notebook again.

'It must have been between about ten o'clock Saturday night and about six or seven Sunday morning. Why do you need to be precise?'

'It's just that when you reported the incident you stated that you wanted a DNA test completed on your evidence. DNA only has a very limited lifespan if it's stored in unfavourable conditions. May I see the bag please?'

'It's in the garden shed. I didn't want to bring it into the house for obvious reasons. It smells a bit.'

With that, they all left the kitchen through the back door and headed to the shed. I hid behind the wall and peered through a gap. Pratt went to the shed and came out with a clear polythene bag.

'I put it in this so you could have a clear look at the evidence. It turns my stomach to think what poor Fang went through.'

Pratt stood there holding the bag at arm's length. Martin stepped forward to look at it closely.

'Yes, you were right all along Mr Pratt. This confirms my suspicions.'

'Yes! I knew it. It's the end for that boy and our troubles. You hear that, dear? They will have to move house now.'

Maureen looked a bit uncomfortable about the whole thing. Martin looked at Pratt.

'Yes it's confirmed Mr Pratt. This is definitely shit.'

'Well we know that officer, and we know it's from that boy, Head, don't we?'

'You seem to be jumping to conclusions here, Mr Pratt. It's definitely shit, but who actually did it is open to conjecture and investigation.'

Pratt was starting to look angry now. He was gripping the bag a bit too tightly. Martin could see and stepped back a bit.

'No it's his, it's got to be. I want a DNA test. That'll prove it was him.'

'We have two problems here, Mr Pratt. Firstly, the DNA; as I mentioned earlier, evidence has to be stored in the correct way to avoid degradation and, most importantly, cross-contamination. Unfortunately you have collected the evidence, in this case excrement, without the proper equipment or knowledge to avoid both. The DNA will have broken down over the last few hours as it's been stored in a hot shed encouraging the growth of harmful bacteria on top of the enzymes and digestive juices in the excrement. There will be contamination from the tortoise itself and also from you as you collected it. So, in a nutshell, a DNA check is out the question.'

'Damn, I knew I should have insisted that you came here straight away and sort this out! But we can't let this criminal get away with this. What can we do, officers?'

'That brings me on to the second problem. You see, I don't think that this was a random drive-by crapping. My recent experience with local drug gangs leads me to suspect that this may be gang-related and that the targeting of your property, or to be more specific, Fang the tortoise, is sending out a message.'

Constable Carter spat a mouthful of tea over the grass at the mention of the drive-by crapping. He was about to

72

question Martin when he was shot another look. He quickly regained his composure and said nothing.

'A drive-by crapping? I've never heard of such a thing, officer. How could we have got mixed up in this?'

Pratt was looking more than a bit perplexed at this development. I must admit I hadn't heard of anything like it. Martin was testing Pratt's gullibility to the limit with this one; I could accept the DNA bollocks but this one was a bit far. Still, I had to admit that he was trying his best to help me out and he was succeeding so far.

'It's a new thing in this country. As with a lot of things, it originated in America and has now been taken on by gangs over here. It's basically gangs marking their territories, much in the way wild animals do in nature. It's this connection to the animals, as they see it, which makes them feel that they are, somehow, wild; beyond the conventional codes and laws as we know them.'

Bloody hell, Martin was beginning to convince me. I could see him on *Crimewatch* next.

'The unfortunate thing about these drive-by incidents is that they tend to use people's pets because it causes distress in the area and word soon gets about. 'Don't mess with us; this is our patch.' Am I making any sense?'

Constable Carter was hopping from one foot to the other. He clearly wasn't sure what was going on and just wanted out of it. I'm sure he could see his fledgling police career being flushed down the pan after a nasty disciplinary hearing.

Pratt was scratching his head. He had thought I'd crapped on his tortoise but was now thinking that Fang was tied up in a gangland drug feud. It just wasn't his day. Perhaps it was going to be mine.

Martin carried on; he now had the momentum and Pratt was on the ropes.

'So, to conclude the second point, it is in fact a much bigger problem than I first thought. It's likely that this gang will return, certainly to the area. We'll have to increase our patrols, to this street in particular, and I think that may scare them off. Would you be happy with that outcome, Mr and Mrs Pratt?'

They both nodded in affirmation and said they would be obliged at the increased police vigilance. Martin had just got the both of them to acknowledge that it wasn't me who had committed the crime; instead it had been a crap-crazed drug gang. Brilliant.

'Now, I would suggest that you dispose of your evidence, Mr Pratt, in whatever way you see fit. And I don't mean throw it over the next door neighbour's fence. Do I make myself clear?'

Pratt nodded like a naughty schoolboy. He was still clutching the bag of stinking shit in front of him. I could smell it from here and it was burning the hairs off the inside of my nose.

'The last thing I need to mention is the question of counselling. Do you think that would be an option, Mr Pratt?'

He was looking a bit shell-shocked now. He had his back to the ropes and couldn't stop the blows raining down on his ego.

'Well, yes I think so. After all I've been through, I think a talk with a trained specialist may do me some good.'

Martin smiled and threw his knockout punch.

'I'm afraid you've got the wrong end of the stick, Sir. The counselling wouldn't be for you; it would be for the real victim of this affair, your tortoise Fang.'

For a moment, I thought Carter was going to piss his pants. He was jumping around like a scalded cat. His hands were grabbing various bits of his anatomy as he showed his distress. He could see the ground opening up in front of him. It had all got too much for him and he made his excuses and said he needed to check in at the station. Martin told him he needed to talk to him before he did. The last thing he wanted was some rookie shouting his mouth off to everyone down at the station about drive-by crappings and tortoise-counselling.

Pratt just stood there, open mouthed; it was all too much for him too.

'We have an animal therapist in the Constabulary who specialises in cases such as this. I'm sure she could help Fang get over the trauma of the last twenty four hours. Mrs Pratt, do you think that would be an option?'

Maureen looked at Martin and his little grin. I'm pretty sure that, at that moment, she suddenly realised what had gone on over the last twenty minutes.

'Could you leave it with me please, officer and I'll discuss it with my husband? Is it possible I could give you a number to contact me if anything comes up?'

'That's very thoughtful of you, Maureen. You can rest assured that my investigation will be in-depth and very probing. I like to root around and get to the bottom of things. There may be a few ups and downs over the next few days but I'll maintain my thrust towards a satisfactory climax to the case.'

Any more innuendoes and Pratt would surely catch on to what was going on between these two. Maureen was practically fizzing at the bunghole. Flirting in front of her husband, with a handsome copper, was obviously turning her on.

'Thank you Martin, I was hoping you would say that. Until later then?' Her tongue was in turbo drive and rubbing all her lipstick off her top lip. Martin wasn't much better; I swear he had a lazy lob-on. Do yourself and your career a favour and get the hell out of there.

'If there's nothing else, then I'd better be off. I hope I've covered everything but if you think of anything else, just ring me at the station. Just one last thing, before I leave, I think I'll just pop next door and have a word with the young gentleman you mentioned earlier. I'm sorry, his name was Richard?'

'Head, Head. See what he has to say for himself. I still find it hard to believe what you've said this morning, officer. It's left me a bit light-headed. I think I need some liver salts and a lie down.'

Pratt was looking decidedly unwell and confused. I think Martin was looking genuinely upset for him; or perhaps it was a pang of guilt?

'Well I'm off then. Goodbye Mr Pratt, Mrs Pratt.'

As he left down the side of the house, Maureen pressed a piece of paper into Martin's hand; I hoped he knew what he was doing. I'd moved into the house when things were wrapping up. I hadn't expected Martin to call in after the interview. Again, I hoped he knew what he was doing.

I heard him call to Carter in the car to join him outside of our house. The doorbell rang and the outline of the two officers could be seen in the porch.

I opened the door to the two of them,

'You'll never take me alive, copper!' I stood in the doorway and clenched my fists, making the angriest face I could.

'You little piece of shit. I'm arresting you on suspicion of having a small cock and an even smaller brain. Put your hands on the wall and prepare to be cuffed. Carter, slap the irons on him and be quick about it.'

Carter just stood there. The day was definitely not going as he'd planned. I looked at him and couldn't help but break into a wide smile and begin to laugh. This confused him even more.

'That's enough of your handcuff fetish, Martin. I'm not one of your kinky girlfriends. Fancy a cuppa?'

Carter looked like the top of his head was going to come off. He just didn't know what was going on.

'Come on in, Steve, and I'll explain.' He put his arm around the young lad and pulled him inside as I made for the kitchen. The kettle was already on.

Martin and the young constable followed me into the kitchen. I made sure the net- curtains were across and all the windows were closed, so Pratt couldn't see or hear what was going on.

'Two teas, milk and no sugar please, Richie.' Martin turned to Steve,

'Steve, I'd like to introduce you to one of my oldest and best friends, Richie.' He didn't use my surname. I walked over and shook his hand; it was a bit clammy but, after all he'd gone through over the last half hour, I couldn't blame him.

'I'm sorry I couldn't be open with you about my friendship with Richie before we came out but, please believe me, I only did it to protect you. The thing is, I wasn't sure how it would pan out with the Pratts. If it went badly, then it would be my ass in a sling and you could walk away from the wreckage without any problem. Am I making myself clear?'

'Not really,' said the nervous young constable.

'What went on today was a lesson in common-sense policing. It's not always as black and white as it first appears. Sometimes you have to use your judgement and apply a few little rules as to what you do and how you do it. It would have been all too easy today to rush around to next door and listen to the pillar of society put the bubble into Richie here, cart him off meaning he receives a criminal record. The end result would be that Richie would now be a convicted criminal and stigmatised for the rest of his life.'

'That's if I crapped on Fang in the first place, Sherlock.' I got that in for Carter's benefit.

'You've got to ask yourself, in everything you do, is what I'm doing, or about to do, reasonable, justifiable and proportionate? If you think that your actions are all of those three then carry on but, don't forget, it's you up there in the witness box and it can be the loneliest place on earth, especially if you're not sure of yourself. Now, am I making myself clear?'

Carter was starting to calm down and he was listening intently. It appeared that he was taking this in. I brought their tea over to them, trying not to interrupt Martin's flow. He should have been a teacher, preferably in a Primary School because I wouldn't trust him with some of the sixth formers knocking around town.

'The bottom line in this instance is that Mr Pratt is a grade 'A' arsehole and has had a downer on Richie, and the rest of his family, for a number of years. Now, I only know that because I know Richie. Even if he was guilty, would the punishment fit the crime? I can safely say, 'No'. For all we knew, Mr Pratt could have been fabricating the whole complaint. So young Steven, never take things at face value. Try to be objective, no matter how compelling the evidence appears, and you might turn out to be a half decent copper. If you only remember one thing from your time with me, then remember what I've just told you and you'll do all right.'

'I take your point, Martin, and thanks for keeping me out of the loop; I appreciate that. There are two things I'm not sure about though. Who are these eco-garden artists and as for drug gang drive-by crappings, well I'd rather not ask. Oh, and what exactly was going on between you and Mrs Pratt?'

Carter had a smile on his face now. I think he'd learned a valuable lesson today about good old-fashioned policing.

'Just read the Intel reports about what goes on in your area, and as for Mrs Pratt, let's just say I was building up a rapport with a subject during an interview.' Martin suddenly got a bit serious.

'None of what went on today is to be discussed down at the station. If word gets out about this, we'll both be in a whole world of shit. Understand?'

Carter nodded knowingly. As he was aware of what went on this morning, he could end up on a fizzer for not reporting Martin's cover-up to a senior officer. Martin turned to me.

'And as for you young Richard, I'd suggest that you wind your neck in or next time you might get it chopped off.'

I looked at him with as innocent an expression as I could muster. He quickly changed the subject.

'Anyway, are you coming out Wednesday for a beer and debrief of Saturday night?'

'Sorry mate, but I've got other plans for Wednesday. We'll have to catch up another time; besides, I'm trying to lay off the booze a bit at the moment. Yesterday taught me a bit of a lesson and I need to look after myself more.'

I explained to them about the God Botherers and being chased by Charlie Ambrose. They were pissing themselves.

'Like I said Richie, wind that neck in a bit because if Charlie had caught you, I might have been involved in a murder investigation today. Listen, we'd better be off and protect society, whoever they are. Take care, mate and catch you soon. No pun intended.'

Martin and Steve left with suitably serious looks on their faces as they walked to their car. Doubtlessly that would change as soon as they drove down the road.

I thought about how lucky I'd been as I went over the last few days in my mind on the walk into work. I'd had a few close calls over the weekend but the tortoise was just stupid. The next time I wound up Pratt, I would have to be a bit cleverer and I had to look out for cameras. He would be even more determined to get me now. He wouldn't buy Martin's bullshit for long and would convince himself that it was indeed me after all.

I often walked to work. It was only a mile or so to the main street and the estate agents. If I left at the usual time, rush hour for most, I would often beat the cars in the mile to the office. The look on some of the drivers' faces as I passed them, stuck in traffic jams, often set me up for the rest of the day. A bit of exercise, a bit of thinking time and it also saved money.

To make things even better, it was a lovely, late summer's day; still pretty warm with no hint of autumn yet.

The Office was set on the high street along with the usual array of banks, other estate agents, and sandwich and charity shops. The charity shops had gradually increased over the last few years. I suppose it's a sign of the times. People couldn't afford the rent and were unwilling to take a gamble opening a business during the current crap economic climate.

There were three estate agents in the street, the biggest of which was directly across from us. Part of a large chain of regional agents, we would often try to gauge the volume of sales they were generating compared to ours. It was certain that they were doing better than us; as a result our managers were putting a lot of pressure on us to improve.

I knew this was affecting Carol. She looked a bit stressed as I walked in.

'Hi Carol, sorry I'm a bit late. Had to sort out a delivery for my mum. I'll make the time up tonight if you want.'

I knew she wouldn't. She just shook her head whilst sipping her coffee and chewing on a large mouthful of doughnut. I smiled at her and sat down at my desk. I glanced across at Tina. She was the receptionist-cum-gopher. Unfortunately, she didn't gopher much as she was a lazy cow. The only thing I knew she'd go for was anything with a pulse in a pair of trousers, usually after she'd downed the best part of a bottle of vodka. She was the ultimate goodtime girl. Her binge drinking made me look like I was a member of the local temperance society. And she liked guys. I reckon that if you took all the cocks she's had and put them in a line, they'd make a handrail all around Wembley stadium.

We didn't get on very well for a couple of reasons. Firstly, as I said, she was lazy. She also took the piss out of Carol, which really cheesed me off. Carol could be too nice for her own good sometimes and one of these times was Tina. She always had an excuse as to why she couldn't do things, so Carol's workload, and to a lesser extent mine, increased. Secondly, I'd turned her down at the Christmas party a couple of years ago. We were both drunk and she offered it to me on a plate but I had a rush of common sense, or possibly self-preservation, and refused. I'm not one for sloppy seconds and sloppy one thousand nine hundred and thirty second's is just too much. I think her gynaecologist must examine her by video link because I couldn't imagine getting that close to her.

'Get everything sorted, Richie?' Carol had finished her coffee and doughnut. She had sugar on her chin and a bit of strawberry jam on the corner of her mouth. It made her look as if she'd been in a fight. I pointed at my mouth and she wiped hers with the back of her hand.

'Thanks love, wouldn't look good to the punters would it? Now, I've got a little job for you this afternoon. A valuation has come up and it's a big one. Michael from head office was going to do it but he's gone sick, so I'd like you to go. It's an old lady who's lived there for years and wants to downsize. From what I remember, it's about seven bedrooms with a big chunk of land and a few outbuildings. If we can get this one, then the heat will be off for a while. What do you think?'

I was quite taken aback by this one. It was a lot of responsibility for someone with not a great deal of experience.

'Love to, just give me the details and appointment time and I'll get over there and do the business. I'll need the car though, as I walked in.'

Carol went off to get the details and I started to get to grips with the day's post and emails. My desk was in the window. For the majority of the time, it wasn't too bad; I could ogle at the young girls as they walked by my vantage point, which was a bonus in the summer. The main trouble was that I had a direct view across the road to the other estate agents, and sat at the window desk, exactly the same as me, was Timothy Sharples. We'd often glare at each other across the street, then I'd laugh and think that with all his public school education and privileges, he'd ended up in the same job as me. The rumour was that his dad had wangled him the job as the boss was a friend of his from the golf club. It also helped that his dad also had a major financial stake in the company. The fact of the matter was that Ena wasn't qualified or intelligent enough to fulfil his dad's expectations. Having him work there was a problem for me, though, as we would meet up on occasions. I was quite cool about it but he wasn't, so I had to be on my guard. I glanced across; he wasn't in his seat. Out doing a valuation or viewing probably.

'Who are you bringing to the awards dinner on Saturday, Richie?'

Tina had finished filing her half-inch long plastic nails. How she could type with nails like that I didn't have a clue. I certainly wasn't taking you; it wasn't much, but I did have a bit of a reputation to keep intact.

'I'm not sure, Tina. I've got so many to choose from, I just don't know which one to take. Much the same as you, probably.'

Only she didn't know the names of the guys she'd been with. One of my mates, who'd been with her, said he knew when she'd had an orgasm because she dropped her chips. Classy.

The problem for me was that I didn't have anyone to take. Sarah was lined up to grace my arm on the estate agents' big night of the year but there was no chance of that now. Perhaps Nicola would come?

'I know who I'm taking but I just can't make my mind up of what to wear. I don't know whether to go classy, you know, all done up with a fancy hairdo or just dress normally. What do you think?'

What I thought was a short skirt, high heels and a cleavage so big and tight you could crack a walnut in it. And as for classy, it would be mutton dressed up as mutton.

'Just go with what you feel comfortable in. Whatever you wear, I'm sure it'll be stunning. Excuse me a minute, I've got to make a couple of phone calls.' I didn't have to really but she was doing my head in. She was starting to do her lashes now.

I got the details from Carol and did what research I could on the house I was to view in the afternoon. It certainly looked impressive but I would guarantee that it would need some work doing on it. I checked the rolls and indeed a single lady lived there. Perhaps her husband had died some time back because I couldn't find a trace of any person other than her for quite a few years.

Research done and post sorted, I grabbed the car keys and set off for the valuation via the sandwich shop. I should have made myself something but, with all the stress in the morning, I didn't get around to it. Besides, the shop butties were better than mine and I got the chance to chat to the girls behind the counter. It was Innuendo City. 'Would you like to see my baps, Richie?' 'Here, feel how fresh and firm they are.' 'Ooh, I do like a nice big cream squirt.' 'You can have my cherry if you like.' It went on and on, but it was funny and harmless and I always left with a smile on my face and an extra big filling in my sandwich.

I ate in the car listening to the radio. I liked the sports channel so I could catch up on the weekend's games and gossip. The chat down the pub always came around to sport so if you weren't up to speed you felt a bit of a gooseberry.

Sandwich finished, and it was time to go. No food spills on my shirt or trousers; big bonus. I didn't want to turn up looking like I'd just come from the soup kitchen having drunk a bottle of cheap cider. As mum said, you only have one chance to make a first impression. Too true.

I rolled into the drive of the big house to find an old white Audi Quattro parked in front of it. I knew at once whose car it was, and just like the Kebab Shop on Saturday night, I knew whose voice it was at once; Timothy Sharples. The old lady was having a number of viewings and Ena was obviously doing this one. I parked up and decided to wait until he came out. I didn't want to knock on the door whilst he was still there.

The wait was only a couple of minutes. Ena was coming out the front door with the old lady, all smiles and laughter. He was as false as a porn star's tits. I didn't wait for him to get into his car; if I had, he would think I was too scared to meet him. I got out and slowly walked to the front door. Ena had turned and was walking towards me and his car. His expression had changed now to one of anger and hatred. I just looked him in the eye and smiled which wound him up even more. The words spat from his mouth.

'What the fuck are you doing here? This is my sale. She didn't tell me she'd asked for any other agents.'

He was obviously upset and more than a little angry. First impressions of the house were that there was a fair lump of commission to be had here.

'I often pop over to see my great aunt during my lunch break. I expect you two must have been talking about me and how she values my input into her affairs.'

Ena was rocked back on his heels by that one. He could see his big fat commission and slaps on his back from the regional manager going for a ball of chalk.

'Now, if you've finished up here, why don't you take a big fuck-off pill before I have you done for trespass.'

He jumped into his car and floored it out of the gravel drive. I walked up to the old lady at the door who was eyeing the deep furrows as he slewed away into the distance.

'My, he left in a hurry. And look at the mess he's made of my driveway.' Ena had not left as good an impression on the lady as he'd left on the drive.

'You just can't get the staff these days, Mrs Edgar. I'm sorry; I'm presuming it is Mrs Edgar? My name's Richard. You spoke to Carol at our estate agency earlier this morning. She couldn't make it, so I'm afraid you're stuck with me.'

As charming as ever. I wondered if that's why she sent me, having talked to the lady earlier.

'Richard? That was my husband's name you know. Sadly he's long gone, but he's still up here.' She tapped the side of her head and smiled.

I took an instant liking to her. She seemed a bit mischievous with a sparkle in her eye that you sometimes see in older people who still have an appetite for life. I wished she really was my great aunt.

'Have you ever lost anyone close to you, Richard?' It wasn't put in a sad way. Just a plain, matter-of-fact question.

'Actually, yes I have. I lost my mother last week in Tesco.' I paused for a second.

'It was in the wines and spirits aisle. It turned out alright though; I found her two minutes later in frozen foods. First signs of dementia, I think.'

It just came out and at first I thought I'd made a huge mistake, but she began to laugh.

'I do love a sense of humour. It's sadly lacking in what friends I have left. All they want to talk about is colostomy bags or how many times they have to get up in the night for a pee. Come in and have a cup of tea and then you can look around my modest little house.'

'First impressions are that it's far from modest, Mrs Edgar, and I'd love that cup of tea.'

She took me into the kitchen and made us both a cup of tea. There were two empty cups on the side; presumably

Sharples had been treated as well. Tea in hand, we went into the front room and sat overlooking the garden. Mrs Edgar then gave me her life story. She pointed out various family members and friends from photographs around the room. She'd certainly had a varied and interesting life. Together with her husband, they had worked and travelled the world in the service of the Foreign Office. She didn't say much as to what they did but concentrated mainly on the countries and cities they'd lived in and visited. There's so much that us youngsters can learn from people like this but, in too many young people's eyes, the elderly are just doddery old farts who smell of cabbage and piss.

Quite simply, I found her fascinating. Before I knew it we had been chatting for over an hour.

'I'm sorry, Mrs Edgar, but I'd better get on and do my valuation or I won't have a job to go back to.' She laughed a lovely little high-pitched warble.

'Don't worry about that. The young man who came earlier has given me a value so you have time for another cup of tea, Richard.'

'With all due respect I'd like to have a look for myself. Call it professional pride. Besides, he might as bad a valuer as he is a driver.'

'Well I'll put the kettle on anyway while you go about your business.' She went off to the kitchen leaving me alone with her photographs and memories and a room full of old black and white photos. By the look of it, Mrs Edgar was quite a stunner in her day.

Time to get to work. It took longer than I thought to get around the house and grounds. The grounds themselves were about two acres with a few outhouses scattered in amongst the trees. Situated where it was, this place was worth about one and a half million as it stood. With planning permission for a few houses in the grounds, you would be looking at considerably more.

'All finished, Mrs Edgar.'

She was pouring another cup of tea for us both as I walked into the kitchen.

'So, how much do you think my little pile would fetch on the current market, Richard?' This sounded like a test rather than a straight-forward question.

I gave her my valuation but qualified it with the costs of some renovation inside and out, as well as explaining the potential value with regards to the land and planning permission. She looked at me for a moment, appraising what I'd told her.

'Did you speak to Mr Sharples as he left?'

'In a manner of speaking. Let's just say we don't send each other Christmas cards anymore; not that we ever did.'

'So he didn't discuss his valuation of my property?'

'No he didn't. Basically we only talk to trade insults. Is there a problem, Mrs Edgar?'

She didn't reply immediately. She was deep in thought for a few moments.

'I'm not really sure, Richard. As I hope you've noticed, I'm not a senile old lady. I still have full use of all my faculties and like to keep abreast of the world around me, including house prices. I've been toying with the idea of selling up and moving to south Devon. My son lives in a little village just outside of Plymouth. It's right on the coast with a lovely little National Trust beach. Wembury; do you know it, Richard?'

'I'm afraid not. I've been to Cornwall a couple of times but never south Devon.'

'Anyway I digress. I didn't tell the other gentleman I was having any other valuations so I presume he assumed his was to be the only one. I deliberately didn't tell you his valuation either.'

I was starting to get a bit uneasy about this. Visions of Miss Marple started to flash through my mind.

'You see Richard, your valuation and Mr Sharples valuation are quite a bit different. In fact, they are very different.'

Sweat was breaking out on my brow and I was starting to feel a bit sick. I was sure I had been pretty much spot on with my valuation but if she didn't agree and sent a complaint to the office; my fireworks would be well and truly pissed on.

'I'm sorry Mrs Edgar, but if you're not happy with my valuation, maybe we could run through it and you could let me know where you disagree with it?'

She looked at me quizzically for a moment.

'No, no Richard, it's not you I'm concerned about; it's Mr Sharples. He has valued my house for exactly one million pounds. He says that it needs substantial renovation which will put off a number of buyers and has priced it to sell. I also asked him about the possibility of building in the grounds. He said it was highly unlikely that I would get permission due to access problems and also the council wouldn't allow the trees to be chopped down. What do you think?'

I knew what I thought; that Timothy Sharples was a lying, conniving little shit. I was reasonably happy with my valuation and so was Mrs Edgar. She knew the value of her house before she called us out; she just wanted a professional confirmation. The fact that Sharples had undervalued her house by half a million pounds had seriously upset her. There was no way he could have made such a fundamental error in valuation. What compounded it were his comments about refurbishment and planning permission. The refurbishment was cosmetic and wouldn't cost a fortune. And as for access and trees, well that was complete bollocks. You could gain access to any new buildings on the land with no problem and the trees could be worked out between the architects and the council.

Sharples was pulling a scam and Mrs Edgar knew it. There had long been rumours about certain agents undervaluing the properties of vulnerable clients. Just go along, promise that you can give them a discounted rate of commission, which in most cases you do anyway, and give them a selling price much less than the market rate. All you have to do then is ring up your dodgy property developer mate who pops round that afternoon with a bundle of cash and the promise of a quick sale. Everyone's happy with the outcome. The developer gets a cheap house and a shed load of profit. The agent gets a big backhander but a reduced sales commission and the seller gets to sell their house quickly but at a big loss to them. The problem for Sharples in this case is that he assumed he was dealing with a stupid old lady and that he would have sole agency. That was obviously why he looked a bit shaken when I turned up.

I explained to Mrs Edgar exactly what I thought was going on. The problem was, all Sharples had to do was say he'd made a mistake in his valuation and there was nothing anyone could do. No comeback at all, just a genuine mistake.

'You knew all of this before you asked me to value the house didn't you, Mrs Edgar?'

'Yes I'm afraid I did. And I'm sorry for keeping you for so long but I had to be sure you weren't in some way in league with Mr Sharples. The problem now is what I do about it; if anything.'

She thought for a minute before continuing.

'Would you do me a favour please, Richard and not mention any of this to anyone? I haven't made up my mind to sell yet but if I do, I will contact you through your office. In the meantime, I have a little bit of thinking to do. Now, I expect you want to get back to work. I've kept you long enough. It's been a pleasure talking to you. It's not often I get new company. If ever you're passing, do call in for a spot of tea and if you ring before you come round I might even bake you a cake.'

I said my goodbyes and sat in the car a bit shell-shocked. What should have been a straightforward valuation had turned into a bag of worms. I'd have to keep my suspicions about Ena to myself for the moment or he could have me for slander. I'd have a word with Martin; he might have some idea if there was anything that anyone could do.

I had a headache. Despite that, my thoughts went to Wednesday night and my date with Nicola. I was getting quite excited. It took me back to my first couple of dates in school when you got butterflies in your stomach and worried about your kissing technique. It was years ago since I would spend hours before a date practising kissing on my arm but I still worried. I remember when my first girlfriend stuck her tongue in my mouth; I thought my eyes would pop out or even worse - she might get pregnant.

There were only a couple of days to go.

Chapter Four

Wednesday came around fairly quickly. I'd been busy in the office but hadn't mentioned the potential problem between Mrs Edgar and Sharples to Carol. There were a couple of times when I'd caught Ena looking over at me from his window desk. He seemed to be deep in thought. I wasn't surprised; I had something on him that could possibly destroy both his career and reputation. The problem for me was that I had no proof beyond his dodgy valuation. I could see him trying to work out what I'd pieced together and what might be the outcome for him. For now, I was keeping my mouth shut and my head down.

I hurried home from the office that evening and had a quick bite to eat, followed by a long shower with lots of smelly shower gel. If the advert was right, then I would be fighting off the girls on my walk across the park to the pub.

Unfortunately for me, there weren't hordes of bikini-clad nymphomaniacs in the park; just a few curious dogs who wanted to sniff my leg. My confidence in the power of advertising was waning, along with my confidence in my personal hygiene. It was too late now. I was already a little late, but I would make that up later by paying for the meal at the Italian.

I hoped she would like the pub. It was an old-fashioned pub which still had all of its original features. The only thing it didn't have was a huge cloud of cigarette smoke. Apart from that, it was pretty much as it was fifty years ago, only with *Sky* TV as well now.

As I got close to the pub, I recognised a car outside; it was Vic's. I knew the lads were out tonight, but we usually went into town. We didn't often go for the quieter pubs because there wasn't enough eye candy about. As I got to the front window, I could hear them talking.

'I tell you what; it was like trying to dance with a barrage balloon. I couldn't get my arms anywhere near around to her back. I reckon if she stood on my feet, I would end up in A&E with them looking like the leftovers of the Sunday chicken roast.'

Devon was in full swing. They must have been there for a little while because both Martin and Devon were on their second pint.

'I think we definitely split the award for Saturday night, Vic. We are the Rhino Hunt champions. You didn't even come close. What was that you were talking to anyway?'

Martin took a swig of beer and waved his hand dismissively.

'It doesn't matter anyway, Vic; we won. Mind you, Richie tried joining in at the end but I'm afraid he didn't try anywhere near hard enough.'

This was all going too far. If Nicola was inside, listening to the three of them, she could get the wrong impression of Saturday. Why the hell did they choose this pub of all nights?

I opened the front door and the three of them watched me walk into the pub. They lifted their glasses and shouted in my direction. All three of them said at the same time, 'Hi Richie, didn't think you were coming out.' 'Beers on you, mate!' 'Come and talk about Saturday.'

I scanned the bar hoping not to see that black shiny hair but my hope was in vain. Sat right behind them, with her back to the door, was Nicola. The hair was unmistakeable. She must have been on time and had probably heard everything they'd been saying for quite a while.

'Hi guys. Listen, I'm not actually here to meet up with you, I'm here to see someone else.'

With that she stood up; still with her back to the four of us. As she slowly turned around to face me, I could see the pain in her eyes. At that moment, I felt the biggest arsehole on the planet. This time, she did have pools in her eyes but these were tears, real tears.

She walked around the tables and stood in front of me, ignoring the other three.

'Is this why you brought me here tonight? To show me off as a prize, what was it, munter? You know I actually thought you were a bit different from the rest and I suppose I was right. You're worse, you callous bastard. How could you be so mean and heartless? I should have listened to my friends.'

The tears were flooding down her face now but she was managing to hold it together, probably through sheer anger unfortunately.

'I can explain Nicola; it's not what it looks like. Please believe me.' I would have gone down on my knees but it was clear it wouldn't have made any difference.

'I hope you rot in hell, you bastard.' She almost spat the words in my face. And with that last show of vitriol, she pushed passed me and left through the nearest door. I ran after her. She was already getting into her car.

'Nicola, please, let me explain.'

I made the mistake of standing in the road by her window. She looked gutted, but it didn't lessen her driving skills. She slammed it into first and let the clutch out. The front tyres bit and she pulled out into the road. I had to jump out of the way or I would have been caught by the rear

94

wheels. My lip reading isn't very good but I'm sure I caught the word 'bastard' as she flashed by.

I stood in the middle of the road watching the car roar away. I don't think I've ever felt so bad or guilty in my life. She must have heard the lads describing Saturday night and figured I'd picked her up as part of Rhino Hunt. What else would she think? Christ, I felt bad. I walked back into the pub and found them staring into their beer, not wanting to make eye contact with me. Finally, Vic spoke up.

'Richie, listen, sorry mate. We had no idea. We didn't recognise her when we came in and we didn't have any idea you were coming out.' They all mumbled sorry over their pints.

'OK lads, I suppose I'm to blame. I should have told you what I was doing but to be honest, I thought you might take the piss out of me. Stupid.'

They could tell I was upset. Devon went to the bar and got a round in. This time, Vic had a softie as he was driving. I didn't have to look in the dictionary this time; the boys were genuinely sympathetic.

'You'll have to ring her and explain, mate. You can't leave her like that.'

Martin was right, but I knew she wouldn't answer her phone. I didn't know where she lived or where she worked. It suddenly dawned on me that I knew absolutely nothing about her. I knew her first name was Nicola, but not her surname. I didn't even know if she lived in town. I knew she drove a red Mini Cooper but I couldn't remember the registration. I knew sweet FA, basically. However, I did have her phone number. She might not answer but I was sure she'd read a text. You always read texts because they're just so impersonal. It cheered me up a bit.

'If any of you say there's plenty more fish in the sea, I swear I'll crap on your tortoise.'

I don't know why I said it. I suppose I didn't want to threaten my best mates with a bit of violence.

Martin laughed but Vic and Devon looked at me and then each other with a bemused expression.

'I'll explain one day soon,' looking at them both in turn.

Martin stood up, finishing his beer.

'And on that note, I'm afraid I've got to leave you chaps. Richie's not the only one with a date tonight. Catch you in the week. And sorry again mate.' He looked me in the eye and meant what he said.

'Who's the lucky girl, Mart?' Dev was more than a little curious. 'It's not one of Cinderella's sisters, is it?'

'Sorry mate, but I can't tell you. If I do, I'll have to kill you.'

I had a sneaky suspicion, so I chipped in,

'Or maybe her stupid husband more like.' Martin shot me a look which just confirmed what I was thinking.

'I hope you know what you're doing mate. Just be careful, OK?'

Martin headed out of the door and started to walk up the road. He didn't have his car, so he must be going to be picked up. If it was who I thought it was, then I was a bit jealous. I bet Mrs Pratt would be a great shag. Living with the most boring guy on the face of the planet, her sex life wouldn't exactly break any bed frames. I bet her husband's idea of adventurous sex was to have a shag on a Tuesday instead of a Saturday. I suddenly felt very lonely.

'What are you boys up to at the weekend?' They both seemed to relax as I'd changed the subject away from Nicola.

Devon was the first to jump in.

'I'm working this coming one mate, so I'm afraid you'll have to count me out of any fuck-ups you've got planned for yourself or any other girlfriends you've got stashed away.'

As soon as he said it, he knew it was the wrong thing.

'Christ, sorry Richie, I didn't mean to say it like that. It just came out.'

'But you did say it Devon and you know what? You're right. I've lost two girls in less than a week and to make things even worse, I haven't got any girlfriends stashed away. I wish I had.'

I explained to them that I had the estate agents' annual bash on Saturday night and, as a result of Sarah dumping me and Nicola thinking I was an insensitive arsehole, my options of taking a ravishing young girl to parade on my arm as eye candy had severely diminished.

'Fancy another beer?' I needed another one but didn't want to drink alone. Vic and Dev looked a bit sheepish. They could tell I was set for self-destruction through alcohol but they didn't want another drink and didn't want me to have one either.

'Sorry mate, I'm driving and I've got work tomorrow and so have you, for that matter.'

Vic was sounding like my mum but he did have a point. I did have work and looking over someone's house smelling like you'd used a pint of lager as aftershave doesn't do your sales' prospects any good.

'I suppose you're right mate. It's not a good idea on a 'school night'. I'd better be off home and think about what I'm going to do about Nicola on the way. Have a safe one this weekend, Dev. Maybe catch up for a few the one after?'

'Sure thing, Richie. You be careful too. You seem to have the Midas touch at the moment but instead of gold everything is turning into shit. Just be careful when you have a piss. Wear gloves or something!'

He had a big smile on his face. He could rip the piss out of me and make it sound like he was doing me a favour. Bastard.

We walked out of the pub. Vic offered me a lift but I fancied a walk across the park to try and focus on what I was going to do about Nicola. Vic was just getting into his car when I had an idea.

'What are you doing Saturday night, Vic?'

He was half into his car when he stopped and thought for a second.

'Come to think of it, nothing as it happens. As the three of you are working or partying, I guess I'm Billy No-mates. Why do you ask?'

'Well, I'd like to take someone along to the dinner but as I've totally fucked up my dance card, I was wondering if you'd like to come along?'

Vic looked a bit surprised. I could tell he was weighing up the pros and cons of the offer. In the main, he would be thinking of the ramifications for me. Me, supposed straight guy, turning up at a dinner with a gay guy, not exactly on his arm, but accompanying him nevertheless.

'Have you thought this through and, in particular, what consequences it could have for your reputation both socially and at work?' It sounded a bit formal.

It was my turn to get the little grey cells working. I could take who the hell I wanted to. If people were so narrow-minded as to talk behind my back and spread rumours then, as far as I was concerned, they could go and boil their heads.

Besides, I would be far more at ease with Vic at the dinner than a young girl who I'd never introduced to any of my work colleagues before.

'I've thought about it, Vic and if you'd like to come along, that would be great. You never know, you might enjoy it.'

'In that case, I'd love to. There's one thing though, I don't look good in a dress and the last time I wore high heels, I sprained my ankle. So if it's alright with you I'll wear a suit and tie.'

He climbed into his car and started the engine. As he pulled away, he wound down the window.

'Give me a text about the times and stuff and I'll see you on Saturday,' and for the second time within an hour I was standing in the road watching a car pull away from me down the road. I couldn't imagine Vic in a dress or high heels; perhaps it's a good thing that some things remain completely private.

I started my slow, solemn walk across the park. My little grey cells weren't working very well when it came to Nicola. All I had was a mobile phone number but I wasn't sure of the next step to take. A text would probably be better than a call. Right, a text it would be then but how should I phrase it and what should I say?

I sat down on a bench to think. It was starting to get dark and people were heading for the exits. A few people were wandering around but I didn't take too much notice. I was wrapped up in my grovelling text to Nicola. It would be electronic protestation.

It began to dawn on me just what a twat I'd been to lose these two girls. I could see the annual awards ceremony in a West End theatre for the *Wanker of the Year*. A famous TV host reading out the nominations might say,

'And the first of this year's nominations is, Richard Head, for losing two gorgeous girls in the space of five days, oh, and asking one of their mums if she fancied having her knickers ripped off. Then, if that wasn't enough, there was the humiliation of the other girl in front of his friends. What an outstanding performance.'

A little later, a lesser-known-celebrity would appear on stage and pull out an envelope with my name inside. I wouldn't make an acceptance speech but at this moment I would certainly accept the award for *Wanker of the Year*. I richly deserved it.

I looked up and saw that a middle-aged guy was wandering towards me out of the gloom. As he got level with me, he stopped and turned in my direction. He looked a bit creepy for my liking.

'Hello, would you like some company?' The words came out very suggestively and I suddenly realised that it was dark and I was alone in a park sitting on a bench doing nothing in particular. I looked up and his hand had gone down to the front of his jeans,

'Sorry mate, but the only solid things I put in my mouth are food and my toothbrush and I'm not cleaning my teeth with that,' nodding to his crotch.

Too much. I'd just invited my gay friend to a work's dinner and now I was being accosted in a dark park. I needed to get home and watch some heterosexual porn on *Freeview* to get some perspective into my sex life, or lack of, at the present moment.

I legged it across the park and crashed through the front door. Mum was watching the TV.

'Hi Mum, is everything ok?'

She looked up from her programme.

'Fine thanks, Richie. You sound a bit out of breath. Is everything alright?'

Mum's intuition, I suppose. She could always suss me out.

'Not really but nothing for you to worry about. Is Sis in?'

Mum explained that she was out at a friend's and would be back later. She made me a cuppa and we chatted for a while but I had to get that text sent to Nicola tonight. For one thing, it would make me feel better, and for another, I hoped it would show her that I did actually have some feelings.

It took me about an hour to complete the message and about a quarter of my monthly text allowance.

I sat in bed looking at the *Send* button. Had I been too grovelling? Did it need a bit more humour or did it just make me out to be a desperate stupid twat? All of them probably, but it didn't stop me finally hitting the *Send* button. It was too late now.

I had basically given Nicola a full explanation of our drunken Saturday night and the Rhino Hunt. I told her about the terrible twins and Martin's and Devon's close call. I tried to convey my feelings from when I first met her and that, despite the misunderstanding in the pub, I wanted to see her again. The truth can be the best option sometimes. I hoped that it would be on this occasion.

There was no point in staring at my phone as I doubted she would ever reply. The closest I would probably get to her again was being chased down the road by a Mini Cooper, with her trying to run me over.

It was late and I needed some sleep.

Just as I was dropping off, I heard the throaty roar of an *E-Type Jag* pull up on the Pratt family's drive. It had to be

Mrs Pratt at this time. Rodney would be tucked up in bed with his hot chocolate watching *Newsnight* by now. The garage door opened and the Jag pulled in. I could hear the click clack of Mrs P's shoes after she had closed the door and walked up to the front of the house. It might have been my imagination but I swear it sounded like she was walking bowlegged.

The first thing I did when I woke up was check my mobile. There were no messages. The text had definitely gone, so either she hadn't read it or wasn't going to reply. Well, at least I'd tried. 'See how the day goes and maybe send another tomorrow,' I thought. Maybe a picture message of me with my cock in a pair of garden shears with the caption 'Can't live without you. Off to become a monk'. I thought of the Nilsson song but as I'd only just met her, it was a bit O.T.T.

I was the first to arrive at work. It was a bit unusual but I thought that it might take my mind off things. Carol arrived shortly after, and then Tina strolled in, late as usual. With the post sorted, it was time for a cup of tea and to get about the day's business. I was going through some paperwork when Tina called over.

'Are you taking your girlfriend on Saturday, Richie?' There was an inflection to her voice, almost a sneer, as if she knew I wasn't taking one. Not a girl anyway. Bitch.

Ever the diplomat, I didn't jump in with 'Fuck off you nosey, fuckin' witch and mind your own fuckin' business!' I just smiled at her and replied in the most nondescript voice I could manage.

'No Tina, I've been let down at the last minute by a couple of girls, so sadly neither of them will have the pleasure of meeting you.'

She looked at me for a minute trying to work out if I was taking the piss.

'So you've been dumped then and can't get anyone to come.'

It was a statement rather than a question. I was going to lose it very soon and diplomacy would be out the window. Try another tack.

'Actually Tina, I may have another friend lined up: Vic, if you must know.' There, no lies or animosity.

'Vic, have we met before?' She was starting to get interested.

'No I don't think you have. You may have met around town or maybe even chased after the same bloke, so if I were you, I'd keep a close eye on your boyfriend on Saturday. I take it you're bringing someone?' Again, no lies, but economical with the facts.

'Yeah 'course I'm bringing someone. His name's Clint, if you must know. He's a bouncer down town. We met the other night outside his club and hit it off straight away. Well to be honest, I'd collapsed outside after too many shots and he helped me get a taxi. He wrote his mobile number on one of my boobs with a message to ring him. Mind, it was a bugger to read the number upside down the following morning.' She seemed genuinely impressed.

'And who said romance was dead? Sounds like quite a catch, Tina.' I was about to inject a bit more sarcasm but Carol evidently had had enough of our banter.

'Haven't you two got anything to do?' It was pointed at Tina rather than me.

'Oh Richie, I nearly forgot, Mrs Edgar rang yesterday evening. She wondered if you could pop in and see her the next time you were passing. I don't suppose it's about putting her house on the market with us is it? We could do with the commission off that sale.'

I wondered what she wanted. It might be about a sale but I had a nagging feeling it might be about Sharples. I still hadn't told anyone about his undervaluation.

'I'm tucked up today but I'll call round tomorrow morning. If it's a sale, I'll ring you straight away.'

That seemed to cheer her up a bit. She was getting anxious about the lack of sales and was also a little nervous about Saturday. She would be meeting other agents as well as our bosses and there was sure to be a bit of professional sniping and point scoring. For my part, I was looking forward to the dinner and presentations. I was under no pressure, not professionally anyway. The only slight problem I had was that Vic was my 'date' for the night. Too late now.

I was particularly looking forward to the speeches and one in particular. Apparently, one of the organisers had picked out Ena as a bright up-and-coming young thing and asked him to give a quick presentation on the market factors in our particular area. No doubt he was going to gloat about his firm's dominance of the market over us smaller agencies.

His selection might have had something to do with the clout his dad had in the area's property development business. He had his finger in a lot of property development pies and the word was that a lot of people were getting very rich on the back of it.

I had a little plan which might upset Mr Sharples' introduction to public speaking. With a bit of luck, a package would arrive either tomorrow or Saturday morning with the seeds - quite literally - of Ena's downfall.

Despite checking my phone for messages all day, I didn't receive any texts from Nicola but I'd received one from Martin. He was on duty and parked up by a local school. He stated that despite all the traffic signs, the only people who drove slowly past the school gates were paedophiles! He didn't elaborate but it didn't sound like he was having a good day.

I walked home after a hard day's work and another head-scratching session about Nicola. She'd received my text but still hadn't answered. Perhaps I should ring just to see if her mobile was switched on or maybe disconnected. I'd wait until I got home and try after dinner. If she'd been out for the day working then there would be more chance of her answering later in the evening.

Mum was still at work when I got home and Sis was upstairs in her room. I shouted up the stairs, but she yelled something about homework which I could just about hear above the strains of Lady Gaga, which really P P P Pissed me off, P P P Pissed me off.

There was a little note on the table telling me where the where-with-all was for tea and to start putting it together should I beat mum home. A little P.S. on the bottom told me there was a small package in my bedroom which had arrived in the early morning's post.

I forgot about dinner and rushed upstairs. There on the bed was a little package addressed to me. It was from a company which specialised in growing and selling speciality chillies.

Most people have heard of the Richter scale for earthquakes or the Beaufort scale for wind speed but not many have heard of the Scolville scale. It's a scale which measures heat; not heat as in Fahrenheit or Centigrade but heat as in how hot to the taste is a chilli pepper. When you mention hot chillies, a lot of people will think of a Scotch Bonnet, but the strength of these on the Scolville scale pales into insignificance compared to what I hoped I had in my little package.

I ripped at the packaging and out fell a small polythene bag which contained a couple of whole dried chillies: Naga chillies. These were probably some of the hottest chillies in the world and they were grown in England, believe it or not. Along with the chillies, there was some paperwork from the company which seemed, at first sight, to contain more health and safety information than anything about my chillies. This was encouraging.

I quickly read through the blurb. It advised handling the chillies with gloves on. If you crush them, then wear a mask and goggles. Above all, avoid contact with unprotected skin. Perfect.

I began to wonder what these little devils would do to you if you actually ate one. A while ago, an old mate of mine got a couple of Nagas off the net for a chilli-eating contest with his mate. His mate ate a whole Naga and was found an hour later in a state of partial paralysis and delirium. Subtle didn't seem to be an adjective which you often heard in the same sentence as Naga chilli.

The front door opened and in came Mum, no doubt anticipating the aroma of cooking but getting an earful of Beyoncé instead.

I rushed downstairs, full of apologies, saying I'd just got in from work and was just about to start dinner. As luck would have it, she had some sell-by-date expired pies which we could have with some quickly knocked-up mash. Not exactly your five a day but cheap, quick and easy. I'd probably pay for it in later life but, right at this moment, I couldn't give a rat's arse.

With a sumptuous meal of pie and mash over, it was time again to think about a text to Nicola. I'd decided that this would be the last one. If she didn't get back to me then I'd tried my best. You never know, I might run into her one night when I least expected it.

The words for the text didn't come easily. In fact they didn't come at all. I was looking at a blank screen. I'd said everything I could say in the previous text and added a little sentiment for good measure but it obviously wasn't enough. There was nothing else to say.

Finally I just tapped out a couple of lines:-

'I'm here if you want to talk. I still want to be your friend. I'm very Patsy Cline. Richard.'

I hoped she'd get the Patsy Cline bit. My mum used to play her records and one in particular had stuck in my mind. The opening lines were, '*I'm sorry. So sorry.*'

I hit *Send* and went off to bed. There was no bowlegged Mrs Pratt arriving home tonight. There was no text either. I slept with a conscience that was a little clearer than the previous night; not much, but a little. I was still in the running for *Wanker of the Year* but today, I thought I might get second place.

I called into work early the next day beating Carol and Tina again. The drive to Mrs Edgar's wasn't too bad traffic-wise but the occasional hold-up gave me a chance to people-watch from a car rather than on foot. I would try and work out what people did and where they were going. You could make up what you wanted because the only way to find out would be to jump out of the car and ask them, which was probably a good way of ending up in a police cell for the morning.

I was just pulling away from a set of traffic lights, about halfway over to Mrs Edgar's, when I noticed a girl walking in the opposite direction. The road was similar to the one where our office was - a selection of banks, sandwich shops and estate agents. The girl looked familiar as well. I strained for a better look and nearly rear-ended the bus in front. She glanced up at the last second and I saw who it was. It was Nicola's friend from the previous Saturday; the one who was giving me a lot of grief and was being very over-protective. I still hadn't worked that one out. Despite my crack at her about her double chin, she looked very smart this morning; if I had to put any money on it, I would say she was on her way to work. And if she was walking, then it couldn't be far from the traffic lights.

A little sense of optimism swept through me. I now had something else to go on other than just a mobile telephone number. The problem was that if Nicola didn't text back then it wouldn't be worth chasing up her friend. I half expected a call-back from her along the lines of Sarah's call on Sunday. It all felt so long ago but not to my ego; that was battered and bruised and resting up in intensive care. The prognosis was not good; it may recover with a dose of T.L.C. but I wasn't sure where I was going to get it from.

Mrs Edgar's house and gardens appeared in front of me. I couldn't remember anything from the traffic lights to where I was now. Auto-pilot had kicked in and got me through the traffic. Concentrate Richard, or you'll have an accident and won't be able to pay the insurance.

I pulled up outside her front door and, as I got to the bottom step, she was at the top to greet me. I could smell the aroma of fruit cake that wafted out from behind her. Despite her age, she had an air of confidence about her; it was a sort of inner strength that seemed to defy her advancing years. I began to wonder if it was some sort of drug you could get on the NHS. If it was, I might ask her for a few.

'How nice of you to come over so soon, Richard. I've just made a cup of tea and I've got a cake in the oven.' She seemed pleased to see me. With her family living away, she probably didn't get too many visitors.

She ushered me through the front door, talking away as she directed me into the front room.

'Now, how long have we got? I've got a few things I need to go over with you and I've got a favour to ask of you as well. I do hope you'll agree to help me.'

I was starting to get a bit intrigued but at the mention of a favour and help, I was apprehensive as well.

'I've got about half an hour before I need to go off for a viewing. Is that enough time for you, Mrs Edgar?'

'Yes, yes Richard. Now enough of this 'Mrs Edgar' business. It's far too formal. You must call me Lyn if we're going to be working together, so to speak.'

Before I could reply, she was out the door and getting tea and cake. I didn't like the sound of this 'working together'. She was making assumptions on my behalf and I wasn't sure what she wanted. A tray of tea and cake preceded her through the door. Before she started off again, I jumped in.

'I don't mean to be rude, Mrs Edgar.' She shot me a glance.

'Sorry, Lyn, but things are rushing ahead here and I'm not sure what you expect of me, or more to the point, what I can actually do for you. If it's about the other day, then I have to be very careful both on a professional and legal footing.'

We both looked at each other for a moment. Me, expectantly, and her, with an analytical expression. She was weighing me up and appeared to come to a decision.

'Firstly Richard, it is about the other day; Mr Timothy Sharples. I strongly suspect that you and Mr Sharples do not get on, on a professional or social level. I would go further to suggest that this animosity between the two of you goes back a number of years, possibly back to your school days.'

She was looking me straight in the eyes, gauging my reactions. I was starting to shift in the chair and feeling more than a bit uncomfortable, all of which was noted by Mrs Edgar.

'Mr Sharples is a dangerous and devious person Richard, and you underestimate him and his associates at your peril. What I am proposing is that we help each other to eliminate a problem that threatens us both - Timothy Sharples. I say threat to me but I believe he is far more of a threat to you. I've only met him once but he tried to steal half a million pounds of my money. If he walked into a bank and robbed them of that money he would spend a long time in jail, wouldn't he?'

I had to agree. She was painting Ena in a whole new light. She carried on.

'I know a little of his family and some of his close associates. That's not enough at the moment, but with your help, I – we - may be able to put some flesh on the bones of Mr Sharples' activities and put a stop to them before anyone else gets hurt.'

I didn't like the bit about getting hurt. However, she must have picked up on my discomfort and immediately clarified herself.

'I mean hurt in financial parlance rather than physical violence.'

'Lyn, I'd like to pick up on that point. As you correctly surmised, Sharples and I go back a long way and he is capable of violence. He's capable of inflicting it himself, if he thinks the odds are stacked in his favour, or he'll get someone else to carry out his dirty work. I've seen it all at first hand.'

It was her turn to fidget a bit at the thought of violence.

'All I am asking of you, Richard, is to keep your eyes open for me and supply me with a few addresses and properties you might come across during your work. It's not illegal or dangerous. You see, I don't think I'm the first gullible old lady that Mr Sharples has short-changed. There are some very desirable large properties in this town and if they could be acquired at a knockdown price and developed, then there would be a substantial profit for all concerned. Do you see where this is going, Richard?'

I certainly did. But I wasn't sure how I fitted in. I nodded an affirmation.

'All I ask of you, Richard, is that you keep your eyes open for properties along the lines of mine, properties that have been developed in the town over the last, say, two years. They probably haven't been on any agents' books other than Sharples' firm and then only on his for a matter of hours, so there will be no record as such. When you see a property, simply write down the address and get it to me however you want. Once I have the property details, all I'll do is a little research to see if my suspicions are correct. There, simple isn't it?'

I couldn't see any problems with her request. It wouldn't put me out in any way and it wasn't dangerous or illegal. If it gave me, or anyone for that matter, the chance to get one over Sharples, then I was up for it. I didn't let on that I would have done it even if it was illegal or dangerous.

'I'm in but I wouldn't ask any questions about Sharples, especially about his dad and businesses. They're friendly with an awful lot of people in this town and very well connected.'

I had the feeling she already knew that.

'There's something I don't understand about this, Lyn. You've only met Sharples once yet it seems like you're undertaking a vendetta against him. And once you start this vendetta, what's going to be the end result?'

'Firstly, Richard, let's not call it a vendetta. Let's call it an investigation; vendetta sounds far too personal. I know I've only met him once but I've met nasty, greedy people like him all through my life, believe me. I just don't like to see the weak and vulnerable suffer. So, if I can turn the tables in this instance and expose these people for what they are, I believe that society will be the better for our actions. Don't you agree?'

I was tempted to replace vendetta with crusade but thought better of it. She really had the bit between her teeth. I don't think I'd underestimated Ena but I was beginning to realise that I'd underestimated this nice little old lady sat before me.

'Now, I've rattled on enough for one day. It's probably about time you got about your business, isn't it Richard?' This was as subtle a kick out the door as I'd ever heard. She was gathering up the cups and herding me out of the house.

'You'll have to excuse me but I've got an old friend coming over soon and I need to tidy up before he arrives. I do hope you understand. Keep in touch, Richard and let's meet up soon. Goodbye.'

And with that, the door was closed behind me.

I wasn't exactly sure what I'd become a party to but as it was all in a good cause, I'd do what I could. I'd start on Monday; I had a bit too much on my plate today - a couple of valuations and a bit of shopping for tomorrow; splashing some cash on a new shirt and tie. You never know, I might be chatted up by a nice young secretary, taken back to her place and have my brains shagged out. I subconsciously looked up at the sky. There were no flying pigs.

Chapter Five

Vic and I met up at one of the town's central pubs for a few pints before the Presentation Dinner, the venue for which was a swish new hotel off the centre. It had a large conference-cum-ballroom which we were using for the evening's festivities. As with all these dinners, I always find it a bit more relaxing to have a few beers beforehand. It loosens you up a bit and it's a lot cheaper than buying drinks at the do. They're always extortionate prices and my pay doesn't run to that. Maybe one of the bosses will buy a drink or two for the hard working staff? Well, there was no chance of that.

We chatted as I scanned the clientele for any familiar faces, but I didn't see anybody I recognised. I was really looking for Nicola or one of her mates. There was still no text back from her and, quite frankly, I'd given up now. Ah well, a few beers tonight and who knows, I might meet up with another nice young nymphomaniac whose father runs a pub.

It was getting on for eight and we were cutting it a bit fine. After four quick pints, we were feeling no pain; just a nice warm glow around you and a sloshing sound in your belly when you walked.

'Come on, Vic, time to drink up and move out. I don't want to be late. I'm quite looking forward to tonight, aren't you?'

We were out of the pub and making the short walk to the hotel.

'To be honest, I'm looking forward to it as well. There'll be a lot of people who I haven't met before and a brief insight into the world of property. It should be interesting. Any fit blokes at these dinners?'

'Vic, mate, don't let me down. I'm already on thin ice all over town so, please just be a model of decorum. However, there's always an eclectic mix at these presentations. Before I forget, we're on a table for eight. Carol, my boss, will be there, along with her husband, Mike. He's a civil servant in the Ministry of Twigs or something. Nice bloke, but he's had a charisma bypass. There's Tina, who you may recognise from around town. She's our receptionist. She'll go for anything on two legs, and most of those on four. Basically, if it's got a pulse, she'll nail it. If we had one, she'd be captain of the Olympic shagging and drinking team. Be careful though, she's not as stupid as she looks. And watch her boyfriend, Clint. He's a bouncer downtown and I don't know much about him other than he's with Tina. Enough said, I suppose. The other two are our mortgage advisor and his missus; they're ok.'

I'd explained to Vic earlier that Ena was giving a speech, but I didn't let on that I had a little surprise for our arch enemy, should the opportunity arise. Time would tell; very shortly, according to my watch. We were a bit late.

We dashed into the hotel lobby and were shown the way to the presentation room. I quickly found our table and we sat down. We were the last to arrive and everyone already had a drink.

Tina and Carol looked at me questioningly. I knew what they wanted to say, 'You've brought a bloke!'

Vic got up and offered to get the first round in. He politely asked around the table, not expecting any takers, but Tina quickly downed what was left in her large glass and asked for another. It was like watching Moby Dick swallow some poor unfortunate seaman, but then again, I think she was well-practised at that.

'Richie, when you said Vic, I thought it was going to be a girl.'

114

Tina was going to go fishing again.

'No Tina, he's definitely a bloke. He's one of my oldest friends, as it happens.'

'But you said that we may have been out on the town chasing the same.....' She was about to say 'blokes' when two lights came on in her head. Firstly, I don't suppose she wanted Clint to know that she was a girl about town, although if he didn't know that by now then he must have the brains of an amoeba. Secondly, she realised that Vic was probably gay.

'You mean that he's, well, you know?' To give Tina her due, she didn't want to say it in company.

'Yes, Tina, he is.'

'But you're not, are you? Why else would you bring him? You don't drive on both sides of the road, do you?' The table was starting to take more than a little interest in our conversation. I needed to change the subject before Vic came back.

'No, Tina, I'm not and I don't. Sorry, but you haven't introduced me to you your boyfriend; Clint, isn't it?'

I offered my hand across the table,

'I've heard a lot about you from Tina. All good, I hasten to add.'

I'm glad I added that rider because he took my hand in what felt like a vice. His hand was like a bunch of bananas. The muscles rippled beneath his suit. This guy did some serious working out and maybe a few 'roids to enhance what the weights couldn't give him. His smile revealed that he wasn't on first-name terms with his dentist. I hoped that his IQ was higher than the amount of teeth on show. When he spoke, I was a bit taken aback; for such a big bloke, his voice didn't fit the frame. It was surprisingly high-pitched, almost feminine, but I wasn't about to point that out to him. My head was particularly fond of my shoulders and I didn't want them to go their separate ways.

'Nice to meet you, mate. You'll have to come by the club one night. Give me a nod and I'll get you in for nothing; call it doorman's perks. Did Tina tell you that's where we met?'

I wasn't sure how much I should know.

'Not really, Clint. She's quite a quiet person at work. You hardly know she's there most of the time. We're particularly proud of her charity work for the homeless and needy. She often finds them a bed for the night.' Bollocks, I'd gone too far again. Clint looked at Tina with a surprised expression.

'She doesn't talk about it, Clint, so it's better not to mention it. She's a real star and we love her to bits.'

I nearly jumped back from the table and beat the imaginary flames that were raging around my arse. Liar, liar, pants on fire.

Tina was giving me a look which would have turned most people to stone. Out the corner of my eye, I could see Carol trying desperately to keep it together.

Vic appeared over her shoulder with our drinks. Tina's eyes lit up at the thought of more alcohol, especially as it was free. My comments seemed to be forgotten for the moment, thank goodness.

A few people were starting to mingle among the tables. I could see Ena at his firm's three tables. They were at the front, near to the stage and the lectern. The wine and beer was flowing and the entire group seemed to be a bit pissed already. I noticed one of the guys at his table; if I wasn't mistaken, it was his dad. Then I spotted another bloke.

'Vic, have a gander at the front row tables. The guy in the middle of the left hand one, isn't that Fido?'

Vic glanced over and smiled as he recognised an old friend. Well, he wasn't exactly a friend. He used to hang around with Ena and his mates when they were at school together. He was a grammar school kid and a full-on geek. As a result, he was picked on unmercifully whenever we got the chance. He was into computers and wore very thick glasses and even Ena and his mates got pissed off with him in the end. But there he was, sat at one of the top tables and obviously well in with the faces.

Fido had a phobia about dogs. Unfortunately, the phobia was caused by the four of us. We caught him in the park on the way home from school. As usual, we took things a bit too far and, as a result, Fido, or Graham, I think his real name is, became petrified of dogs. In a nutshell, we decided that he shouldn't be crossing through our territory. He needed to be shown a lesson and made to be an example to other trespassers. Unfortunately, kids of twelve and thirteen can be very cruel indeed. Earlier in the day, we'd had a history lesson about the Wild West and in particular, the red Indians. Of course, the teacher touched upon some of the methods of torture they would employ against the settlers and soldiers they captured. I remember he only did this to keep the lads' attention.

We caught Fido and decided to torture him. Martin, for some strange reason, had a jar of beef stock in his haversack. We debagged Fido and tied him on the ground between four small trees using the belts that secured the trees to their wooden stakes. Martin then got his jar of thick brown stock and poured it all over Fido's meat and two veg. Devon managed to entice two rather large dogs away from their owners and, before you knew it, they were lapping up the thick beefy liquid off poor Fido's nether regions. He still had his school blazer on, and was naked from the waist down, shouting and pleading at the dogs to stop licking his bollocks. I can still remember his screams as we ran away across the park laughing our heads off. We weren't laughing later that evening when the police knocked on all our doors and read us the riot act. If we'd been any older, we would have really been in the shit; big time. Neither did we laugh years later, when we found out the psychological damage we'd caused him. Nevertheless, we still called him Fido, just for old time's sake.

All the other tables in the room were full and people were starting to throw drinks down their necks at an alarming rate. It was obvious that a lot of tables were on free drinks supplied by their companies. Unfortunately, our sales over the year dictated that we wouldn't be so fortunate tonight. The bosses were probably drinking on the business and no doubt it would be written off against some expense account with tax relief claimed somewhere along the line. Later in the evening, Vic and I might have to do a bit of minesweeping for a few drinks - pinching drinks off very drunk people or waiting for someone to put theirs down when they go off to the loo. It's relatively risk-free and saves a fortune.

Our host for the evening was walking on to the stage, and up to the microphone. He was the regional manager for one of the local agencies and, as it was his company's turn this year to make all the arrangements; the dubious honour and workload had fallen to him. A very polite round of applause welcomed him onto the stage with just the odd heckle. The night was obviously young. Give it a couple of hours and the odd tomato or roast spud might get launched onto the stage.

He kicked off with the usual thanks to everyone for coming and how great the hotel had been for staging this year's presentations and how supportive his staff had been and.....

.....after about three or four minutes the entire audience was rapidly losing the will to live. This guy could bore for Britain. His voice, after a while, was like fingernails being dragged across a blackboard. Everyone was shifting uncomfortably in their chairs and looking at their watches. If Martin used this guy to question suspects, they'd be begging to confess after a couple of minutes. Unfortunately, it would be deemed as inadmissible due to the confession being given under duress or torture. I'd go for torture.

The poor guy eventually got the message that he'd lost his audience as half of them were talking amongst themselves. He wound up rather quickly after a particularly poor joke about an estate agent's wife, a pig and a tube of hair remover. When no one laughed it was the final straw.

The food started to arrive at the tables.

'Thank fuck for that. I'm fuckin' starving.' Tina's fork nearly went into the back of the waiter's hand as he put the starter down in front of her. She got a heavily sarcastic 'Bon appetit' from him as she stuffed a huge piece of melon and Parma ham into her mouth. It was so big that, for a moment, she looked just like the Joker as it wedged across her teeth and gums.

Polite conversation flowed around the table as everybody tried to ignore Tina's empty glass. Every few seconds, she'd pick it up and drain an imaginary few drops out of it before banging it on the table. It developed into a game of poker. Who would blink first? Eventually it was Clint who bought her a drink. Carol also took the opportunity to put a couple of bottles of wine on the table just before the main course.

The rest of the meal passed without any real incident. The only thing of note was that Clint took off his jacket to reveal his huge, tattooed arms. You wouldn't want to tangle with this guy; I reckon on a good day he could bench-press an elephant. It looked as if he came from a good family because all of his tattoos were spelt correctly and it would appear that he loved his mum and dad.

As the meal drew to an end, I became increasingly interested in the three top tables and in particular, Ena's. For my windup to work, my timing would have to be spot on. I fumbled with the two little airtight jars I had in my jacket pocket.

The drinks were flowing on their table. Ena was to make a small speech before the proper presentations. I would have to gauge when his speech was about to start and time my 'chance' meeting with him. I could see that he was getting a bit nervous. He kept looking at a couple of sheets of paper which would probably be his speech or prompts. His index and forefingers constantly pulled at his shirt collar to try and cool himself down. Words of encouragement and wine came in a steady stream from the group around him. It wouldn't be long now.

The tables had all been cleared and the Master of Ceremonies for the evening was getting himself together. He would be up on stage for a minute, and then invite Ena to come up and do his bit, before the cake and arse really started. It was time for a piss. I wanted to meet Ena on his way in to the toilets for his nervous pee before his speech. Judging by how much he'd drunk in the last fifteen minutes, without a piss, his back teeth must be floating by now.

I hurried through the tables towards the loos. Ena still hadn't got up. Once in the loos, I headed for the nearest trap and pulled out my two jars. Thirty seconds later and no one had come in behind me. It was now or never. I left the trap and headed out of the door slowly, as I needed to meet Ena on his way in. As I walked across the carpet towards the hall, he was walking towards me. His top lip curled when he recognised me.

'Thought you'd be here somewhere, you little shit. Stuck with the rest of your loser pals in the cheap seats, I suppose.'

He stood there waiting for me to take the bait. However, it wasn't me who was going to take the bait, old chum; not tonight.

I stood in front of him and pulled a resigned and downbeat look on my face. A sort of 'Yeah, you're right, Mr Top Table, sir. I bow before your superior intellect and bank balance.'

'Listen, Tim, I know we've had our differences over the years, but I know how important this is for all of us tonight. If your speech goes well then we could all benefit, so, good luck.'

He looked a bit shocked; even more so when I grabbed his hand and shook it. Before he could reply, I was off across the hall, but not to my table; I took a quick detour across to the other toilets to wash my right hand.

As I got back to the table, Vic was giving me the evils. He was perplexed, angry and aghast, all at once.

'What the fuck was that all about? Shaking Ena's hand? That fucker hates us and you're getting all matey with him.'

I got a bit closer to his ear so nobody could hear me.

'Sorry, Vic but needs must. Hopefully in a couple of minutes, you'll get some idea about what I was doing. It might not be pretty but it sure as hell will be funny.'

The opening speech was well under way when Ena got back to his seat. A quick look at his notes and a few deep breaths showed how nervous he was. With a bit of luck, he'll be starting to sweat a bit under his designer threads. Those little pores would be opening up to let the sweat glands do their business.

Ena was invited up for his speech on the local area and, quite possibly, the ritual humiliation of his company's competitors. He seemed to be walking a bit gingerly as he made his way up to the lectern. With his notes placed in front of him, next to a glass of water, he started addressing his audience.

'Ladies and Gentlemen, it is indeed an honour, for both me and my company, to be invited here to make this short presentation.'

I noticed a sudden line of sweat forming across his brow and top lip. His feet and knees turned in on themselves, as if he was suddenly trying to squash his balls between his inner thighs. His voice went up very slightly.

'This has been a difficult year for the whole of our profession, as market factors have bitten into every aspect of all businesses. Despite this, our branch has had a particularly good year due to a combination of hard work, team ethics and a sound knowledge of our local market.'

His voice was starting to quiver now and he was gripping on to the lectern with both hands. There was no blood in his knuckles as the pain was starting to build. The sweat was also building on his face and he looked increasingly like someone in a sauna. This was working a treat.

'Excuse me a minute.' He took a swig of water and mopped his brow with the back of his sleeve, leaving a dark stain on his grey suit.

'As I was saying, we have had a good year. Unfortunately this can't be said for some of the smaller agencies, whooooo.....' His right hand went down to his crotch and he began to scratch and rub furiously. He was bending at right angles to the lectern with his arse poking out behind him. To make things worse, he was scratching at his balls, making loud moaning groans which were being picked up by the microphone.

People on all the tables were starting to look at each other to see if anyone knew what was happening. Either this bloke was on drugs, or he got off on spanking his bishop in public.

Ena pulled himself together for one last effort. He was obviously in pain, but he needed to carry on.

'The smaller agencies that cannot compare with our service and expertiiiiiiiiiiiiiiiiiiise........Oh fuckin' hell, oh God, oh God!'

He was down on his knees now; both hands still holding on desperately to the lectern. They didn't stay there long. He began by ripping his trouser belt off and undoing his trousers. He then pulled the top of his pants out to inspect the source of his pain. Reaching up he grabbed the glass of water and poured it down his pants onto his crown jewels. Ladies were starting to gasp in shock while husbands and boyfriends put their hands over their partners' eyes. He reached up again and this time he poured the whole pitcher of water over his groin.

Ena wasn't going to carry on. He was rolling around on the floor, clawing at his bollocks, screaming at the top of his voice.

'You bastard, you bastard, I'm going to kill you. Oh God, Oh God. Help me someone please, help me, I'm on fire!'

I didn't have a clue what he could mean!

Victor was looking at me in awe and admiration.

'How the fuck did you do that? I think you must be some kind of witch doctor. Remind me never to piss you off.'

I looked around the table. Nobody had picked up on Vic's remarks. They were all too interested in what was unfolding on the stage. Ena was screaming in agony. His entourage had rushed up to help him but they didn't have a clue what was going on. Eventually he was carried out to the toilets by his dad and friends. The screams didn't stop until the toilet door shut behind them.

'Sod this, I'm off to see what's happening in the bogs,' and with that Vic hurried away to satisfy his curiosity. As he opened the toilet door a piercing scream washed over the hall. Ena was in a whole world of pain. Perhaps I'd gone over the top again? More screams from the loos; maybe I had.

It was too late now and I was very pleased with myself because my plan had worked perfectly. I wasn't a witch doctor as Vic had alluded to; I just had a devious mind and a bit of a righteous streak in me.

How had I done it? I'd used a small jar of very finely ground Naga chilli, another jar of barrier cream and a bit of time for planning.

I knew that Ena would have to have a nervous piss before his speech. The only thing was the timing. I went to the loo before him. Once in the trap, I covered my hands with the barrier cream, then put the finely ground Naga chilli powder over my right hand, in particular the areas of the hand which Ena's fingers would clasp if we shook hands. Chilli powder applied, it all depended on meeting him on his way for his piss. As luck would have it, or perfect timing, I met Ena just outside. It was then easy to grasp his hand and wish him luck. He then has his nervous pee and applies the powder to his cock, which in turn transfers it to his bollocks. After that, it was up to his sweat glands to open up and do the rest.

As soon as he was up on the stage, I knew he would be sweating like a pig. As his glands opened, the chilli powder went to work; a little too well for my liking. Perhaps some of the powder went into his Jap's eye; now that would be painful. It must have felt like he was dipping his crown jewels into a deep fat fryer.

The only thing I had to do was to wash off the powder and cream from my hands in the other toilets before going back to the table. What happened next will be talked about in estate agents' circles for a few years. I think I may have left scars on poor Ena's ego and reputation but at least you can't see these.

Everyone was talking amongst themselves at the tables. After the initial shock of seeing Ena writhing around in pain, most were starting to giggle and laugh at his obvious discomfort. Isn't it odd how we can find fun at someone else's expense when they're obviously in pain or trouble? If we didn't, then we wouldn't have a lot of the popular TV shows nowadays.

Another cry of agony came from Ena's now-sore throat. I glanced up to see Vic walking back to the table from the toilet. It was obvious that he was trying not to laugh.

'Fuck me, that poor bastard is in a really shit state.' Everyone on the table was leaning towards Vic so they wouldn't miss anything, anticipating his next description of pain and degradation. Tina was nodding and asking for more.

'He's got his wedding tackle out in the sink and his mates are spraying liquid soap all over his bollocks. Ena's scrubbing away like a mad thing, screaming as he rubs but with all the rubbing and itching; he's got an enormous boner! His mates, and his dad, are all trying to look the other way but there are mirrors everywhere. If he isn't careful, he's going to go off like a nine-litre foam fire extinguisher.'

It was finally too much. We all fell about at the vision of Ena giving himself a soapy hand-job in front of his dad and bosses. People from the other tables were looking over but we were too far gone.

We were saved by the host introducing the next speaker. And from then on, it was all a bit rushed and embarrassed. It was as if everyone knew that this evening would be remembered for reasons other than who had received their various awards and accolades. Finally, the speeches ground to a halt, and everyone gave a sigh of relief. It was time to get shit-faced and try not to get caught slagging off your boss or workmates.

After two hours of punishing her liver, Tina finally decided it was time for her to waddle off to the toilet. Unfortunately, she didn't leave the table straight away. She decided to stretch her arms and back before she left. The result was really quite effective. Most of the guys who could see her manoeuvred for a better ogle.

As she stretched her arms, her silky shirt looked alarmingly small as it strained against her silicone fun-bags. I shut my eyes because I didn't want to lose one when her buttons shot off like a bullet. Then, she stretched her back, pushing her hips forward. When she stood up, I thought her trousers were tight but now they looked like they were tattooed on. Her crutch suddenly looked like someone had pushed a camel's toe down the front of her trousers. It was too much for one of the guys on the table behind me. He choked on his lager, spitting it out across the tablecloth and ending up with a coughing fit. With her back-stretch finished, Tina stood straight and looked around the room to see if her exhibition had had the desired effect. She smiled slightly; it obviously had. Her crutch had now transformed into what looked scarily like the bonnet of a VW Beetle. It just didn't have squashed flies and bugs on it.

Clint sat next to her, looking her up and down. It was like Pavlov's dog dribbling all down the front of his shirt.

Tina finally left the table and headed for the loos. A lot of guys still had their eyes on her and she knew it. Tits out, arse in; she was walking like she had a couple of fifty pence pieces clenched between the cheeks of her arse.

'Well, that appears to be the end of the entertainment for the evening.' Clint shot me a glance. 'I think that's all the speeches done, so if you'll excuse me, I'm going for a mingle.'

'I'll join you, mate. You never know who you'll meet.' Vic and I left the table and headed for the bar.

When we were out of earshot, Vic finally asked me.

'Richie, just what did you do to Ena? And how did you do it?'

'If I tell you, I'll have to kill you. I'll explain it all down the pub in the week. For the moment, neither of us has got a clue what happened, no matter who asks. I'm afraid things went a bit better than I expected and, as a result, there are going to be some very pissed-off people about tonight.'

As if on cue, the toilet door opened and Ena was led out towards the front door. He was walking very gingerly and was obviously still in a lot of pain. Behind him came his dad; he looked very pissed-off. Not surprising when you think that his son had just been publicly humiliated in front of his peers. Vic must have been reading my mind.

'I think we'll have to keep out of his way tonight, Richie. He's going to be looking to blame this on someone and I'm afraid you're the usual suspect.'

We could see Ena being helped into a car outside the hotel. Unfortunately, his dad didn't go with him; he came back in with his cronies and returned to their table. They looked in a much more sombre mood than before. I wasn't looking forward to meeting Sharples Senior but somehow I knew it was inevitable if I hung around much longer. To be honest, I didn't give a flying fuck. I wasn't going to be intimidated by some jumped-up pseudo upper-class twat, senior or junior.

'How about we get a drink and float around the tables? You never know, Vic, you could meet your future civil partner, or whatever they call it these days.'

'That sounds like commitment to me, mate. The only commitment I have is to get my rocks off by the time I've got to get up and go to work. Men never look the same in the morning, do they?'

'How the hell would I know, Vic? Now women, that's a different story. Unfortunately the only ones I've found that look the same are pig-ugly to start with. So the moral of this story is that neither of us has any, correct?'

I glanced at Vic as I picked up our drinks off the bar. He was nodding with a smile on his face which I took to be an agreement with my statement. His eyes were busy scanning the room for a potential partner for the night. I didn't know any gay estate agents, but then I didn't have the sixth sense that gay people seemed to have for recognising a potential partner. Martin called it 'gaydar'. Heterosexuals didn't possess it; it just seems to be an innate gift given to gay people.

As my gaydar wasn't working, I left Vic to find someone who wanted to play clackers with his bollocks and then concentrated on the female of the species. There were quite a few to choose from. The drink was flowing and most people were starting to get a bit pissed. I looked over at our

128

table and everyone seemed animated. I guess they had stayed as a group because no one really had anything to brag about to the other agents. I felt a bit sad about that if I'm honest. Still, another couple of drinks and I wouldn't give a toss.

'I'm going to have a bit of a wander, Vic. Want to come or are you all right on your own?'

He was concentrating on a small group near to the dance floor. The DJ was just about to start up and the lights were being dimmed.

'You carry on, Richie, I'm OK. Just let me know when you're leaving, alright?' He was being protective.

I really needed to talk to a nice young lady. It had been nearly a week and my confidence was starting to take a knock. I'd have a wander around and you never know your luck.

I only got a few paces towards the dance floor when my path was blocked by a middle-aged guy in a very expensive suit. His chest was puffed up to try to look imposing but he didn't need to; he looked very angry and nasty.

'Richard Head?' It was the first time I'd met and spoken to Ena's dad.

'Yes, sir, how can I help you?' He looked me in the eyes,

'That's easy, sonny; you can be found in the gutter with your face smashed to a bloody pulp and both your arms and legs broken.'

He leaned forward so he was now in my personal space. He was trying to intimidate me, maybe even goad me into doing something stupid. If that's what he wanted, he'd picked on the wrong bloke.

'Although we haven't formally met, I take it that you're Tim's father. And from your aggressive tone and posture, I take it that you think I had something to do with your son's performance this evening. Let's get something straight right from the start, Mr Sharples, Timothy has hated me from the age of twelve. Why, I don't really know. We were adversaries at school and took the field against each other many times in different sports. But what's brought about this level of animosity and hatred against me and my friends, I can't for the life of me explain. Perhaps that's something you can help me with, Mr Sharples?'

I took a deep breath. I'd taken myself a bit by surprise, as well as Ena's dad. He looked like he was struggling a bit for a comeback. For one second, I thought he was going to have a go at me. He was rocking on his feet and clenching his fists and I got the impression people just didn't speak to him like that. Then he seemed to gather himself again.

'You listen here, you smarmy little shit; I know it was you who fucked my lad up tonight and you're going to pay. You mess with my lad and you mess with me.'

He was starting to go red in the face.

'You have no idea who you're messing with, do you, sonny? It might be tonight or it might be in a few weeks, but when it happens, you're going to wish you'd never fucked with my family.'

He seemed quite pleased with himself, trying to intimidate a young nobody who, by rights, should be shit-scared.

'Mr Sharples, I wouldn't fuck with your family even if they had bags over their heads, or even if I had one over mine, just in case yours fell off. So do us both a favour and take your vicious family vendetta and shove it up your arse.'

It only took a split second, but I was ready for him. He was a bit different to his lad in that he was prepared to have a go, even if the odds weren't five to one in his favour.

I'd shifted my weight onto the balls of my feet and had my left hand to my cheek and right hand at my left elbow. A thinking pose, you could say. From this position, if you turned your palms to the front, you are immediately in a defensive posture. Left protecting head and right protecting heart, stomach and vitals.

In that split second, I thought old man Sharples' head was going to explode. He'd gone crimson and completely lost his composure. He lunged at me, throwing a looping right as he came.

It was pretty easy to slide away to the left under his haymaker and out of trouble. As he slipped by, I gave him a little help with both hands to send him on his way. The only trouble was that his way was blocked by a table full of drinks with four drunks sitting around it.

He couldn't stop himself and took the lot out in one go. Glasses, bodies, chairs and the table went everywhere. They were all shouting at each other whilst inspecting the damage. It was my cue to melt into the background and watch things from a safe distance. I didn't want to meet Sharples Senior again tonight, or ever, come to that. Despite being quite pleased with myself in the way I'd handled things, I instinctively knew that I'd made a powerful enemy. He would be true to his word in that he would try to fuck me up. I'd have to be very careful over the next few weeks or until things came to a head, preferably not mine.

The five of them were standing up now and Sharples seemed to be calming everyone down. It appeared that he was managing this with promises of copious amounts of alcohol. I was mingling with a crowd at the back of the room, ready to duck out of sight if the need arose. Luckily, it didn't. It seemed that discretion was the better part of valour as Sharples made for the exit after sorting his new friends out. Just before he left, he called Fido over and was talking into his ear for a few seconds. Fido's face split into a large grin and he nodded an affirmative. With that, he was out of the door. I suddenly got a nervous knot in the pit of my stomach; those two scheming bastards were talking about me and I really didn't want to know what it was they were discussing. The trouble was, I had a pretty good idea.

'Just a little word of advice, mate, you don't want to go messing around with that bloke. He's trouble, or more to the point, his mates are. Some quite handy fuckers if I remember rightly. I've seen 'em down at the clubs.'

I turned around to see Clint behind me.

'Did you see what happened?' I could tell he was in work mode. He was switched on and a bit tense. Christ, I hope he wasn't working for Sharples; I haven't made a will and there's so much I still wanted to do in life.

'All of it, mate. I was on the way back to the table. You know, I was getting another drink for Tina. I've been a few feet away just in case a couple of his hangers-on tried to jump you from behind. I've seen it before from him. You must have really pissed him off for him to have a go at you. And I have to say you handled yourself really well. Most people would have been taken out by his charge. Who taught you?'

I was looking at Clint in a different light. He was talking like a professional; like someone who was very good at his trade and who had analysed the situation perfectly. I was also very grateful that he'd covered my arse. If I'd been jumped, I wouldn't have stood a chance.

'My mate, Martin mainly; he's a copper. They do this personal safety training. Stance, blocks, punches and holds. He then shows me what moves he's learnt. Comes in handy sometimes. Also, my granddad was a boxer and I remember when I was a little kid, him throwing punches and me trying to stop them. It hurt but I've still got the reflexes.'

'Well, it shows. If ever you want a job, just let me know. We can always do with a good little 'un; it takes the punters by surprise.'

He was actually serious about the job. Me, a bouncer? I didn't think so, but just think of the girls you'd meet.

'Thanks for looking out for me tonight, Clint, I really appreciate it. If there's anything I can do for you, just name it and I'll see what I can do.'

He thought about it for a second,

'Now that you mention it, there is. Any chance of putting in a good word about me with Tina, when you get the chance? You see, I really fancy her and, well, a word from you might make a lot of difference.'

'It would be my pleasure, mate.'

He grasped my hand and shook it until the bones cracked. With that, he was off with his drinks and back to the table. A sudden thought crossed my mind; I wonder if he'd ever heard of Naga chillies? I glanced nervously at my hand.

It had been quite a productive evening so far. I'd managed to fuck up both Sharples, junior and senior, and gained another enemy as a result. I really was making a total fuck-up of my life. I'd lost two girls and gained two enemies. Wonderful.

I looked around the room and saw Vic chatting to the manager of a local agency. I didn't really know him but he was renowned for his dress sense. He must be mid-thirties and, as far as I could remember, there was no scandal surrounding him at all, which was unusual for a manager. My gaydar wasn't picking anything up but, as he was whispering into Vic's ear, you didn't have to be Einstein to realise what the implications were. I made my way over, and Vic saw me coming.

'Terence, I'd like to introduce you to my old friend, Richard. I think you might know him as he works for one of your rivals. In fact it was him who invited me here tonight. Richie, Terence, Terence, Richie.'

Terence looked me up and down and smiled.

'Richard, I've heard a lot about you in the work circles and I'm glad we could meet at last. Saw you have a bit of a contretemps with young Sharples' father earlier. I hope things are all right?'

Terence and Vic were a bit in each other's personal spaces as they both waited for my reply. Everyone had had a fair amount to drink and the evening was degenerating into a free-for-all. I got the distinct impression that I wouldn't be sharing a taxi home with Vic tonight.

'Just a bit of a misunderstanding, Terence. He seemed to think I had something to do with his lad falling apart on the stage. Must have been something the poor lad ate. Anyway, as you two seem to be getting on famously, I'll leave you to it.'

Terence put on a false show of dismay at my intended departure,

'No, no, Richard, please stay and join us for a chat and maybe we could all go around to my place after for a little drink? What do you think, Victor?'

Victor's very short show of dismay was far from contrived. He was shocked that Terence had proposed a threesome after no more than a minute of meeting me. Terence's gaydar must be in for repair.

'Terence, I don't think that would be Richie's scene, if you get my meaning.'

'Oh, Richard, I'm so sorry. Please don't take offence. I should have been a bit more discreet. Anyway, mum's the word, if that's alright?'

'No problem, Terence, mum's the word. I might need a favour from you one day, you never know.'

Terence was looking a bit relieved. I'm sure he didn't want any rumours being spread around about his sexuality.

'If you must leave us, Richard, then grab a drink from the bar and put it on my tab. I think the two of us will end up having that drink later. I think I'm developing a bit of a cold. Maybe later, I'll have a little Vic rubbed on my chest?'

He gave a smile to his prospective partner. Vic just rolled his eyes and gave me a resigned look.

'On that note, I'll leave you two to your own devices. See you in the week, Vic, and I'll take a cab home. I don't think it's an option to walk the streets tonight.'

I took up Terence's offer of a free drink. I very nearly treated myself to a double brandy but in the end I settled for a beer. I still had some morals left.

Standing at the bar, I thought I was the only relatively sober one there. To make things worse, there wasn't a single attractive girl who wasn't playing tonsil tennis or having her arse groped on the dance floor. It was time to go home.

I popped over to our table and said my goodbyes and waved at Vic and Terence. I hoped that Vic knew what he was doing. He was a big boy now though.

There were a few cabs for hire outside the hotel, which was a bonus. I didn't want to walk any distance. I knew Sharples would try something but maybe not this quickly. Better to be safe than sorry, though.

A tenner for the taxi and I was home in a few minutes. Another Saturday night over and another mini-disaster. At least I wouldn't wake up in the morning with a raging hangover this time. Mum would be surprised.

It was up the stairs and 'hello bed'.

Chapter Six

I got my usual cuppa from Mum in the morning. She seemed quite cheery today. I wondered what she'd been up to last night. She didn't go out much, but then she couldn't afford it really. I knew she was going out with some friends from work; perhaps she'd met a bloke.

Two things came to mind; both of which formed an image which I quickly erased from my mind. Firstly, it was the image of a fat, bald bloke who was going to be my step-dad. That was my worst nightmare. The second was the thought of my mum having a sex life. It just didn't seem right that your mum, or dad (if you've got one) still 'did it' after having kids. It just shouldn't be allowed.

Just think of the trauma it puts on us poor kids.

'And what did you get up to last night, young man? Not a lot, judging by the lack of aromas in your bedroom this morning. It usually smells like you've marinated yourself in beer and garlic chilli sauce and then followed through after an enormous fart.'

'Mum, please! Go and wash your mouth out with soapy water. That's what Gran would say, isn't it?'

I was a bit shocked at her language. This wasn't like her at all. Perhaps she'd been on drugs last night? She smiled at the thought of her mum telling her off all those years ago. Nostalgia ain't what it used to be.

'Have a good night, at your awards last night? I bet it was quite an occasion.'

Mum was hovering at the end of the bed. There was a little bit of pride in her voice. Her special soldier was going to an awards ceremony. It didn't matter that I hadn't won anything; in her eyes I'd achieved something. It was something for her to be proud of, despite all the crap she'd endured over the last few years. I didn't want to burst her bubble.

'It was quite an evening.' I sat up a bit and slurped a mouthful of tea.

'Yes, quite a night indeed. I'm afraid I didn't win an award for the mantelpiece but I tried my best. Anyway, it probably wasn't as good as your evening; you sound in a very good mood this morning.'

She flashed a smile and I swear she blushed a bit. Bollocks, I might be getting a step-dad.

'Just a few friends from work and a couple of drinks around the town. But it was nice to get out and relax for once.' She started to leave my room. The conversation was over.

'Your breakfast is nearly ready if you want it hot; otherwise I'll put it in the oven if you want a lie-in.'

The door shut and I was left with my images of step-dads and Ena with his self-basting bollocks.

I fancied a bit of breakfast so I had a quick shower and went down to the kitchen for 'heart attack on a plate'. Sis was up and about. I tried to spark up a bit of a conversation but I didn't get anywhere. She was just a grumpy teenager. She went off mumbling something about going out for the night with her mates and disappeared to her room.

I suppose I was the same at her age, but without the makeup and periods. I was grateful I didn't have either.

After my full-English, I did the washing up and decided to cut the grass for Mum before embarking on the rest of the day. I got the old lawn mower out and dragged it around to the front. Rodney was already out cleaning his beloved Jag.

'Morning, Mr Pratt, lovely day for a spot of gardening.' I just loved being civil to the old bastard. It didn't give him any room to move.

He glanced up from polishing the bonnet and grunted in my direction. This turned into a sneer when he saw the state of our mower. His, of course, was a top-of-the-range which actually put stripes on the lawn. Mind you, his lawn didn't have a tribe of pygmies living in it, or any weeds unknown to science.

I flashed the mower up and sent a sheet of smoky exhaust drifting over him and the car. He burst into an exaggerated cough and waved at the smoke with his polishing cloth.

I fought manfully against the couple of weeks' growth, thinking about what to do in the afternoon. I decided on the option of visiting Martin at his mum and dad's, then popping into the pub on the way home for a couple of pints and catching the Sunday late-afternoon footie.

I'd got about halfway through the lawn when a bit of a commotion started on Pratt's drive. Rodney was cleaning the inside of his car when he suddenly started shouting for Mo to come out at once. He seemed very pissed off about something. I switched the mower off and played about with the cutters, so I could earwig what was going on.

'What on earth is this, Maureen? Footprints on the inside of the windscreen? What have you been doing to my car?'

Now that he'd mentioned them, I could clearly see a load of prints on the screen. They were all over the inside. I thought back to Martin leaving the pub early when we'd met up during the week. Surely not; not in her husband's pride and joy? Then it suddenly began to make a bit of sense. What better way to get back at the miserable old git than by getting your brains shagged out in your husband's first love? I bet it made her feel naughty at the same time. That'd be quite an aphrodisiac.

Maureen stood there like a naughty schoolgirl; hands clasped in front of her and head slightly bowed. She glanced over to me, knowing that I was listening to her chastisement. She started to colour up, either with embarrassment or having a bollocking administered by her twat of a husband.

'Just look, they're all over the inside. And the dash is all dirty as well.'

He started to clean the inside of the screen. If it was Martin, then it looked like he had a good time. A bit of classic car shagging. I reckon that the car and Maureen were about the same age.

Maureen began her defence. She'd had enough of being belittled and if she wanted to use it as a shagging-wagon in the future, she'd better come up with a good excuse.

'Actually, Rodney, if you'd asked me properly, instead of berating me in public, I could have told you the whole story very easily. As it is, I'm very angry and upset.'

She paused for effect, wiping her eyes and sniffing. She was very good, I'll give her that.

'It was your car that caused the problem. It started to lose power on the way to the gym and judder. Eventually it stopped and it took ages to get going. As I was late, I decided to change there in the car because I wouldn't have time in the gym and I'd be late for my class. The trouble was that I was wearing those stupid jeans and I needed a bit of leverage. I'm sorry, but I had to put my feet on the dash and they must have slipped on to the screen. I know I should have told you about the problems but I've just been too busy; sorry.'

It was plausible, but a complete crock of shit. You don't need leverage to take them off; it's getting them on that's the problem. Anyway, I've never seen her in jeans. If Rodney thought about it for too long, he'd twig and Mo would be in the shit.

I switched the mower to *off* and pulled the cord a few times. The mower just turned over a couple of times with a puff of exhaust for good measure. Rodney glanced over to see what I was doing. He was scratching his head, obviously not sure about Mo's explanation.

I turned the mower slightly on its side and played underneath. I then started it up and jumped back with a scream of pain.

'Aaaah, aaaah, fuckin' hell, I've lost my finger. For fuck's sake, help me!'

I made a scene in the garden and jumped about holding my hand. I held my middle finger of my right hand down against the palm, with the other three and thumb pointing upwards. Both of them were looking at me now in horror. Mo had her hand to her mouth.

I stopped screaming and jumping about and stood still.

'It's OK, don't panic, I've found it.'

With that, I pulled the fingers and thumb down and extended the supposed missing middle finger towards Rodney.

He was looking over at me but it took a few seconds before he realised what I had done. For the second time in about twelve hours, I had made a guy go crimson with rage. I was getting good at this. But it had the desired effect; Mo used the opportunity to disappear back indoors and leave her accuser to vent his anger on another target - me.

Having saved the day, I just stood there and smiled. I didn't want Mo getting into any trouble and I'd probably earned a pint off Martin. It wouldn't do him a lot of good being named in a divorce court.

'Sorry, Mr Pratt, I just thought I'd break the ice a bit. Life can get a bit too serious at times, don't you agree?'

I swear I heard him tell me to 'fuck off' over the mower's engine. That was a first. I really was getting good at this.

He went back to cleaning his beloved car and I cut the rest of the grass. I'd had enough of middle-aged man-baiting, so it was time to pop round and see Martin. Perhaps he might fill me in on the dirty dashboard and my even dirtier neighbour.

Martin's parents' house was a good forty-five minute walk away. It was in what was once an affluent area of town but, over the last few years, it had been taken over by increasing numbers of immigrants. Victorian terraced houses and quite a few Georgian villas and townhouses with lots of good-sized rooms, which could easily be converted into flats for a nice little earner. Being fairly close to the centre of town, it was the first area to see an influx of immigrants looking for a future in England. As a result, it was now an area which typified the Government's idea of a multicultural society. Nobody knew their neighbours, let alone talked to them, even if they spoke the same language.

Martin's parents had lived there since they got married. They liked their house and its proximity to the town, but in recent years the vast majority of their friends had moved away to the suburbs, or even abroad, in search of a better life. This was a bit ironic, as their friends had been replaced by people doing the exactly the same thing.

I liked Martin's parents. They were as down-to-earth as they come. Martin's dad had worked in the Merchant Navy all his life. He was now retired but it hadn't taken the edge off his earthy humour. You had to watch him, or he'd stitch you up like a kipper. He hadn't lost his taste for a drink either. I'd made the mistake of going out with him and Martin round to their local; I'd never do that again. He'd stand at the bar and tell you story after story of his adventures at sea, all the while throwing beer and rum down his neck and yours. The result was always the same; before very long, you were absolutely shitfaced, singing dirty songs with some new-found seedy friends in an even seedier bar.

Martin's mum had worked in a variety of local factories and was as hard and worldly-wise as they came. She'd seen most things in her time and had done most as well. She was a hard woman, and also a hard drinker like her husband.

As I walked up their street, the first thing that always hit me was the smell. It was the smell of food, or food being cooked, to be more precise. There was a whole variety of aromas which assaulted the nasal passages as you walked up the road; food from all over the world. It always made me hungry.

I saw their next-door neighbours unloading their car as I got close to the house. It was a young couple, most likely Indian. The girl was an absolute stunner; she was about twenty five, with long black hair and a fabulous figure. I swear girls can sense when a bloke is staring at their arse. She immediately turned around and stared at me. I was just admiring your jeans, honest! No, it would never work. I just shrugged, said hello and smiled at her on my way up to her neighbour's front door. She actually flashed a smile at me showing off a set of lovely white teeth. Perhaps there was something in this multiculturalism after all.

I knocked on the door and waited. I looked up the road in the opposite direction to the Indian girl; I couldn't be caught ogling at her arse twice. A few doors up, I saw that the God Botherers were working their way down the street in the direction of Martin's parents' house. This was too good an opportunity to miss.

The door opened to reveal a ruddy and unshaven Mr Bormann Senior.

'Hello, Mr Bormann; is Martin in?'

He smiled as if to show off a set of teeth which had seen better years; years of assault from nicotine and various types of alcohol and sugar. I wondered how long it would take him to get through a steak these days.

'He is, son, but he's just dropping the kids off at the pool.' I stared at him with a quizzical look on my face. I really didn't have a clue what he was on about.

'He's having a crap, taking a dump, giving birth to a flock of sparrows. Christ, don't they teach you kids the Queen's English anymore?'

Although he came across as gruff, he had a smile on his face. He liked to shock and took pleasure in watching people's reactions. I remember him saying in the pub that when he was at sea, the main topics of conversation were the three S's - sex, sport and shit. I suppose it was the same the world over, although I wasn't sure about the shit part! It wasn't my cup of hot chocolate.

'Well, you might as well come in and have a cuppa while you're waiting for him, or do you want anything a bit stronger?' He had a little glint in his eye which I'd seen before; once bitten, so to speak.

'No thanks, Mr B. It's a bit early for me. But don't worry about me; if you fancy one, you carry on.'

He looked a little disappointed as he led me into the kitchen. He was looking for a drinking buddy, but I wasn't going to play. He'd probably go down to the pub soon anyway.

'Oh, before I forget, Mr B, you'll probably get a knock at the door soon from a young couple with their kids. It's a bloody cheek if you ask me; selling double glazing on a Sunday afternoon. Shouldn't be allowed. I'm not one for religion but they should keep Sunday special.'

He grunted his agreement and disappeared into the front room to catch up with the *Eastenders* omnibus.

I sat in the kitchen waiting for Martin. The flush was going every few seconds, coupled with a bit of swearing. It sounded like he was having trouble and Mr B was shouting that he'd break it. He finally emerged.

'Bloody flush, it's never worked properly. I'm always left with a Moray turd poking his little head out from round the U-bend, staring at me with his little sweetcorn eyes. Just won't bloody flush away. If I use the loo again while he's still there, I get this feeling he's going to jump up and take a bite out of my chocolate starfish. Bastard.'

He was just like his old man; always talking about sex, sport and shit.

'And what brings the infamous tortoise-violator over to this neck of the woods then?' He went about making himself a cuppa whilst seeing if I would bite at his crude expressions and having a dig about my nocturnal scat fest.

'Nothing much mate, just brought some insurance papers for you to sign regarding some damage to an *E-Type's* dashboard, windscreen and stains to the upholstery.'

I let the statement hang in the air whilst looking at Martin over the rim of my mug. He started to scratch his back then realised what he was doing. He actually coloured up for a second.

'Fancy a walk around the estate, old chap?' And with that he left the kitchen and went into the back garden with his cuppa. We sat in the garden, or what passes for a garden in this area. It was just a few square feet of grass, overlooked by the neighbouring houses.

'So, am I going to be blackmailed or bollocked? Quite frankly, I think I deserve either one, or possibly both.' Martin actually sounded contrite, which was very unusual for him. Usually, if it had a pulse, he would shag it without a second thought.

'Sod it, on second thoughts, do your worst. It was one of the best shags I've had for a long time.'

I glanced up from my tea to see him staring into the distance with a wistful smile on his face. It must have been good.

'I'm not here to judge, mate. I'm not your conscience and I'm not your mother but you're sailing very close to the wind with this one. Firstly, she's part of a police investigation; your investigation, in fact. I'm sure there's a rule somewhere which states that you shouldn't shag a witness's brains out. And secondly, her old man may be a complete tosspot, but he's not stupid. I actually saw the aftermath of your *E-Type* eroticism and was witness to Mo's inquisition. If I hadn't jumped in when I did, I'm sure he would have twigged.'

I explained about Rodney cleaning the car and finding the marks all over the inside and Mo's feeble excuse about changing her clothes. He thanked me for my intervention, saying that he didn't want her to get into any trouble but reminding me that she was more than a willing participant; in fact, she was more the instigator than he was.

146

'Look, Richie, I'm not going to go into graphic details at the moment. Maybe down the pub on Tuesday night, if you're up for a pint. But not now, mate. I know I've been a bit stupid and possibly put my job at risk but, believe you me, it was worth it. Would I do it again? I'm not really sure but I'd definitely think about it. Anyway, that's enough of that for the moment.'

He'd drawn a line under that topic of conversation and was obviously a bit touchy about it. I wasn't sure why but now wasn't the time to pry or he might try one of his holds or punches on me. He was scratching his back again then realised I'd picked up on it and stopped.

An uncomfortable silence followed, which was thankfully broken by the sound of the front door bell. I had an idea who it might be. I'd probably go straight to hell when my time came, for stitching up God's emissaries two weekends in a row.

'Tell you what, let's take our tea into the kitchen and listen in on the callers. It might lighten your mood a little.'

'What have you been up to now, Richie? If you've stitched up my old man, you'd better be a fast runner and have a long memory because he'll get you, sure as eggs. He might even join up with Devon's old man and form a lynching party. I heard what you did to him and he's spitting feathers.' He was smiling, which was a bit of a relief. I didn't like seeing any of my mates in any sort of bother.

'In that case, I'd better not have another cuppa because I may be legging it up the road in a minute. If my guess is correct, Devon's dad's mates are at the front door and your old man thinks they're double glazing salesmen.'

'Shit, this I've got to listen to.'

We crept into the kitchen just as Martin's dad answered the door. I noticed he'd opened a big bottle of cider, most of

147

which was now gone. By squinting through the gap between kitchen door and frame, we could just see the front door. Mr B sounded a bit miffed to say the least. Someone had come between his drink and the *Eastenders* omnibus. Heaven help them, although it probably would.

'What the bloody-hell do you want on a sodding Sunday afternoon?'

No, he wasn't happy. He stood in the doorway looking at the bemused family of God Botherers. They probably expect a little bit of hassle in the course of their vocation, but not a full frontal verbal assault from someone who looks the epitome of a life spent contravening every Commandment going. Still, I suppose they look upon it as a bit of a challenge.

'I've already got double glazing and it works fine. It keeps the rain and wind out, the heat and sound in, which is handy because the missus gets a bit noisy when it comes to a bit of hanky-panky on the front room sofa on a Saturday night.'

He followed up his appraisal of the benefits of modern window technology with a few knowing taps on the side of his nose with his right index finger. He'd obviously had a drink because he was slurring just a bit. The cider wasn't the only drink he'd had today. Martin had his head in both hands. It was obvious that he was like me; he couldn't imagine his parents still 'at it' when they should be enjoying Saga holidays and eating cholesterol-busting spreads.

Mr B's gaze shifted to the two kids. He looked at them for a couple of seconds and probably realised what he'd just said. He shifted from foot to foot in slight embarrassment.

'Sorry, kids, but you shouldn't be out selling windows with your mum and dad when people are trying to relax on their day off.'

The parents were looking down at their two kids with a smile of pride on their lips. It was obvious that they saw what they were doing, and what they were subjecting their kids to, as a sort of rite of passage. It was something they had to endure from people like Mr B; people who didn't know any better because they didn't live their lives in the service or the calling of their Lord. He wasn't to be pitied; he just didn't know any better.

I had a sudden vision of missionaries setting out across Africa in the 19th century. Their calling must have been the same; to convert people, tribes, and ultimately, nations, to Christianity. The difference was that I don't think they ever encountered a Mr B at the door of his mud hut, drinking a pint of cider in a string vest and smoking a roll-up.

'We're here, Sir, to explain a new window of opportunity for you; a new way to bring light into your life and to reach levels of fulfilment you never dreamt of before.'

'Bloody hell, I've heard all about this new thermal energy saving glass and it's not for me. You may save on electricity, but I don't need it. Nor do I need a five-point locking system either come to that. If anyone breaks into my house I'll brain 'em. Anyway, what are you doing out on a Sunday with your kids going door-to-door?'

The wife jumped in before her husband. He was starting to look a bit sceptical. This wasn't going as planned.

'We find it's the best day to find people in, so that we can talk and explain what we are trying to do; to offer people a real alternative to what they have at the moment. We offer enlightenment, and advice on how to achieve it, and we travel as a family, as our children will one day carry on our work in the community. The Lord guides us in our work.'

She looked down at her two children and then to her husband. Pride shone in her eyes.

'If the good Lord guides you then let him guide you next door. I don't want windows and I don't want your holy stained glass windows. Sell 'em some windows next door and tell 'em to keep 'em shut to keep those bloody awful smells in. Bloody fed up, we are.'

He'd obviously had enough. *Eastenders* waits for no man; unless you've got a *record* button, that is.

Father Botherer was starting to put things together.

'Sir, you seem to have the wrong end of the stick, so to speak. We are not window sellers. We are trying to spread the word of the Lord and enlighten people regarding his teachings.'

It was Mr B's turn to look a bit perplexed. He was starting to twig as well.

'So you're not double glazing salesmen? You're out bothering devout fully-paid-up atheists like me on a Sunday afternoon while *Eastenders* is on. Bloody hell, I bet I missed the old lady falling down the bloody stairs and breaking her neck. I've been looking forward to that all bloody week. Anyway, why did you say you were selling windows?'

'We didn't, sir. You just seemed to assume it.'

They looked at one another for a moment. The scene was interrupted by the sound of juvenile sniggers coming from behind the door. Martin and I were wetting our pants with laughter and couldn't keep it in any longer.

Mr B looked at us through the crack between the door and frame. He had the sudden realisation that he'd been stitched up. Not only had he missed his TV programme but he'd also missed valuable drinking time. He turned back to the family.

'I don't care what you're selling; I'm not bloody interested. If you want lost souls then this is the street for you.

Most of the buggers here don't know what country they're in, let alone which town. And as for religion, just mind out for the sacrificial goats and stone idols at number twenty four. Now there's a challenge for you.'

He stepped into the house and closed the door on the bewildered family; not before the father had caught a glimpse of me as I came out from behind the door. In that split second of eye contact, I could see his recognition of me and his humiliation, at my instigation, for a second Sunday. I actually felt a little sorry for him; just a little.

That soon changed when I saw the look on Martin's dad's face. He was starting to make what sounded like little growling noises whilst the colour built up in his face. The pressure was obviously building as he let out a long squeaky fart which had escaped past his increasingly clenched arse cheeks.

Time to go; I'd smelt one of Mr B's farts before. The hairs were just beginning to grow back on the inside of my nose and I wasn't taking any chances on this one. He'd been drinking cider most of the afternoon and his guts were probably in turmoil.

We both made a dash for the back garden, quickly followed by a hail of insults and verbal abuse. He didn't follow us out the back. The lure of a broken society portrayed on the TV was far too much for him.

'Dev's dad last Sunday, and now mine? You're sailing very close to the wind, my friend. They're going to get you sooner or later. You may be quick and you may be savvy but these old buggers have got a lifetime of experience and they will get their revenge. Those who live by the sword, Richie, but I don't expect it'll come to that. No, they'll probably just cut off your bollocks and use them as a paperweight.'

I was sailing a bit close to the wind. I was sure that Dev's and Martin's dads would eke out a bit of revenge at some time or other but I wasn't worried about that. I quickly reflected on last night and the retribution the Sharples would no doubt be planning to exact. A little shiver ran down my back.

'Well, if it's a bit of afters they want, then I'm afraid they'll have to join the queue.'

Martin glanced up from his now-cold tea. He was asking a question with his raised eyebrow. I took a deep breath and filled him in on the events of the night before. I told him all the gory details, including Victor copping off with a manager from another company. His eyebrows danced while I went through Ena's humiliation and only appeared to calm down when he went into fits of laughter at Ena's expense. He began to get a bit serious when I came to the end of the evening and explained about Ena's dad, our fight, and his very brief conversation with Fido.

'You really are a prize wanker. You know that, don't you?'

It was a rhetorical question, but I could tell he really thought that I was a wanker for what I'd done, and the really bad thing was that I couldn't disagree with him. I'd fucked up again.

'I can understand you having a pop at Ena every now and again, but you've crossed a line in the sand. You've gone too far this time, mate and they're going to come after you, and it's going to hurt.'

He let the words sink in for a moment, hoping they might have some sort of sobering effect on me. It was a bit of a wake-up call to get me out of my serial wanker mode.

'I pick up on the odd bit of gossip and whispers while I'm out and one I've heard more than a few times is that you don't piss on old man Sharples' fireworks. He's a nasty bit of work. But what's more worrying for you, Richie is that his hired helpers are an awful lot nastier. You're going to have to be very careful over the next few weeks or otherwise you're going to be eating your Sunday lunch through a straw, and you'd better think about how you can adapt your house for wheelchair access.'

His tone had become very serious; almost parental. I was being advised and told off all at once. Fuck it, he was right. I was a wanker and I had fucked up big-time, but it was too late. I'd enjoyed seeing Ena writhing in public testicular torture. I'd enjoyed getting the better of his old man when he tried to separate my head from my shoulders. But the price both Martin and I thought I might have to pay for a brief moment of glory over these arseholes probably wasn't worth it. They'd be coming for me, coming hard and coming soon.

I had a sudden thought about Mrs Edgar and her evaluation of the Sharples. It was all becoming a bit clearer now. But what wasn't obvious was how a little old lady could be so concise in her summing up of someone she'd never met. It was a little ray of light at the end of what was becoming a very dark tunnel. I'd have to sort some things out with her very soon if I had any hope of getting the odds back in my favour.

Martin broke the sombre mood between us.

'Fancy a beer, mate? You look like you could do with one.'

I'd had a reality check and it wasn't looking good. I'd lost two girls within a few days and I'd probably got a contract out on me! That's not bad for a junior estate agent.

Martin came out from the kitchen with a couple of cold bottles of lager. By the sound of it, we weren't the only people to be enjoying an alfresco moment. There was the chink of glasses and plates from nearby gardens and the smell of roasting meats and exotic spices wafting over the garden fences. Martin seemed to read my mind. He glanced over the neighbouring fences and wrinkled his nose.

'If you shut your eyes, you could imagine you were in any country in the world, apart from England.'

There was a melancholy tone to his voice that I'd never heard before; a real sadness.

'Sorry, Martin, but it's the way of the world. Things change and we have to adapt. Nothing stays the same forever.'

He quickly turned to meet my gaze. His melancholy had been replaced by a fearsome stare.

'Why the fuck should we have to adapt?' He kept my gaze in a sort of challenge. He'd issued a statement, not a question.

'I know what you think, Richie; that I'm a fuckin' rabid racist that would have anyone who's not of white Anglo-Saxon descent strung up from the nearest lamp post with a burning tyre around their neck. I'm right, aren't I?'

He didn't wait for a reply. He took a mouthful of beer and sat down next to me and carried on.

'I'm not a racist; I'm a realist. I can't afford to be a racist in my job because, if I was, I wouldn't last five minutes with all the pink and fluffy bullshit that you have to work with and around these days. You wouldn't believe some of the things I see and hear, and am increasingly told to do. The newspapers wouldn't even print them because they'd be shouted down as racist or more likely, it would scare the crap out of the majority of the population.'

He was on a roll and I had the feeling I should just shut up and listen.

154

'Twenty or thirty years ago, my mum and dad knew and spoke to the vast majority of people in this street. Most were white and working class, what you'd now call the salt of the earth, probably. There were a few coloured families and everyone got along with them because they rolled up their sleeves and they made themselves a part of the community. Some of them may even have come over with Dev's family. I've got nothing against them or anybody else who wants to come to this country to start a better life and are prepared to work for it. I've got nothing against anyone who comes to this country because they've been persecuted in their own lands and are here to genuinely seek asylum. I've got no problem with that at all.'

He took another swig of beer. He was calming down and it seemed that he needed to get it off his chest. I just drank alongside him and nodded knowingly, but I wasn't sure at what yet.

'My great granddad fought in the First World War. He was in the First Fourth Gloucester's and was in the trenches on the first day of the Somme. I can't imagine what it was like. He was sixteen, for God's sake. My granddad was in the Second World War in the RAF. He wouldn't, or couldn't, talk about his experiences. I'm by no means a scholar on either war but from what I've read, been told and seen on TV, we owe a huge debt to the people from the far-flung lands around the world that answered our call for help and fought alongside our boys. The Empire's troops, from lands that were pink on the map to mark them as part of our once great Empire. Indians, Africans, Nepalese, Fijians and more; they all fought alongside the larger Empire countries like Australia, Canada, South Africa and New Zealand. If their country was pink on the map of the world, and their King or Queen sat in Buck' Palace, then a lot of lads, and women, signed up to shed their blood on behalf of a grateful nation. Millions fought on our side during many wars and hundreds of thousands died, so we could keep our way of life. It's a debt, I for one, will never forget.'

Martin's voice was getting a bit reedy and I swear there was a bit of a tear in his eyes. Mine too, if the truth be told.

'No, mate, I've not got a problem with people coming to this land, because we owe a debt of gratitude to a lot of people from a lot of nations. What pisses me off is what's become of our society as a whole due to the scandalous immigration policy we've had over the last ten or so years. I've heard it described as a multicultural society; absolute bollocks. Unfettered, wholesale immigration which, in my humble opinion, was designed to totally destabilise the whole fabric of British society. And do you know what? Whoever dreamt up the policies and framework that's allowed so many people in must be extremely chuffed indeed because, from what I can see every day when I step out onto the street, it's worked beyond their wildest dreams.' Martin took a big swig from his bottle,

'Fuck me, I'm having a right old rant here, aren't I?'

He looked at his bottle and then at mine. They were both empty.

'Fancy the other leg? I'm sorry, but I'm not finished yet.'

It was an offer that I couldn't refuse. Besides, I didn't want to be disrespectful or I might end up with a horse's head in my bed.

Martin quickly came back with another beer. He took a large swig, gave a big barf that sounded like a rutting red deer and swung straight back into his take on multicultural Britain.

'Just look at this street. My mum and dad are probably the only white people who live here now. All their old friends have moved away. If you asked them when was the last time

156

they spoke to a neighbour, let alone go around for a drink or a bite to eat, it's probably so long ago, they can't remember. Nobody talks to anyone else; they just keep themselves to themselves. The only people who may talk are those from the same country or maybe even the same region. There's no integration at all. No incentive to learn English or even to get a bloody job. You and I pay for most of the people in this street and their extended family back home in whichever bloody country they came from. That's the thing that pisses me off. They're not asylum seekers; they haven't even come here in search of a new life. All they're here for is a house and lifestyle paid for by the British taxpayer; you and I. We should all go down to the local tattoo parlour and have MUG tattooed on our foreheads because that's what we all are.'

Martin's voice had gone up an octave or two and he was getting red in the face. It was like a pressure cooker on the hob with the steam steadily hissing out of the pressure-relief valve; only in this case, it was his ears.

'When I'm out on the street, I see the real consequences of this so-called utopia of multiculturalism - the nirvana of equal opportunities and diversity. Well, it's a crock of shit championed by pink and fluffy zealots who haven't got the intelligence or aptitude to get a proper job. The result is that you get hit around the head with the big diversity stick until you've been hit so many times, you just can't get up again. I feel sorry for the people who dare voice an opinion against these stupid draconian laws. They get branded as racists, troublemakers and nonconformists; a branding which makes them pariahs in our current society.'

'I see a side to their policies which they don't want to see; a side which they won't acknowledge exists, because it fucks up their utopian dream. They won't acknowledge that some people from the old Soviet bloc countries work cash-in-hand and send their money home. There's no input to the

157

economy there. There's no acknowledgement that a few of them are involved in Class A drug importation, distribution and large-scale people-trafficking and prostitution. There's no acknowledgement that some people from the Indian sub-continent are involved in Class A drug importations, money-laundering, local and international terrorism and have an aversion to paying the correct amount of tax due to the Exchequer.'

This was a side of Martin I hadn't seen before. It wasn't a rant, but more of an outpouring of his frustrations that had built up over a period of time. I was his best friend and this was the first time I'd heard him so passionate about something. I'd always had him down as a racist but it was dawning on me that he was far from it. He was a patriot, that was clear, but it went further than that. He was not averse to immigration. He wanted people here who would contribute to society, no matter what their ethnicity might be, people who would embrace British culture, whilst retaining their heritage, and have a positive impact upon British society.

After all, most people on these islands have a bit of Scandinavian or French blood running through their veins. The gene pool was spiced up a bit as a result of a few rapes and pillages from the Vikings and the odd 'conquest' from the Norman Barons. So, in the current age, where travel is quick and easy and national frontiers are often just a post by the side of the road, it was inevitable that we have some influx of people wanting to live here and start a new life.

I knew exactly why Martin was upset; it was the same for him and millions of others. British culture would never be the same again. Most of us knew and most were afraid to say it. The mass immigration of the last few years had irrevocably changed our society. Whether it will be for the better, I suppose only time will tell.

We sat drinking our beer. Music started up from a nearby garden where perfumed smoke was rising up from a stove or barbeque. It was the sound of sitars, drums and bongos accompanied by the lilting lyrics of an Indian girl. It was ironic after Martin's outpouring. It became very prophetic when a hail of what sounded like Slavic insults was hurled in the direction of the bhangra garden, closely followed by a couple of empty cans of cheap lager. The music was turned down immediately.

'See what I mean, Richie; you might as well be in another country. Sorry to load up on you, mate but it's just that I can't talk at work. When it comes to stuff like this, you just can't trust anyone. One little whisper to one of the bosses and I'll be shining my arse on a chair for a couple of years counting paperclips and staring at the secretaries' shirt potatoes.'

He'd come down from his pulpit and he was Martin again. We'd soon be chatting about the three S's and laughing again. It was good that he'd got things off his chest and I felt that I knew him a bit better.

'Anyway, have you heard from Vic today, or is he having reconstructive surgery on his chocolate starfish?'

It hadn't taken long, had it? He'd made me choke on my beer a few seconds after crying into it, reflecting on the demise of Englishness as I once knew it.

We talked about the previous night again, but in a little more detail. He particularly picked up on Tina and what she was almost wearing. I got the distinct impression that Martin may be a notch on her bedpost, which had probably been whittled down to the size of a toothpick by now.

'Yeah, I know Tina, who doesn't? It's said that there are only two certainties in life - death and Tina. From what I've heard, Tina is a better bet.'

I didn't press things. If Martin wanted to elaborate, he would. It appeared that Tina and Mrs Pratt were filed away in the 'Shags I've had' folder and not in 'Pending'.

'Have you heard from that girl you picked up last Saturday, or has she put a contract out on you as well as the Sharples? You ought to be careful, Richie. She might give Ena a ring and get some discount. After seeing her in the pub the other night, I'm surprised she hasn't rung up *Directory Enquiries* and asked for 'Assassins R Us' or 'Retribution 4 U.' She'd probably qualify for Buy One Get One Free, as over the last week you seem to have transformed yourself into a Grade A arsehole.'

Despite the seriousness of my situation, I couldn't help laugh at Martin's take on my current predicament. It also made me think of Nicola. I hadn't heard from her despite my text; I probably never would again. Fuck, today was like Alton Towers; a bit of a rollercoaster with ups and downs all day. Time for another beer in the hope of an alcohol-induced amnesia.

Sadly, common sense prevailed as we both realised a session wasn't in order. We both had work in the morning and turning up half drunk wasn't in the best interest of career enhancement for either of us.

I left the smell of exotic roasted spices wafting across the gardens and said my goodbyes to Mr B as I passed the front room.

'I'm a bit like an elephant, young Richie. Thick, grey, wrinkly skin, brown shitty teeth and a fuckin' long memory. So boil your head on the way out and watch your back 'cos if I don't get you, some other fucker will. Nice to see you, by the way, and do call round again when you've got a lot less time.'

He followed up his slightly veiled threat with a rasping cider-charged fart which rattled the windows. Maybe he did need new double glazing after all. It was a good time to go.

I caught a glimpse of his belly straining at his string vest as he lounged in his chair watching some banal American shite on the TV. The canned laughter just seemed to add a bit of sadness to the scene. There wasn't anything in the least bit cheery about watching a bloke who you admired, for all his faults, drinking himself into an early grave. We got outside before Mr B's trouser-cough advanced down the hall like a green fog.

'Nice to see you, Richie. See you in the week and we can catch up properly on last weekend. Dev owes us a couple of beers, as he's spent the last few days rescuing old ladies' cats from the tops of trees or dealing with saucepans stuck on little boys' heads.'

'Or more likely rescuing little boys stuck in old ladies!'

We both knew it was a cheap joke on Dev's account as neither of us wanted or could do his job. But then, as all his mates said, he had a lot of experience handling a very big hose. Lucky bastard.

I walked out into the street, closely followed by Martin. The same Indian couple I'd seen earlier were just getting into their car. I was immediately staring at her arse again. It was like two boiled eggs in a handkerchief; absolutely perfect. I sensed Martin was staring too.

I heard a polite cough and looked up at her face to see her looking over her shoulder at the two of us with a broad smile on her face. Her long black hair was flowing down her back as she slid her way into the front seat. There wasn't a hint of embarrassment on her face and no ring on her left hand. She gave the impression of being a very confident young lady.

The car pulled away and left the two of us reminiscing over a perfect gluteus maximus.

'If I was giving her marks out of two, I'd definitely give her one.'

Martin had heard it before but he still followed up with the punch line, as he had many times before.

'I can safely say Richie, that I'd give her one too.'

We both laughed and waved our goodbyes as I wandered down the street and headed for home. It was too late to head for the pub and catch the football. I was a bit rung out after listening to Martin and sinking a few beers. I'd need a clear head for tomorrow and the days to come.

A lot had happened today, some good, and some not so good. But in the end, I think I'd learnt a lot about some of the people around me and maybe a bit about myself.

Sigmund Freud, eat your heart out. It was time for home and a bite to eat before bed. The coming week was going to be very interesting.

Chapter Seven

I enjoyed the walk into work. It gave me time to reflect on a few things and draw up some sort of plan to combat anything which I thought the Sharples' might use to come at me.

Mrs Edgar was at the forefront of my plans. For some reason that I couldn't explain, I had the idea that she might be my salvation. I'd hardly met the old lady, but she'd already made a marked impression on me. I'd have to get cracking on her request for property details in the area, so she could carry out her research. I had no idea at this stage what she was going to do, or how she would use her findings. She wasn't exactly Mother Teresa, but I hoped that she had a direct line to someone of a slightly lesser importance.

At the same time, I didn't want to put my all eggs into one basket. I still had a few mates who might be able to help me. Martin was an obvious one; they knew that Martin was a copper, especially Ena, as the two of them have had a number of run-ins over the years. In Ena's case, they were mostly runaways. Vic and Dev would watch my back, but they didn't carry the same clout that Martin did as a copper, even though they did carry a punch.

My thoughts ran back to Saturday night and the meeting with Clint, following my little sparring session with Sharples Senior. I couldn't help but be impressed by his willingness to cover my back and to jump in if needed. I'd hardly met the bloke, but, like Mrs Edgar, I had this sense that I could trust him. What a pair to have on your side; an old lady and a tattooed bouncer made strange bed-mates.

I needed Clint's help and I'd have to go through Tina to get it, in a manner of speaking. I certainly didn't want to be Martin's or Clint's custard cousin.

I thought of what the Sharples' might have planned for me, or more correctly, what Fido had arranged on their behalf. As far as my job went, I was pretty bombproof. I didn't handle cash and I'd kept my nose clean since I'd been at the Agency. I had no skeletons in the closet and, if they did get me sacked, it wouldn't be the end of the world.

No, it would be violence. Unfortunately, it would be directed at me. I had no assets in the world that they could destroy or affect.

I was looking at a good battering. What I was unsure about was how extensive the battering would be. I'd had beatings before, but a few loose teeth, cuts and scrapes were nothing to what I thought they were planning. Ena had been seriously humiliated in front of his peers and Mr Sharples had suffered directly at my hands, again in public. I had besmirched the family honour and, in their eyes, I had to pay. They had a reputation to uphold within their fraternity as people you don't fuck about with. Fortunately, after my brief conversation with Clint on Saturday, I might have an 'in' to their associates. The Sharples' would be looking for muscle and Clint just might have big enough ears to give me a bit of warning.

A sudden chill hit me; what if it was Clint that took the job? There weren't enough windows in our house for me to lick over the next fifty years; I'd be cabbaged.

I arrived at the office with thoughts of Clint attacking me from behind with a heavy blunt weapon. It was a vision which Vic would probably find arousing but it scared the shit out of me. I quickly put it out of my mind and opened the office door to another week of viewings and phone calls.

Carol had already arrived but Tina was yet to show up. She was invariably late on a Monday morning after her exertions over the weekend.

'Morning, Carol. Did anything happen at the do on Saturday, after I left?'

I tried to sound matter-of-fact, but a bit of anxiety showed through in my voice. After all, I'd had a fight at the year's most prestigious awards ceremony and possibly brought the Agency into disrepute slightly. I hoped the big bosses hadn't seen anything.

She smiled at me, sensing my nervousness. I'm sure most women are witches in their spare time. I found their ability to read minds and pick up on the slightest inflection a bit scary, and Carol was no exception.

'Not really, Richie. There was a knockdown in the seventh, then a bad cut over the left eye had the corner-men working overtime, but apart from that, it was down to the judges' cards and a unanimous points' decision.'

She was enjoying this. It wasn't a bollocking but just her making me squirm for a few moments. She cut in before I could come back on her teasing.

'If you're worried about your little fracas with Sharples Senior, then no, nothing happened of note. Apparently very few people saw it and those who did were pissed and thought Sharples was as well. And from what I could pick up from the scuttlebutt after you left, I don't think he'll be following it up. After all, he was the one who swung first, wasn't he?'

It was a leading question. It was her way of asking me if it was true and, if the shit did hit the fan, should she back me up? It was true but there would be a follow-up. I didn't want to think about that bit.

'For what it's worth, he swung first and I ducked out the way. He crashed into a couple of tables, and a few drunks, and I slipped away. That's about it, really. Anyway, what have I got on this week?'

165

I hoped she'd go along with my none-too-subtle change of subject. Thankfully, she did, explaining that I had a few visits and viewings lined up and the post was on my desk.

I wandered over and sat down. It was still busy outside. The roads were jammed and a few frantic workers were dashing to work having missed their nine o'clock start time. A slight movement from across the road caught my eye. It was Ena, sat at his desk and staring directly at me. If looks could kill, I'd be six foot under again. It was a look that I was unfortunately getting all too used to. His stare was pure malevolence. As I met his stare, he seemed to mellow a little, almost imperceptibly. The hard lines around his mouth and eyes softened as he was no doubt imagining my forthcoming demise.

I turned back to my work and decided to take the initiative from Ena. As I did so, Terence walked passed my window. I say walked, but it was more of a painful shuffle. There was sweat on his brow and he was obviously in pain. It was as if he was clenching a couple of ten pence pieces between the cheeks of his arse. I needed help from Clint and maybe I could call in a favour from Terence. After all, he'd been in the business a lot longer than I had and, if anyone knew the type of buildings, Mrs Edgar was looking for, then he would.

As I mulled over my approach to Clint and Terence, Tina made a rather subdued entrance. I'd seen her rough before but never in this state. Carol gave her a long, hard stare before issuing a rather gruff 'Good Morning'. Tina's reply was almost painful. She seemed to be in a worse state than Terence. It was the perfect time to get some help.

'You look like you need some strong coffee, Tina. Do you want me to flash you one up?'

She dropped her chin to her chest and looked over her dark sunglasses at me suspiciously. After all, I wasn't in the

166

habit of helping the lazy cow but, in this instance, I really didn't have any other option.

A few seconds followed as she furrowed her brow but, eventually, her immediate needs overcame her suspicion.

'I'd love one thanks, Richie, strong and black with two sugars.'

I wandered out to the kitchen and asked Carol if she wanted one too. She looked at me quizzically and I smiled back. A brief nod and back to her work. She knew I was up to something, but would go with the flow.

I came back with the coffees, placed one in front of Tina and sat on the side of her desk.

'Did you have a good night Saturday, Tina? You looked like you were enjoying yourself.'

She'd taken her glasses off whilst I was making her coffee, but her chin still went down to her chest as she looked at me. I'd never sat on the end of her desk before and had never been this nice to her either. I suppose she had good reason to be suspicious.

'Yeah, I had a really good time as it happens. I had way too much to drink. Clint and I drank into Sunday evening without a stop. Between you and me, I feel as rough as a badger's arse.'

I was a couple of feet away, but I swear I could smell alcohol leaching out of her pores.

'To be honest, I'm glad I left a little early. I've had a bit too much lately.'

There was a bit of a pause, but she didn't come back as to why I left, so maybe she didn't know the full story.

'He's a really nice guy, your Clint. We had a bit of a chat over the evening and I was surprised at how well we got on and how much we have in common. He seems to be quite taken with you, Tina. He was asking all sorts of questions about you.'

I really had her interest now. A bit of colour was emerging on her cheeks.

'What sort of questions?'

'Well, what sort of food you like, what you do in your lunch breaks; just general stuff really. I think he was trying to get a bit of a picture of you.'

She answered before she realised what she'd said.

'He's got enough of those already.' Her hand went up to her mouth.

'Shit, you didn't hear that, OK?'

I nodded.

'Anyway, I was thinking, do you think Clint would like to come out for a beer with me and the lads one day in the week? I know he's busy most weekends with his job, so maybe a quiet beer sometime. The only thing is that I haven't got a number for him. Any chance you could text it to me and I'll give him a ring to see if he's up for it?'

After a brief think, she explained that he'd probably like a pint with someone else other than his usual mates. However, it wasn't possible for me to ring him until at least this evening, as he was in bed with a hangover.

Carol's curiosity was only partly satisfied. She'd probably twigged that I wanted Clint's number, but she'd have to surmise for herself why I wanted it. There was nothing I could do on the Clint front for the moment, so maybe I could have a quiet word with Terence to sound him out.

I finished off my post and planned my visits and appointments to give me a bit of time with Terence before lunch. I knew he worked alone on Monday mornings, with his secretary coming in this afternoon.

An hour later, I was a couple of hundred yards up the road, stood in front of Terence's agency. He was sat at his desk but he seemed to be unusually high in his chair. As I went in, I noticed that he was sitting on a couple of big foam cushions.

There was a look of panic on Terence's face as he squirmed uncomfortably on his cushions at my unexpected arrival.

'My God, what do you want? You've been talking to Victor, haven't you? It was all a big mistake; believe me, a big mistake.'

He sat there on his foam throne, eyes wide open, vigorously shaking his head. Something wasn't right and I didn't think I wanted to know; certainly not now anyway.

'Sorry Terence, but you've got me at a bit of a disadvantage. I haven't got a clue what you're on about.'

He seemed to relax a bit, sinking down into his cushions.

'As I said on Saturday night, mum's the word. What happens behind closed doors is no business of mine unless people want to talk about it. And I haven't seen or spoken to Victor since I left the two of you at the awards. So, I hope that clears that up.'

I couldn't have been plainer. I wasn't there to blackmail him; just to ask for a little favour. No bodily fluids would be involved at all.

Terence just sank further down into his chair. Obviously, something had happened on Saturday night about which Terence was being very defensive. He didn't want to talk about it and it appeared from his discomfort that whatever took place had been very painful. A few things sprang to mind and I began to feel very uncomfortable. I'll just lay my cards on the table and be on my way.

'I'm sorry, Richard, it's just that I'm not, um, entirely myself at the moment,'

He shifted awkwardly in his chair and I noticed the sheen of sweat on his brow again.

'Anyway, what can I do for you?'

Without any preamble, I explained that I was looking for particular properties in the area that fitted Mrs Edgar's brief. Once I'd explained what I needed, he asked why but I declined as politely as I could.

'It's better for all concerned that you don't know, Terence. If you do manage to come up with any properties and feel happy to pass them on to me, then I'll guarantee your anonymity. I won't divulge where I got the information from; in fact, I'll say I came up with them myself. If my suspicions are correct, you'll be better off not getting involved in any way but you'll probably benefit from the end results. I'm afraid that's all I can say, but your help, and your trust, will be greatly appreciated.'

He looked at me from his foam cushions, weighing up what I'd just asked him to do. His reply didn't take long.

'Young man, I will assist you in any way I can and I appreciate your promise of anonymity. I'm not sure what you're up to but I would like to help. You have intrigued me no end. You know, I thought you'd come on an entirely different matter.'

His whole manner had changed since I walked in and he was back to the usual Terence. Quite what he was worried about, I didn't really know, but the next time I had a chat with Vic, I was sure I'd get a much better idea.

We arranged to meet later in the week when he would pass me details of any properties that fitted the bill, either from his agency's portfolio or his local knowledge.

I walked back to the office in a much better frame of mind than earlier in the day. I was beginning to take the initiative. Sitting and waiting for a severe beating wasn't an option. Terence was now on-board, even though he didn't know why. It must have been my charming personality, the promise of absolute discretion or, more likely, my perfect arse that had swayed him.

Tina was looking slightly better by the time I got back. She'd tidied up her makeup a bit and some colour was returning to her cheeks.

'Clint's up and about, if you want to ring him. I told him you might give him a bell later.'

I thanked her and sat at my desk working out my next move. The sooner I rang Clint, the more time it would give him (that's if he decided to help me) to pick up any rumours or gossip flying around about me and the Sharples'.

I made my excuses and headed for the nearby park, where I picked a remote bench away from the lunch-goers and MILFs with their pushchairs and screaming kids.

Clint answered his mobile after a couple of rings. He wasn't that surprised to hear from me, having spoken with Tina, but he did sound a little worse for wear.

'You all right, mate? I'll ring back another time when you've got your head in gear, if you like.'

He said much the same as Tina had earlier in the day. It sounded like they'd had quite a weekend.

'What can I do for you, Richie? I expect you've heard enough about our lost weekend. Mind, if you do hear anything about what we got up to, let me know 'cos I can't remember a bloody thing.'

I reminded him about Saturday night and my tumble with old man Sharples and him watching my back. Thankfully, he remembered all of it. That made things an awful lot easier for me.

'To cut to the chase, Clint, I feel a bit like a dead man walking at the moment.'

His grunt of affirmation didn't make me feel any better. I got that feeling in the pit of my stomach which is closely followed by saliva flooding into your mouth. You're going to puke.

'After what I did to old man Sharples, and his boy, on Saturday night, I reckon they're going to come after me sooner rather than later. It won't be them specifically, but some hired muscle.'

Another grunt from down the line followed by a long pensive, 'Hmmmmm,' Clint was trying to guess my next question. I was pretty sure he wouldn't want to get too involved in a face-to-face front-up with some goons hired by Sharples. He had a business and a reputation to look after. Besides, if he openly backed me, he was well aware of the connections Sharples had and I reckon I came a very poor second. I put him out of his misery,

'Listen Clint, I know you work with, and meet, a lot of people who are connected to the Sharples family and I'm not asking you to take sides or help me out in a bundle.'

I could hear the loud exhalation of breath down the other end of the phone. He was obviously relieved.

'No, it's just that I have no idea who or what I'm dealing with here. All I'm asking for is if you hear anything about me or if someone may have taken on a 'job' after the weekend, is there any chance of tipping me a wink? I don't want you asking any questions because that would be too obvious and I don't want you to get involved. So, any chance you could help and maybe save me from a beasting?'

There was a short pause. He was weighing up his options.

'I'll see what I can do, Richie, but I can't promise anything. If the word goes out, it may only go to a couple of people. It's not exactly going to be advertised on the back pages of the *Sun* or on *Sky Sports News*. These things are usually kept quiet, for obvious reasons. If I hear anything though, I'll ring you, okay?'

It was my time to grunt an affirmation. I wasn't feeling on top of the world. He must have picked up on that.

'I'm working tonight at a private party downtown. All sorts of Herberts are going. You never know, I might hear something. In the meantime, watch your back very carefully. It'll probably be two blokes. They won't stand out very much but they'll be handy. There'd be no witnesses and nothing to trace. It'll be fists, boots, something blunt and heavy or, if you're very unlucky, it might be a knife. Just look out for anything out of the ordinary. Try to stay near people or crowds and don't get isolated. Oh, and don't be afraid to run; don't be stupid by tooling yourself up. You're just as likely to have them used back on you rather than you getting the chance of using them on them. It's a big sentence, don't forget. The one who turns and runs away lives to fight another day.'

He made a lot of sense and I was getting a few things in perspective. Clint was nowhere near as thick as I'd first pegged him for.

'Listen, Richie, I've got to go. I feel like shit and I've got to work, so I'll see you soon, eh? Oh, and good luck.'

He certainly didn't pull any punches. I immediately winced at the inadvertent pun. Whichever way I looked at it, I was in trouble.

I started to nibble on my lunch but the sandwich had lost its appeal as I had lost my appetite. I wasn't in the mood for food. I glanced around the park with a hint of fear and an even bigger dose of paranoia, thanks to Clint's précis of my predicament. Everyone looked dodgy. Even the MILFs dragging their kids around while they were trying to smoke a fag were looking at me as if there was a price on my head. Christ, this was starting to get to me.

In the middle of my paranoid delusions my phone chirped in my pocket. It was a text; I didn't get many texts. The only texts I ever received were from my mates joking about the latest footballer to get caught hanging out with a wannabe celebrity or with a bad ethnic joke that was likely to offend about half of the world's population.

I checked my phone half-heartedly but I got one of those shocks that send your heart into little palpitations. The name on the screen was Nicola. Bloody hell! What a surprise!

It was last Wednesday that I'd texted her after our disastrous meeting at the pub. After five days of silence, I didn't think I'd ever hear from her again. Yet, here she was getting back to me.

My negative frame of mind, or more likely my desperate situation, took over from my initial state of shock and mild euphoria. I bet she's texted me to give me another bollocking or to tell me that I've won a week-long guilt trip at a rundown seaside resort.

I opened the text with more than a bit of trepidation. Fuck it, I was right. The first two words were 'YOU BASTARD'.

They leapt out of the screen at me. I swear that I flinched backwards when I read them; smacked in the mouth by text. I'd settle for that right now but I'd hoped for better, at the very least, just not in capitals. It was like she was shouting at me.

I read on. The capitals stopped and she started to explain her feelings after receiving my text last week. To be honest, it seemed to be a bit of an outpouring. I wasn't yet sure of what though. She explained how hurt she was after listening to the lads in the pub; how she'd been stressed lately and had taken it out on me. She had every right to do that in my view, so I couldn't argue there.

What was encouraging for me was that she said she'd thought about my explanation on the night and my subsequent texts and came to the conclusion that I wasn't a complete and utter arsehole after all, and that I may be a nice bloke with good intentions, despite the Rhino Hunt incident. Well, that's a result then.

But having been built up, I soon came crashing down. The end of her text didn't exactly fill me with optimism. I kept reading the last few lines over and over, trying to make some sense of them, but I kept coming up blank.

'I'm going away for a few months. So, please don't try to contact me again. I don't know if I will ever see you again, so no Vera Lynn moments for us! And remember that fat people have feelings as well. Nic. X'

There was something I wasn't picking up on. However, there was a kiss at the end. I may be a bastard, but I got a kiss.

I suddenly felt great. All the concerns of the last couple of days fell away and I felt like a little kid on his first date again. I know she said not to, but I had to send her another text:

'YOU'RE RIGHT. Thanks for getting back. Sorry about the misunderstanding. I really would like to see you when you get back, hopefully with no friends in the background! And remember that bastards have feelings as well. Richie. X'

I couldn't believe I put a kiss. Who said that romance was dead? On reflection, I think it was my last two girlfriends, but it's the thought that counts, isn't it?

Tina and Carol both looked up as I whistled my way into the office. Tina was her usual discreet self.

'Fuck me; you look as happy as a dog with two dicks. For you to be that happy there must have been a girl involved. I bet I'm right, you little stud-muffin you.'

I was right; I'm working in a witches' coven. It was also a bit endearing coming from Tina. I was glad I'd taken the time to have a little chat with her, even though I did it for my own benefit.

'Well if you must know I've just had a text from a very nice young lady who I met the other night.'

Carol and Tina gave me a teasing 'Ooooohhh' in unison. I went a bit red and my collar suddenly became very tight around my neck.

'The bad news is she's going away for a while and I don't know if I'll get to see her again. Bummer, hey?'

'Top tip, Richie, if a girl tells you she's going away for a while, you've either been dumped or she's hiding something. Judging by your mood, I reckon she's not told you everything and she's holding something back.'

Both Carol and I were staring at Tina after her words of worldly wisdom. Carol broke the silence,

'Christ, check out the amateur psychologist with the love-bite necklace.'

It was Tina's turn to blush.

'What? I was just saying that 'cos all girls do it. I'm telling you there's something else. Now if you'll excuse me, I've got a bit to catch up on. Can't gossip all day with the likes of you lot.'

With that, she went back to her computer. This was another side of Tina I hadn't seen before.

She'd made me think about Nicola's text again and she was right; there was something else; something I was missing. I'd certainly had to change my perceptions of a few people over the last few days and I wondered if the next few days would be the same. I'd probably discover that Tina was in fact an ex-SAS trooper who'd had a sex change and was now an assassin for hire.

It was time to get back to saving my skin. I'd scammed the office car for a couple of hours in the afternoon so, after my chats with Clint and Terence, it was time to visit Mrs Edgar and give her a sitrep. I'd been watching too many American action films to actually think I'd give her a sitrep.

'Damn straight, bring it on, mo'fo', outstanding, hoorah!'

All I'd get was, 'Do you want a cup of tea?' Never mind, nothing wrong with a nice cup of tea and I was sure to get one round at Mrs E's.

I pulled up outside Mrs Edgar's house early in the afternoon to find the tail-end of a black Jaguar disappearing out of the other gate. I remember her saying that she didn't get many visitors, so I was a bit intrigued. She was at the front door as I walked across her drive; you could still see the faint lines where Ena had wheel-spun away before our first meeting.

'You're not still seeing other estate agents are you, Mrs Edgar?'

She shot me a stern look.

'Sorry, Lyn, I still don't feel comfortable calling you by your Christian name.'

I thought she was going to give me a little hug for a moment because she changed in an instant. She was back to the little old lady with the never-ending pot of tea and the EU cake mountain.

'No estate agents, Richard. Just an old friend popping around to see if I'm OK and if I need anything. Such a sweet young man, reminds me so much of my husband when he was about his age.'

She had a brief, wistful look in her eyes, followed by a long sigh. I guess she must miss her husband and her youth.

She quickly took me by the upper arm, just above the elbow, and easily manoeuvred me into the front room. She would have made a great bouncer.

'Now, young man, let's have a cup of tea and a slice of cake and you can tell me all about what's been happening to you since the last time we met.'

She must have picked up on my sudden deflation. The chin to the chest, the shoulders rounding, and an even bigger sigh than hers. I shrank to the size of a small child in a couple of seconds.

'Oh dear, that bad? I'll get the tea while you think of a way to sugar-coat it for me. I do so hate disappointments, don't you?'

178

She was off to the kitchen and back in a flash with a slice of cake that was so big that it would cost you a fortune in excess baggage if you tried to take it on a plane. She got straight to the point, her voice felt like a scalpel as she told me what to do.

'Right, Richard, no flim-flam or dilly-dallying. Tell me, warts and all, how bad it is. Tell me everything, no matter how trivial you think it might be, and maybe we might be able to salvage something from the obviously poor situation you find yourself in.'

I felt like the pupil and she was the teacher. So, without a moment's hesitation, I opened up to an old lady I hardly knew. I'd never even been as open with my mum as I was over the next half an hour or so with Mrs Edgar.

She said very little. There was just the odd prompt and word of encouragement throughout the whole of my confession; at least that's what it felt like. I had the impression that she was in control of me. At the end, I felt a bit drained, almost abused or violated in a strange sort of way. I couldn't put my finger on it, but it was almost like I had been expertly interrogated. She made us another cup of tea.

'Well, Richard, I can see that we need to work a lot faster than I had first anticipated.'

She wasn't talking to me; she was talking to herself; to an alter ego with a bit of steel and resolve that came through in her voice and belied her age.

'You really have got yourself into a frightful pickle, haven't you?' It wasn't a question; it was a statement.

'Right, in situations like this, I was always taught to pick out the positives. Forget the factors over which you have no control and concentrate on those which you can influence.'

I nodded a bit, but wasn't sure where she was going.

'On the positive side, you know they will be coming, and I agree with you in that it will be sooner rather than later. From what I hear, Mr Sharples is not a patient man. You also have an asset in Mr Clint. It wouldn't appear that he is compromised, as he didn't have to come to your assistance on Saturday, so his help may be invaluable in giving us an early warning. Martin is also a positive but, unfortunately, I fear his assistance may be after-the-event. I'm afraid the majority of it is down to you, Richard. You will have to act accordingly when the moment arises, and arise it will.'

I looked at her face. I tried to recall all the girls in the early *James Bond* movies, but she wasn't there. I was being lectured, and taught, in the art of self-preservation by someone who should smell of cabbage and piss and being served food through a straw. It was as if she was Miss Marple on steroids.

'You'll have to break your routines and habits. For the next few days, you cannot be predictable. For example, alter your times of getting to and then leaving work; lunch breaks also. If you have a regular commitment in the evenings, then change it.'

She then went through basically everything that Clint had advised, but then she got a bit heavy.

'When the time comes, you mustn't hesitate. Make your mind up and act immediately. If that means running, then run and don't look back. It slows you down and you can fall. If you decide to fight, then be sure. You must be decisive. Remember, people can't fight if they can't see or can't breathe. If you achieve one or the other, the odds are stacked in your favour. If you achieve both, then it's game over, as they say. Now, any questions?'

I was a bit shell shocked.

'Yes, just how does a nice little old lady know all this stuff and why do you want to help me so much?'

She just gave me a little smile.

'Firstly, Richard, I wasn't always a little old lady. I had a life once, a long time ago. It was quite a boring life, but I picked up a few things along the way that I thought might come in useful. Secondly, as to why I'm helping you, let's just say I've taken a shine to you, in a matronly way, of course. And I've taken a particular dislike to the Sharples' and their associates. One other thing you may like to bear in mind - the last thing that young Sharples will be expecting is an overt action on your part.'

'What? You mean take the fight to him?'

'Yes, that's exactly what I mean. It's the last thing he'll be expecting. It could very well work to your advantage in that they would become very annoyed and, hopefully, very sloppy. Circumvent their planning and make them rush, but if you do decide to do anything, be very careful.'

She had a point. Ena's guard would be down; he's probably still scratching his bollocks after Saturday night. Besides, I liked fucking Ena over so much; it should be in the Olympics.

I took on everything that she'd run through and I suppose I felt a bit happier. I then described my meeting with Terence and, when she questioned his reliability, I explained his little secret and my suspicions about some problems on Saturday.

'Well, each to their own, I suppose. I rely on your judgement regarding Terence and the properties but I would suggest if anyone else becomes involved, you let me know first.'

This was my first telling off. It was time to go and practise some anti-surveillance moves. Actually, I was going to drive around the block twice then park up and have a sandwich. Jason Bourne, eat your heart out.

Having satisfied my annoying inner demons that Colombian motorcycle hit-men weren't following me, I dumped the car and got back to the office via a circuitous route.

It suddenly felt a lot more serious than when I'd arrived in the office some eight hours earlier. I scanned the street only to find Ena looking over at me from the shadows.

What do you know, you bastard? Well, bring it on. I felt more determined than ever to beat Ena, once and for all, but it would take a lot of work and probably a lot of bottle. Talking of which, I needed a drink.

I explained to Carol that my mum had been taken ill and that my movements may be a bit erratic over the next few days. She didn't ask any questions but she gave me a Roger Moore eyebrow. She didn't believe me. With that, I made my excuses and legged it out of the back door. This caused another raised eyebrow.

I'd been watching Ena from the corner of my eye. He was involved in a conversation with his boss and he wasn't giving me the evils anymore, so it was time to take the fight to the old enemy. This wouldn't be a person but a car; an old German Audi Quattro.

The next stop was a small Indian deli' situated a couple of streets behind the office. It was handy because it was very close to where Ena parked his car.

The deli' sold a variety of curry powders. I chose a nice hot one that was particularly aromatic. If it was cooked up, I bet it would make a lovely curry but I had other plans.

I had a pang of conscience, as this would be the second time in three days that Ena was going to be in a whole world of chilli-induced pain. It lasted for what must have been about three milliseconds. Fuck him.

Sixty seconds later, I was walking towards Ena's car. As I approached it, I took the metal lid off the curry can and put the plastic cover back on for the last fifty metres. I was ready. There was no one else in the street and I'd only need about five seconds.

Older cars tend to have a big air-intake grill between the bonnet and the windscreen. Below this is the main intake for the air vents into the car, in particular the vents on the dash.

I reached the Audi and had a quick look around; it was all clear. Off came the lid and I spread the powder across the width of the grill then brushed in the remainder left on the top down into the intake with my hand. Five seconds and I was done. There was no sign at all of Mumbai's favourite curry powder. Hopefully, it would be a recipe for disaster for poor Ena. Just to make sure that I really pissed him off, I went around to the driver's door, stuck a matchstick in the lock and snapped it off. Perfect.

There was a small park just across the road with a number of small bushes for me to hide behind. I suddenly had visions of my being arrested as a suspected paedo' for lurking in the bushes. It was a chance that I was willing to take, because I didn't want to miss this.

Luckily, it was a hot day. I was counting on him using his forced air as soon as he got into the car and not when he was actually driving. That could be a big problem for me if he took off and smashed into something or someone as a result of my prank.

I didn't have long to wait for Ena. The cocky bastard came whistling down the road, no doubt imagining my imminent demise. Well, I was about to spice up his life.

He got to his door and tried his key in the lock. Then he tried again; no joy. He bent down and looked at it, following up with a stream of mostly single-syllable words. He gave up on the driver's door and went around to the passenger side. From my vantage point in the bushes, I could see his relief at finally getting into his car. He was suitably wound-up as he climbed over the gear stick and prepared to start up.

What happened next appeared to be in slow motion, as I had been anticipating it so much. The key went into the ignition and then I could hear the first few cranks of the engine. What followed was beyond all of my expectations. I'd heard about this curry storm down at the pub but I'd never seen it, until now.

The engine had kicked into life and so had the electrics. Ena hadn't got any of his windows down yet, so he was enclosed in his icon of many a crime series from the Eighties. The powerful fan sucked the air through the grill and dragged the curry powder into the car. With pure German efficiency, one second I could see him, all red-faced and angry, then the next he was engulfed in a cloud of Saturday- night takeaway.

I could hear the screams from where I was, about thirty metres away. I had a sudden recollection of the same sounds from the estate agents' dinner. Poor fucker was having a really bad run.

The next thing that happened was the driver's door burst open, emitting a large cloud of brown dust. This was quickly followed by an apparition. Ena had lost all his colour and so had his clothes. They'd taken on the colour of the curry powder, a sort of shitty brown yellow. The powder on his face had turned to a paste, like a curry face pack, as it had mixed with the sweat and tears streaming from his eyes. He looked

184

like some sort of satanic beast or something out of *Doctor Who*; it could be *Doctor Who and the Curry Creature* or *Doctor Who meets the Balti Beast*.

He fell to the floor clutching at his eyes and mouth. I was glad I'd gone for the hot one; it was having the desired effect.

By now he was rolling around in the middle of the road. A car came down and just drove around him. I thought it was a sad reflection of society as a whole that someone could simply ignore a person so obviously in need. There again, I was the one in the bushes, glorying in someone else's pain, and I was revelling in it.

Ena was screaming like he had done on Saturday, squealing like a little piggy.

Front doors were starting to open and people were coming out to see what was going on. He would have made a good professional footballer because he was rolling over and over. The difference was that he was actually in pain and wasn't feigning it at all.

As I left my front row seat in the bushes, people were coming out of their houses with pans and buckets of water and throwing them over a distressed Ena Tikka Masala. I glanced back to see him lying in a pool of what looked like diarrhoea; it was just shitty brown water. He was still tinged with yellow from the curry powder. I thought that if this stuff can fuck-up your outsides so much, what on earth does it do to your stomach and intestines? I swear he looked just like Homer Simpson but without the big belly.

Mrs Edgar would be proud of me. I'd got my retaliation in first and, to be honest, I'd enjoyed it possibly a bit more than I should have done.

Daddy would know soon enough and would probably unleash the dogs. Like Fido, I could see Ena developing a phobia, only this time for chilli. Whatever they'd planned for me would happen very soon and I'd have to be on my toes. I just hoped that I'd goaded them enough into making a mistake.

It was time to go home and get tooled up, despite everyone advising me to the contrary. I wasn't going down without a fight.

As I jumped on the bus home, I had visions of Ena sat in his car in about a year's time and still smelling the curry powder as it leached out of his carpets and upholstery. He could always decorate the inside of the car with flock wallpaper and have sitar music on the CD player.

'Would you like lime pickle with that, sir?'

Chapter Eight

Ena didn't turn up for work the following day. I kept glancing across at his empty chair but he didn't show. I suppose looking like a cross between Homer Simpson and someone with renal failure didn't exactly entice you to get up and go to work. He didn't turn up on Wednesday either. I must have really fucked him over. I felt a bit like I'd pissed myself wearing black trousers; it gave me a nice warm feeling, but no one would notice and I certainly couldn't tell anyone.

Overall, I felt happy with myself. So much so, that I fancied a bevy with the boys and Wednesday night was our usual midweek get-together, if none of us had anything else on.

I rang each of the lads. Devon and Martin were well up for a couple of pints but Vic was surprisingly reticent. He didn't sound too good on the phone. Perhaps he had a bit of a cold, as he sounded a bit nasally. I eventually managed to persuade him when I promised to tell him about my run-ins with Ena and his dad over the weekend and on Monday.

On top of my normal work at the agency, I was steadily compiling a list of properties for Mrs Edgar. Once I got on a roll, and knew what I was looking for, it became quite easy.

I concentrated on certain areas which had the sort of larger properties that needed a bit of refurbishment and would invariably have older occupants. I was surprising myself with the number of suitable properties I was coming across. They weren't hard to find. Quite a few still had *For Sale* signs outside, advertising one- or two-bedroom flats in what were very big houses. It seemed to me that someone was maximising their profits by splitting up the houses into apartments and, in some instances, developing the extensive grounds as well.

I still hadn't got anything back from Terence and I was beginning to think he wasn't going to help me. Maybe I'd see Vic tonight and would actually be able to blackmail Terence into giving me a bit of information. How true that would turn out to be.

I dropped my results around to Mrs Edgar before heading home for tea, a shower and a brisk walk to the pub. I had second thoughts about the walk and jumped on the bus to get around the park to the pub. The last time I was there was when I had my ill-fated meeting with Nicola. I still hadn't heard back from her following my last text, but I was still grateful that she'd actually contacted me after her humiliation at the hands of my mates; perhaps all wasn't lost.

I got off the bus around the corner from the pub and my phone rang as I touched the pavement. I hoicked it out of my jeans' pocket and glanced at the display. It was Clint. My current state of positivity took an immediate knock as Clint's reality-pill hit home. If he was calling me, he must have news.

I'd always been a positive person. When Dad left at my tender young age, I'd had to adopt that frame of mind to keep us going and to keep Mum and Sis happy. It would have been very easy to slip into a 'woe is me' attitude and think that life was just a bowl of toenails, but that wasn't for me. I'd always try to take the positives from a situation and to appear happy and upbeat at all times.

Well, just at this moment quite a few negative thoughts came flooding into my mind, but a faint heart never fucked a pig, as they say.

I took a deep breath and pressed the *answer* button.

'Hello, mate, what can I do for you?'

'Unfortunately, there's nothing you can do for me, but you're going to have to do a lot for yourself. You're going to have to do this one all on your own this time.'

Clint came across as serious. This didn't sound good.

'Is it that bad? It feels like you've just pissed on my fireworks. Who, or what, have I got to look forward to?'

Look at the positives. At least it wasn't Clint coming for me. He wouldn't be ringing me up if he was.

'It's bad in as much as things are happening, and from what I hear, it won't be very long before someone comes calling with a wedge of cash in one hand and a lump of lead in the other. It sounds like you've really pissed off the Sharples' big-time.'

I thought back to Monday night with Ena emerging from a Saharan curry storm and subsequently rolling about in a pool of Indian gravy. I guess that did the trick. Mrs Edgar's plan was coming to fruition, but I just hoped that I could cope with the forthcoming shit-storm.

'I've been keeping my ear to the ground and there's been so many jungle drums going off, I've nearly got my head stood on. To cut it short, it seems Sharples wants you done very quickly and he's been cutting a few corners to get a crew together. He's not being very subtle.'

Monday definitely worked.

'The concrete stuff I've got comes from someone close, so it seems kosher. I was chatting to one of the lads on the door last night and it would seem that Sharples, or to be more precise, one of his gophers, has got hold of a couple of lads to do a job. He didn't know what it was about but it sounded like the money was good. The word was they want someone FUBARed, like now.'

I guessed the gopher would be Fido. If I got fucked up big-style and lived through it, I'd be putting more than liquid beef-stock on his bollocks. It'd be more like two crocodile clips wired up to the mains.

'The crew are brothers by the name of Miliband. Not the Labour MPs, I can assure you. These boys won't try and talk you to death, just beat the fuck out of you. The Chuckle Brothers aren't known for knives, so that's a good thing, but they're not very bright and enjoy dishing out a beasting.'

It looked like I was going to get beaten to death by New Labour.

'That's all I've got, Richie; hope it helps. And please, no matter how it goes, keep my name out of it or I might end up in Intensive Care in the bed next to you. I'm only joking, mate.'

He was winding-up the call. Did I have any questions for him before he hung up?

'What do these guys look like?' He gave a short chuckle.

'That's easy mate. Let's say they stand out in a crowd. They're not big; average height and a bit wiry. White but look a bit grey. Probably all the drugs they chuck down their necks with gallons of cold Euro-fizz and roll-ups.'

I wondered how they stood out. They seemed like most lads you saw out on a Saturday night.

'The thing is they're covered in tats. One has a tattoo of a bat on his forehead and the other one has a line around his neck with 'cut here' tattooed on the side. They've also got loads of tats on their arms. Not good ones like mine. Looks like most of them were done in prison with a bit of ink and a pin. Like I said, these boys are not known for their subtlety.

They must have really hated their parents when they were young.'

'Thanks for this mate. I really appreciate it. If I get through this, I'll owe you one big-time.'

'Best of luck and watch your back. See you soon, and hopefully not on the front page of the local rag.' With that, the phone went dead. I really did appreciate what he'd done. He'd gone out on a limb for me, albeit a very large, muscular, tattooed limb, but a limb all the same.

The pros were that I now knew who was coming for me and it would be very soon. The cons, or ex-cons to be precise, were that I had two nutters on my case and they might not stop to see if I was still breathing while they were using my head as a football. Perhaps Mum would install some raspberry-flavoured windows in the house so I would enjoy licking them.

I needed a beer to calm my nerves. I was soon stood at the bar and downed my first pint of vitamin B complex like there was no tomorrow. This was as bad a Freudian slip as I could wish for.

I was the first one to arrive at the pub, despite my call from Clint holding me up. I got myself another beer and took a table at the back so we could chat and not be overheard. It wasn't long before Dev and Martin strolled in. They could have been brothers.

I wandered over and bought them a beer. As we walked over to the table, Martin picked up on my fragile state.

'Are you OK, mate? You seem a bit preoccupied with something.'

He knew full well what a mess I was in, so it was him breaking the ice to get me chatting and maybe to reassure me a bit. I took a deep breath; I was ready to go through the whole scenario for Dev's benefit, but Martin cut me short.

'You don't have to go through the whole lot, Richie. I've brought Dev up to speed on the way over. Like me, he thinks you're a complete wanker and have got yourself into a whole world of shit. What the fuck were you thinking of?'

Dev put his pint down after a long swig. It left a big white moustache on his upper lip. I was about to get a bollocking from Morgan Freeman!

'Before you say anything, Dev, it just seemed like a good idea at the time. But things have escalated a bit since Saturday night and, yes, I'm in a whole world of shit.'

I explained about Monday and how I'd got my retaliation in first in an attempt to bring out Sharples a bit quicker in the hope that he'd make a mistake. I could see they really enjoyed the thought of Ena being locked in his car surrounded by a swirling cloud of curry powder and emerging looking like a jaundiced Chinaman.

'All I can say, Richie, is that I hope I never get on the wrong side of you. You really can be an evil little bugger, can't you?'

There was a hint of admiration in his voice but it was tinged with more than a bit of concern. To add to this, I went on to tell them about the Chuckle Brothers. When Dev spoke again, all hint of admiration had gone. There was just concern; grave concern.

'Fuck me man, you've done it this time. Old man Sharples is going to have your bollocks sawn off with a blunt knife and use them as a paperweight on his big mahogany desk.'

He was looking at me with his big brown eyes, shaking his head at the same time. What concerned me at the time was that I might be dragging them into it as well. I hadn't thought of that one when I was hatching my plans. I'd won Wanker of the Year by a mile.

'I know the Milibands and they're just as you described them; thick but dangerous. If you want, I can make a quick phone call, an anonymous one from a phone box down the road, and get them picked up. Sometimes the phone is mightier than the sword; untraceable and a lot less messy. It gets someone else to do the work for you. Just make up a story about them having a couple of kilos of weed and they get their front door busted. Knowing them, they'll have a bit of gear around the house so they'll get locked up. What do you say?

I thought about it for a moment.

'No thanks Martin. I prefer it the way it is.'

'What, that you're going to get your head rearranged by a couple of Neanderthals? I can stop this within a few hours.'

'I might not have a few hours Mart. At least, in this way, I know who's out there gunning for me. It gives me a bit of an edge. If they're picked up, I'm blind again. Besides that, the next lot might not be as 'nice' as these two. No Martin, I'll stick with what I've got.'

Martin thought about it for a second.

'I think you're completely round the fuckin' bend, but you've got a point. Right, it's time for another beer. Same again?'

Martin took our glasses and went for three more of the same. There was still no sign of Vic, which was a bit unusual. He was usually the first here, but then, he didn't sound too well on the phone.

To give Devon his due, he did try to reassure me that things would work out and he'd be there if I needed him. I

193

couldn't help getting the feeling he thought he was talking to a man on death row, just as the minister and the guards were walking down to the cell to cart him away.

They weren't hollow words but we both knew there wasn't a lot, if anything, he could do. The Chuckle Brothers weren't thick enough to wander into the pub and exact retribution in the middle of the local quiz night.

'Three of England's finest beers. It puts hair on your chest and a couple of inches on your belly. Cheers.'

We all lifted our glasses and took a big, long gulp. We needed a drink after a rather serious few minutes. I needed a piss and started to get up just as Devon did.

'I need a nervous piss. Were you on your way too, Richie?'

Sod it, this was a bit awkward.

'No Dev, just need to stretch and keep supple for the big fight.'

He smiled back weakly and wandered off to the bogs.

'So you've got an inferiority complex too, mate?'

Martin smiled across the table as he waited to see what affect his cutting observation would have.

'Too bloody right; I thought I was the only one, but you as well, hey?'

'Yeah, too right. It didn't used to bother me but as I get older I'm starting to suffer from White Man's Willy Syndrome. I just worry that it's not big enough. And having a squirt next to Dev just doesn't do your self-confidence any good at all.'

Martin smiled and I could tell that he had the same paranoia as me.

'You know, in most toilets, they have the normal height piss-pots and then you've got the lower ones?'

'The kids' ones, you mean?'

'Well, my theory is that they're not for kids. They're for lucky buggers like Dev. It's so that he can have a piss and not have his bell-end dragging in the fag ends and smelly sugar cubes when he has a piss.'

We both cracked up at our vision of Dev's fortune.

'It's like a baby's arm holding a big purple plum.'

Dev came back to the table to find us in a better mood.

'What's tickled you two while I've been pumping my bilges?'

Martin came to my assistance.

'Nothing mate, we were just discussing life's lottery and male insecurity in general. Best you don't know.'

He gave us a quizzical look and shrugged his broad shoulders as he took his seat. There must have been something in our manner that gave him an inkling as to what we were chatting about or maybe it was my reluctance to share a urinal.

'It's as the girls say, boys, 'Once you've had black, there's no going back.'

It was his turn to smile. I took advantage of our improved mood,

'Anyway Martin, talking about people completely round the bend, what's the story about you and my next door neighbour? Come clean mate or it'll eat you up. Besides, it's time we had a laugh at your expense. What was it like, polishing old Pratt's leather seats with his wife's arse?'

I wasn't sure if Martin would want to talk about it after his reticence on Sunday afternoon.

'As the cat's out of the bag, I might as well fill you in on the gory details. You perverts, can't a man have any secrets?'

Devon licked his lips with his pink tongue in anticipation.

'Not with us mate. We might pick up a few tips.' Dev was sitting on the edge of his stool whilst Martin gave another involuntary scratch of his back.

'Number one tip is never get involved with that lady unless you've got a very high pain threshold. My back's cut to ribbons and my bollocks still feel like they've been sucked out through my Jap's eye.'

This was going to be interesting.

Martin ran through how he'd rung her up after their meeting concerning Rodney's complaint about Fang getting crapped on. Dev was as unimpressed with my nocturnal habits as he was with Martin's.

They'd arranged to meet up the road from the pub after our last get-together. She'd be driving as it was the only way she could get out of the house without raising Rodney's suspicion.

'Well, when she turned up in a spanking old *E-Type,* I couldn't believe my luck. The trouble was, as soon as I got in, I knew I was in trouble. Firstly, she stuck her tongue so far down my throat I thought she was after my dinner. Secondly, there's no bloody room in the car for what she had in mind. I had visions of ending up in A&E in about two hours' time, having the cigarette lighter surgically removed from my arse.'

He went on to explain that she drove to a wood just outside of town and that she had to be home in about three hours as Rodney thought she was at the gym.

'When she said she only had three hours, I panicked a bit. I'd never done yoga or seen any of Houdini's contortions. There then followed the next bit of trouble. She was wearing jeans, very tight ones, and, in a nutshell, they were bloody difficult to get off. It was like a snake sloughing its skin. She was wriggling this way and that and in the end she had her feet up on the dash with me pulling them down.'

We were starting to enjoy this. I was seeing Mrs Pratt in a different light; in the dark to be more exact.

'Once her jeans were off, it all kicked off. She just went mad for it. I dapped my hand on her pussy and that set her off. She just went absolutely fuckin' wild, literally. I swear she's got an epileptic clitoris.'

Dev and I were in fits by now. We were revelling in Martin's obvious discomfort as he laid himself bare, along with Mrs Pratt.

'After nearly castrating myself on the gear stick, I finally got over to her side. Well, almost. You can't do it with a steering wheel in the way, so we went back to my side, eventually. If she'd slipped she'd have put it in reverse. That's when it got a bit wild. It was like trying to shag Edward Scissorhands. She's got fuckin' nails like Freddie Kruger.'

It was all getting a bit too much for us. I was feeling physically sick because I was laughing so much.

'My back's like a lace curtain. Fifty lashes strapped to grating would have been less painful and bloody, I can tell you.'

Martin took a well-earned swig of beer and scratched his back again.

'Overall, I can only describe it as heaven and hell. If shagging an octopus on heat for two hours floats your boat, then she's the one for you. As for me, once was enough.'

I thought back to her walking back from the garage. I imagined a cowboy making his way back to his bunkhouse after two weeks in the saddle. She couldn't have stopped a pig in an alleyway last Wednesday night, that's for sure. Mind you, Martin hadn't come out of their woodland frolic much better.

Dev managed a breath in between his almost uncontrollable laughter.

'Sounds like you deserve a Purple Heart for wounds received on the battlefield, Mart.'

'It sounds more like he got a Purple Knob and a back looking like a road map.' I couldn't help rubbing it in.

We needed more beer and then, I'd make a quick call to Vic. Where the bloody hell was he? He was missing all the fun.

'More beer, chaps? Do you want Scratchings with yours, Mart?'

If looks could kill.

'In fact, I think I will; just to be awkward and so you spend some money on me, you bastard.'

I made it to the bar just as Vic walked in. Christ, he looked a bloody mess, quite literally.

He clocked me at the bar and walked over a bit sheepishly.

'Fancy a beer, Vic? Looks like you need one. What the hell happened to you?'

His face was a mess. His nose was obviously broken and there was a strap over it to help him to breathe. No wonder he sounded a bit nasal over the phone. He had two big black eyes, probably as the result of the impact on his nose.

'You don't want to know mate, believe me.'

'Course we bloody do. One of our mates gets beaten up, and then we're all involved. Did that Terence do this to you?'

I was angry that my mate had been whacked, on my night out too.

'No Richie, it wasn't Terence. It's a bit more disturbing than that.'

He didn't wait for a reply as he turned and headed to our table. The other two lads had seen him come in and, by the looks on their faces, they shared my consternation.

'What the fuck happened to you?' The question came out in unison.

'To be honest guys, I don't really want to talk about it. It's too embarrassing and painful, so if it's alright with you, can we just leave it?'

Martin was the first to jump in.

'Sorry Vic, but you can't just come in all bashed and bruised and ask us not to delve. As embarrassing and as painful as it might be, it seems that this is the night for opening up your soul and facing public ridicule and humiliation. I should know because I've just done it.'

I quickly filled Vic in about Martin's gymnastic and masochist encounter in the front seat of a classic English sports car. He tried to laugh but he was soon wincing in pain from his broken nose.

'OK, but it doesn't go any further. I've got someone else's dignity to think of as well as my own. The trouble is, after I've told you what happened, I don't think I'll have any dignity left to speak about.'

Dev's tongue was out again and he'd slid to the front of his stool. Martin, too, was waiting with bated breath. Dev's description of us was probably correct; I was beginning to think that we were all perverts.

'Firstly, don't ask me for the name of the other guy, please, and keep this strictly between ourselves.'

Vic shot me a warning glance and I did the same to Martin. I was sure I'd mentioned to him about Vic picking Terence up on Saturday.

He took a big mouthful of beer for a bit of Dutch courage and started to tell his story. I wasn't sure why they called it Dutch courage. Why not English courage? After all, in Nelson's time our boys fought with at least a pint of rum in their bellies. It's a wonder how they managed to aim straight after that, let alone fight hand-to-hand with murderous weapons.

Vic left out how he met his partner for the night and just referred to him as 'this bloke'. After leaving the hotel, Vic went back to this bloke's place and, after a few drinks, got down to whatever blokes get down to in the privacy of their own home. Vic was, thankfully for three fully-signed-up heterosexual males, scant on detail during his tale. All three of us were keen not to show our embarrassment, but we had our legs and knees tightly together, quietly squirming on our stools.

'Then it started to get a bit freaky. The bloke asked if I'd like to see one of his pets. Well, I needed a bit of a break, so I said yes. Before you could say Pets' Corner, he came back with a little beige gerbil. That was OK; I quite like animals, but he had a small plastic tube. I'm not a pervert, lads, but I knew where this was going, so to speak, and I wasn't comfortable with it. Nor was he, a few minutes later.'

All four of us were becoming increasingly uncomfortable. We'd heard about this sort of sexual practice but when it gets this close to home, one of your best mates, then it somehow seems all the more distasteful. Still, it's best not to judge before you've heard the full story. Perhaps the bloke thumped Vic because he didn't want to take part in his sordid sex play?

'I won't go into the full details but you can all imagine what happened next.'

We all nodded and our knees and butt-cheeks clamped together like a set of lock gates. In fact, my cheeks were tighter than the space shuttle's outer hatch.

'To be honest, it seemed a bit rude at the time not to go along with his fetish.' Embarrassment was written all over Vic's face but in his defence, we had pushed him into telling us.

''A bit rude' certainly comes close, mate. A bit fuckin' weird comes a bit closer.' Martin spoke for us all.

'The problems started when Fluffy wouldn't come out.'

It was Dev's turn to butt in.

'Hang on, Vic; you're saying that this chutney ferret's name is Fluffy? For Christ's sake, I've heard it all now.'

Fluffy broke the mood of disquiet.

'Yes, Dev it's called Fluffy and Fluffy was at the other end of the tube. And I don't need to explain where that was, do I?'

That shut Dev up for the moment.

'After a couple of minutes, the bloke started to get more than a bit anxious. Those little buggers have got sharp teeth

201

and I don't think he wanted Fluffy doing some colon caving or grazing on his Chalfont St Giles, so he started to panic. He starts screaming and shouting for me to get Fluffy out.'

We were starting to laugh now. My stomach was still hurting from Martin's story.

'Well, the first thing I thought of was to try and entice Fluffy out with a bit of food, so I ran to his cage and got a handful of seed. Big mistake. Most of it fell into the tube and, for all I know, I thought the bloke might have a pumpkin patch growing in his lower colon in a couple of weeks' time. So, on to plan B. Perhaps if I could see him then I could hook him out. That was the second, last, and biggest mistake.'

I wasn't sure where this was going, but I was about to find out.

'The bloke was a smoker so the nearest source of light I had was his lighter. I should have known better, I suppose, but I flashed up the lighter and put it to the end of the tube. The next thing I knew was a bright orangey blue flash followed by a hollow woomph.'

It was all too much for me. I'd have to get to the hospital and have my sides stitched back up. The other two were in just the same state as I was. Vic was also starting to see the funny side but his nose was obviously hurting.

'Like you said, Richie, it looks like I'll have to get a dictionary if I want sympathy. It's between shit and syphilis, isn't it?'

I was beyond his sarcasm.

'Sorry, mate, just carry on. Don't mind me.'

'The next thing was a sickening blow to my nose and what felt like little pellets. Christ, it hurt. At first I thought it was the explosion but then I saw Fluffy lying on the floor surrounded by loads of seed. Poor little bugger had been shot out of the tube straight into my nose along with his food.'

Dev was holding his stomach. I thought he was going to be sick.

'Tell you what, mate, it was a good job Fluffy didn't have a crash helmet and cape on. You'd really be a mess then.' But honestly, I couldn't see the Amazing Fluffy act in Pets' Corner.

Martin fell to the floor. He'd had enough. Everyone in the pub was staring at us by this time but they could boil their heads as far as we were concerned. We were enjoying this too much, despite the physical pain of our laughter. Vic continued,

'I thought I'd got a bit of concussion but the bloke's screams quickly brought me around. He sounded like he was in agony. When I glanced over, the tube had gone but he was in a mess. His arse looked like a squashed ripe tomato.'

All three of us were on the floor now. Like three little beetles with our arms and legs thrashing around, gasping for air.

'Stop it, Vic; stop it for a couple of minutes. Let us get our breath back and have a beer for God's sake, no more.'

I needed a rest and more beer. I was drinking far too much for a school night but I was having a good time. Sod it. You've only got one life, so make the most of it.

We pulled ourselves together and recovered from our excesses at each other's expense. Once we'd recovered, it was back to Vic.

'What happened next in your epic tale of bestiality and modern weaponry, Vic?'

Martin was keen to see how it finished up. So, it was back to the edges of our stools.

'After the cannonball and scattergun fired out of his arse, we were both totally fucked up. I was bleeding like a stuck pig and his arse was in ribbons. We couldn't call an ambulance, because of his neighbours and I couldn't drive, because I was a bit pissed.'

'Why didn't you call a vet? He could have sorted you all out at the same time,' chimed Martin.

'Ha fuckin' ha. The only thing we could do was clean ourselves up and call a fast black to get us to the hospital. So, that's what we did. Twenty minutes later, we were on our way to the local hospital with me holding a towel to my nose and the bloke with a cold wet towel strapped between his legs looking like a fat forty-year-old baby.'

We'd started to crack up again. Poor Vic, he'd need a bigger dictionary.

'How the hell did you explain it to the A&E doctors and nurses? It's not every day they get to treat an exploding sphincter and wounds caused by pumpkin seed shrapnel and a flying furry animal.'

'No, that was a bit difficult. We'd talked about the spontaneous combustion of his arse whilst sitting on a hot radiator after eating a vindaloo but we didn't think they'd believe us. So in the end, we came up with the idea that he threw a cigarette down the loo whilst he was having a dump. Unfortunately, there was bleach in the bog which exploded and caused his injuries. They seemed to buy that one. Not entirely though, because there were a few raised eyebrows, but in the end I think they thought it wise not to investigate further.'

'Sounds like Sherlock Holmes and the case of the wrecked rectum. What do you say, Watson?' Martin was on a roll.

'Alimentary, my dear Holmes.' I couldn't help myself.

'I'm trying hard here, guys. Cut me a bit of slack. Anyway, I'm nearly finished.'

Vic said he told the nurses that he'd fallen over in his rush to the toilet and bashed his face on a door, hence his damaged face.

'Well, that's quite a story, Vic. I'm genuinely sorry about your nose and your mate's exploding prolapse. One question remains, perhaps the biggest of all. What happened to Fluffy? If he's dead, I'm off to the RSPCA and reporting you both for animal cruelty.'

To be honest, none of us were sure if Martin was being serious. After all, he was a copper, but I wasn't sure if he was an animal lover or not.

'Fluffy lived to fight another day. He came around while we were waiting for the taxi. I'd thought he croaked it, but he shook himself off and wandered off to his cage. I don't think that bloke or Fluffy will be playing that game again and I doubt if there'll be any toilet-roll tubes chucked in his cage either. It'd send the poor little bugger into a panic after that episode.'

It was time to change the subject and move on, for all our sakes.

'So, can we say that's the end of the greatest circus act to hit town for years?'

I raised my glass and everyone nodded.

'To the demise of Victor and the flying gerbils! I'm just glad I wasn't there to see it.'

'I'll drink to that,' said Vic, drawing a line under his revelations. I had realised who the victim was by now; poor old Terence would be sitting on his pillows for a couple of weeks yet. I just hoped it didn't stop him from getting his list up together and onto my desk.

Dev had the last word.

'I'm off to the Zoo tomorrow, chaps, because I feel a bit left out. Victor's got his gerbil. Martin's got his octopus and Richie; you've got your two gorillas. I think I deserve a pet.'

We sat around chatting over a couple more pints. There was nothing to compare with the first hour or so but we still enjoyed ourselves. We caught up on each other's work and just had a general natter. It's surprising to me that nobody seems happy in their own job nowadays. We all seemed to be under pressure to produce more with fewer resources. I began to wonder if it was just us being negative, but the more we chatted, it would seem that all our mates were the same as us.

Dev was playing on Saturday afternoon and was gearing up for his trial in the next few weeks. We'd had such a good night, so we arranged to meet up and watch Dev, have a few beers in the clubhouse bar and then hit the town.

I was having such a good time with the lads that I'd completely forgotten all my immediate problems. So had the other three. We were all full of bonhomie and beer and none of us had our thinking heads on.

We all went our separate ways after bidding our farewells outside the pub. By the time I began to think of things other than beer, gerbils and *E-Type Jags,* I was on my own, well, , across the park, on my way home. I was about halfway across and totally screwed. There was no point in turning around. I might as well carry on as quickly as I could.

I was frightened. It was dark and there was no one about, thank goodness. The slight fear and a few pints had the effect of heightening my senses, or so it felt. I could feel my heartbeat thumping in my chest. I turned my head slightly to improve my night vision a bit; trying to use the cones on the sides of the eyes to pick up any movement ahead of me. Every little rustle in the trees set me on edge and I began to sweat. I wasn't enjoying this one little bit.

I'd quickened my step, but hadn't broken into a run. If there was someone hiding behind a tree, I wouldn't be able to react in time and I'd easily end up on the ground. Fatal, especially with two of them. Just one little touch and I'd be over. A quick walk was best. I could react quickly if I needed to and at least I'd worn my trainers. I reckoned I could outrun them but I didn't think I could outfight two of them.

I was nearly across the park. A flood of relief seemed to course through my body. How could I have been so stupid? That was easy - alcohol as usual. I wished my mates were with me.

The sweat was pouring off me by now and it wasn't just from the pace I setting myself. I was hot and stressed, but a sudden, icy chill ran down my back.

I could see the edge of the park ahead, at the end of the dark tarmac path, which contrasted with the grass on either side. Two big brick pillars marked my exit, but they were bigger than usual. I noticed a slight movement by the left hand pillar, then another movement from the opposite one as two shadows detached themselves from the dark bricks and started to move towards me.

I knew instantly who it was: The Chuckle Brothers.

I slowed my walk, but it was too late; I was almost on them. Doubt swept through my mind. Perhaps it wasn't them? Maybe it was just a couple of youngsters out thieving or tagging? It was a fatal hesitation on my part. Before I knew it, we were almost face-to-face and my chance to run had gone.

They were side-by-side and if I turned and tried to run they'd be on my back before I could get away. Too late; they'd stopped, blocking my path.

The moonlight picked out the tattoo of a bat on the forehead of the one on the left. Shaven-head, leather jacket, jeans and big boots. They'd hurt. I could just make out the tattooed line on the neck of his brother. He had big boots on as well.

My heart seemed to slow and the blood drained from my extremities as my chin went into my chest. It was the fight or flight reaction, except I didn't really have the option of flight. Still, I might be an angel soon.

For a second, we all stood still in front of each other. I slipped my hands into my jacket pockets, but turned to a slightly oblique angle to them, left foot forward. I started to remember my training from Martin. Fighting stance, but I had my hands in my pockets.

Batman on the left broke the short silence as he pulled a pack of ciggies from his jacket pocket.

'Got a light, mate?' It was a surprisingly high-pitched voice, just like Clint and not what I expected from hired muscle.

I started to pull my right hand from my pocket as if to comply with his falsetto request.

'How much is Sharples paying you?'

They'd been about to jump me but my question knocked them back momentarily. I could see both sets of eyes open wide for a second and their gaping mouths. It was the chance I needed.

I'd thought about Clint's advice that I shouldn't tool myself up. It was good advice but it came from a guy well versed in rearranging a person's physiology. The more I'd thought about it, and weighed that up against my lack of fighting attributes, the more I came to the conclusion that I needed a bit of an edge. I would tool myself up but not in the way Clint had envisaged.

My right-hand was now out of my pocket. In it was a small squeezy bottle with the cap already off. As I squeezed the bottle into the face of the right-hand brother, I remembered the advice given to me by Mrs Edgar. If they can't see or they can't breathe, then they can't fight. Well, let's see if it works in practice.

The contents of the bottle hit him full in the face, flooding into his eyes, nose, and open mouth. He screamed instantly and his hands tore at his face. Little brother was totally fucked. He fell to his knees in agony.

I hadn't used all the Naga chilli on Ena. I'd kept the majority of it under my bed; you never know when you might need it next. I thought I might even cook with it one day. But tonight, I put it to another use. Mixed and diluted with water, it was still a powerful weapon. I'd thought about using it as a powder puff but I guessed some of it might end up in my eyes. That would leave three blind guys fighting in the park in the dark. No, a spray would go further and I could direct it. And if I got stopped by the coppers, I could say it's for my next Thai meal. The trouble was it was a small bottle and I'd used it all on one guy. Too much adrenalin pumping through me for my own good.

One Miliband down, one to go. I'd evened the odds, but this guy looked mean. I suppose I'd be a bit pissed off if I saw my brother running screaming into the distance and throwing himself into the boating lake.

'You'll pay for that, you little shit.' His voice had got even higher in his rage.

We faced each other in the pale moonlight. I could see the white of what was left of his teeth glinting as his top lip had curled above them. I'd dropped my empty bottle on the floor and adopted a fighting stance. I'd need another kind of bottle now. Hands up and open, arms slightly bent and left foot forward. Martin would be pleased, but only if I got out of this in one piece.

His head and face were starting to sweat and beads ran over his tattoo; the bat suddenly looked darker.

Before I knew it, the bat was rushing towards me out of the darkness, at frightening speed. He'd bent over at the waist and was charging at me with his arms out and fists clenched. Martin had told me that open hands and bent arms gave you more power than a clenched fist. Good information, but I didn't want to put it to the test.

I slid back slightly, and then tried to slip away left under his now-swinging right. It glanced off the top of my head and I saw stars immediately. I went for a straight-arm hammer-fist into his chest as I slipped away, but his blow had ruined my balance and my intended blow just grazed the right side of his ribs. There was no damage done to him and I'd shown my hand. He knew I could fight a bit and would be more careful and calculated next time.

I spun around to face him again. My head was clearing, but I knew I'd been caught by one.

'Is that all you've got, you slippery little fucker?' He was gathering himself for another go.

He rushed at me again; not as fast as last time, but his hands were still wide. He was nearly on me and I feinted left. He swung his right arm a bit lower this time to try and catch me as I tried to slip away.

I came off my left foot to move inside his right arm and drove towards him. As I did so, I bent my left arm and

210

smashed my elbow and forearm into the side of his head. I felt a few bones crack, hopefully not in my arm. If I'd broken something, I was fucked.

My smash had hurt him, but his momentum and wide arms gathered me up in his charge. I was forced back by his weight and I couldn't slip out. In a second, I was crashing into the tarmac on my side with his full weight on top of me. I was winded, but, luckily for me, he had been hurt by my smash.

We lay prone on the floor. He was the first to react with an attempted head-butt to the side of my head. I saw it coming and my chin went to my chest. It caught me high, but still hurt like hell. I needed to get up, or I was history.

Then he was above me, pushing his body up on both arms as he tried to get some leverage into his punches that would be raining down on my head in a second or so. It was the only chance I would have.

I twisted left so I was directly underneath him. His right arm was cocked, about to rearrange my smile. I reached up with both hands and grabbed the front of his jacket, pulling him into me. He wasn't expecting that. For a moment our faces were pressed against each other and I could smell the sweat, beer and cigarettes on his breath. I doubted if this guy had a girlfriend.

As I'd pulled him down, I brought my right leg up. With all my strength, I twisted and pushed to the left, with both arms thrusting upwards as I did. It worked. He went flying off and landed on his back. Martin said at this point I should run away, but two blows to the head had slowed me down. I hadn't hurt him and he would catch me, no problem. We both got up and faced off again.

'I'm getting pissed off with your little tricks. You shouldn't have been so clever.'

He was reaching around his back as he spoke. I knew what he was doing and an icy dread spread through my body.

His right arm came back around and I caught a glint of stainless steel flashing in the moonlight. This was the first time I'd faced a knife, or any other weapon. I had to do something or I was sushi. I needed a weapon and I needed to keep him away from me. I thought about my jacket around my left hand and arm, but that wouldn't keep him off. It would merely delay the inevitable. I needed something else.

There was nothing on the floor. No branches or stones just grass or tarmac. That was no good. I'd have to think fast, as he was starting to circle me. I could see the sweat glistening on his head. Then, I had a bit of inspiration. I did have a weapon on me and one that would keep him off and maybe do a bit of damage - my nice big-buckled belt.

I reached down, quickly undid the buckle and slipped it from around my waist. I just hoped my trousers didn't fall down. This wasn't a *Carry On* film; it was a lot more serious.

My trousers held and I began to whirl the belt around my head. The heavy buckle whizzed through the air over my head. I now had a reach on him and a substantial weapon.

We circled around each other in the dark. He was making all the aggressive moves, but, each time he came forward, I aimed a swing at his head. I didn't hit him, but it kept him and his butcher's knife away.

He was getting more and more frustrated. He was being paid to give me a proper beating, but it wasn't working out as he and his brother had no doubt envisaged. Jump me in the park on the way back from the pub and a few hundred quid to spend on a few bags of gear, ciggies and piss. If he fucked this up, he'd probably be on the end of a beating himself.

He lunged closer this time. I didn't want to hit his arm for fear of wrapping the belt around it. I wanted to hit his head, face or eyes to inflict the maximum damage.

My arm was getting tired, so I began to move towards the exit of the park. I inched sideways and backwards but Miliband tried to block me off every time I made a move. I still had a way to go and there were no houses nearby to attract any attention by shouting. I'd have to think of something else.

'Still doing your brother's dirty work every time he shits his pants, Miliband?'

You could still hear the brother's wails as he splashed about in the pond some way off in the darkness. Miliband baulked at the mention of his name. His anonymity had been stripped away as if a searchlight had been shone on him. This wasn't turning out well for the brothers. He dropped his guard for a split-second and I stepped in.

The buckle caught him on the side of the head with a solid clunk. He swayed to his right but stayed up. Bollocks. I thought that he was probably dosed up on amphets.

I stepped in quickly and swung again, clipping his nose this time. Hell of an effect, as claret burst from his damaged nose and onto his face and chest. The trouble was that I was aiming for his eyes.

He was getting increasingly angry and desperate. He couldn't get near me, because of my belt and he was getting tired. So was I, for that matter. By now, after just a few minutes of pure adrenalin, I was cream-crackered.

Miliband suddenly drew back his arm and threw the knife at me. I didn't know what he was doing at first. Surely he wouldn't sacrifice his weapon on the slim odds of hitting me somewhere vital? My question was answered by the faint whir of the rotating blade and a solid whack to the forehead.

I reeled back, blood streaming into my left eye. He'd been lucky. So much for slim odds. I was in trouble and he knew it too.

He came at me again but much more slowly this time. It was much more calculated, because he knew his prey was badly wounded. I tried swinging a fist into his side, but he blocked it a bit too easily for comfort. I couldn't see out of my left eye and, unfortunately, that's where his next blow came from - a big right to the side of my face. I went down like a sack of shit. I lay on my back, watching as he bent down and picked up his knife. I thought I was going to cry. All the old clichés came to mind, 'I'm too young to die,' 'Live fast, die young,' and a few more. Total bollocks. The plain truth was that I was scared; absolutely terrified. And there was nothing I could do.

With my good eye I thought I caught a movement behind Miliband. It was probably his brother to perform the coup de gras.

The next thing I saw was the blur of a white hand chopping into Miliband's shoulder an inch or two from his neck. He let out an anguished and painful grunt as he collapsed to his knees. As he fell, I saw a shadowy figure stood behind him. It sure as hell wasn't Miliband's brother but I couldn't make him out as the moon was directly behind him. He moved to Miliband's side and grabbed the other side of his head with both hands driving his knee into the ribcage. The explosion of breath and spittle showered over my bloody face. He still smelt rank.

The figure held Miliband up as if he didn't want him to fall, and then he looked down at me.

'Are you well enough to make it home, Richard?'

I was too stunned to ask an immediate question; maybe something along the lines of, 'Who the fuck are you?' Instead,

I wiped some blood from my face and eye and did a quick assessment of my wounds. Cut to my forehead from the knife, big lump on the side of my head from the head-butt, arm and leg on my right side bruised from the fall and twisted right knee which was starting to give me a lot of pain. I'd got away lightly on the face of it.

'Bit bashed and bruised, but I can make it.' I said, in obvious discomfort.

'Good, just wait one minute while I have a little chat with Mr Miliband here.'

How the fuck did this bloke know who he was? I really didn't care too much. If he hadn't come along, I'd be dead meat.

He hooked a couple of fingers under Miliband's lower jaw. I remember Martin telling me about a pressure point there; he even tried it on me to show how painful it could be. It was bloody excruciating.

Miliband was still on his knees and in bad shape. The stranger lifted his fingers slightly and Miliband's eyes bulged in pain. He was too fucked-up to get to his feet, despite his pain.

'Now, listen to me very carefully.' He bent down slightly to talk softly into his victim's ear, as if to emphasise his point.

'As far as everyone here is concerned, you fulfilled your contract for Mr Sharples and his associate. You'll ring and tell him that Richard took a severe beating and you cut him up a bit, which is, in fact, somewhere near the truth. You will tell your brother exactly the same story. Do you understand me?'

Miliband was still hanging off the two fingers. He tried to nod his head but just impaled himself further. He ended up grunting an affirmative.

'If you tell Sharples anything to the contrary, or if you, or your brother, come within half a mile of Richard again, I will take great pleasure in breaking every bone in your body and then throwing you in the river. It would give me even greater pleasure to see scum like you try to save yourself as your bones grate together and slice up your innards, whilst you drown in screaming agony.'

I don't know about Miliband, but this bloke was frightening the life out of me and he was on my side. Miliband must have a gusset full of peanut butter by now.

'Now I suggest you follow my request to the letter and hurry off and rescue your brother from the lake. We wouldn't want him to drown, would we?'

More grunting followed by short painful breaths as he was lifted to his feet while yet more pressure was applied to his lower jaw.

'Run along now, there's a good chap.'

And with that, Miliband hobbled and shuffled away towards the lake and his brother. The stranger turned towards me. He just looked like a normal youngish chap, maybe five years older than me. He wasn't well built; he wasn't small; just completely average. He wasn't even sweating. The thing I did notice was his accent. It was posh, but not affected, well-educated, with no accent; not the sort of bloke you'd expect to be in the park at this hour and definitely not a vigilante; he couldn't be, because he knew me and the two brothers. I managed to get myself together a little bit.

'I don't know who you are, but thank you for saving my arse. I thought I was a goner.'

He just nodded and lifted his hand slightly in a brief acknowledgement of my thanks.

'Just who the hell are you and how come you know so much?'

'Some questions are better left unanswered, Richard. Let's just say I happened to be in the neighbourhood and came to a friend's assistance. Now, I would suggest you go home, call a taxi to take you to the hospital and have a few stitches put in that wound of yours and get yourself checked over.'

The blood was running down my face again and I was starting to ache all over.

'But…'

'You won't have to worry about those two again, I can assure you. You'll be perfectly safe on the way home; that's if you don't annoy Mr Pratt again.'

I was completely stunned.

'I would strongly suggest that you follow the story I've just told to Mr Miliband. If you don't, Mr Sharples will be back again and the next time, you might not be so lucky. Now off you go, young man.'

It felt odd being called young man by a guy only just older than me but somehow he exuded confidence and authority. I wasn't going to argue in my state.

'Just one question. Why me? You know so much about me. Why me?'

He looked at me like a teacher to a pupil.

'You really don't have a clue do you, Richard?'

He chuckled for a second.

'You have some very influential friends, Richard, and you don't even know it. Now, off home before both of us are arrested.'

He turned on his heels and was about to leave when he called over his shoulder.

'By the way, what was in that spray? It was very effective.'

I just tapped the side of my nose a couple of times and smiled. It was reciprocated and then he was off across the park. I was left alone in the dark. I felt exhausted and drained, not to mention beaten up. Even the squeals from the pond had disappeared into the night.

I hurried home in a considerable amount of pain. I kept thinking about who could be my guardian angel and what did he mean by saying that I had influential friends? I didn't have a bloody clue. Still, with a bit of luck, Sharples would be satisfied and call off the dogs.

By the time I got home, I was covered in blood and stiff all over. My knee had swelled up and I couldn't bend it. I managed to open the front door, although it took a massive effort, and I staggered into the hall to find Mum coming out of the sitting room. It was the loudest, shrillest scream I think I've ever heard. Her hands went to her mouth in horror at the sight of her little boy all mangled and bruised. Mind you, I must have looked half-dead with all the blood and other damage.

'Mum, don't panic, I'm all right. It just looks bad. I'm OK, honest.'

It was the last thing I remember. One second, I was looking at the anguish on my mum's face, then the next, everything started to go black and I felt myself falling to the floor.

Chapter Nine

I woke up to see a white curtain hanging at the end of my bed. I had a weird taste in my mouth and there were strange smells. They were hospital smells of boiled vegetables, disinfectant and old people. I didn't really mind hospitals; it was just the fact that they're always full of ill people and, unfortunately for me, on this occasion, I wasn't visiting anybody. It was me who was ill, or injured in this case. I wondered how long I'd been here. I had no idea of the time or even what day it was.

I remembered back to the fight in the park and my less-than-forthcoming saviour. The walk home was still clear in my mind, as was frightening my mum half-to-death with what must have looked like my death-mask. That was it.

My head was thumping and I could feel the stitches in my head wound. The rest of me ached, especially my knee. I tentatively moved my head a bit to see either side of my bed. I was alone and, thankfully, I wasn't hooked up to any machinery. There was no monitor showing my heart rate as a series of wizard's hats. I couldn't be that bad then.

I quickly assessed my situation. The first thing to cross my mind was that I had all the time in the world, so I might as well do things at my own leisure. Lie back and think of England and its dark underbelly of criminals, like the Milibands and the Sharples', even though they were from different social backgrounds, adopting different methods. However, in the end, the result is the same; they want what you've got and they'll take it any way they can. All in all, despite my injuries, I saw my situation as very positive. As far as I could see, thanks to the stranger and my decision to fight the Milibands, the Sharples' would probably be satisfied with their retribution. The mere fact that I was in hospital would

219

indicate to Sharples that the Milibands had done their job effectively. Unless they blabbed, and I didn't think they would, then I was OK. I certainly wasn't going to come across as anything other than a hapless punchbag.

This was a massive plus. Now I could concentrate on Mrs Edgar's plan and maybe exact a large slice of revenge. I didn't want a violent revenge. I'd now seen it from both angles and I'd come to the conclusion that violence was a very short-term solution. I wanted to hit the Sharples' where it would really hurt them. I'd prefer to attack their values, or the things they valued above all others, like their reputation, both in the criminal world and the non-criminal society in general, and where it would hurt them most, their pockets.

I had also picked up an ally. How, I don't know, but to be honest, I didn't care at the moment. As Terence would say, 'Mum's the word.'

A curtain suddenly swished back to reveal a very pretty nurse at the end of my bed. This reminded me of an experience I'd enjoyed a couple of years ago, although today, the nurse had clothes on, and I wasn't in any fit state to raise a big smile, let alone anything else.

'Hello, Richard. It's nice to see you're back with us.'

She unhooked a clipboard from the bottom of the bed and came up to my side. Her name tag told me that her name was Margaret. She was about thirty, with short blonde hair and had a great figure. I just loved how a nurse's uniform showed off their best features. Perhaps I could raise a smile after all.

She bent towards me and looked into my eyes.

'Have you been awake for long, Richard?' She had a lovely voice as well.

'Maybe ten minutes, nurse, or can I call you Margaret? It's my mother's name and it really suits you.'

A broad smile revealed a lovely set of white teeth.

'Why, thank you Richard, and you can call me Margaret. A lot of people are worried about you. You've had loads of phone calls, especially from your mum. She's been ringing almost every half an hour. What's her name? Mary, isn't it?'

I felt as if I'd been caught with my trousers down and spanked over the end of the bed. She must have thought that I was a total dick.

'Sorry Margaret; force of habit when I meet a very pretty girl. I just go into autopilot and try and chat her up.' Blimey, I was being honest. Maybe it was the bang on the head.

'Get in their knickers more like.' She started writing on the clipboard and made a show of the wedding ring on her left hand. I'd been very expertly put in my place. I'd hoped for a cuddle in the bathroom but was more likely to get a bed bath with barbed wire gloves.

'You're in hospital, Richard, not the local pub, so let's get things on a professional footing shall we?'

I nodded like a naughty schoolboy caught with a copy of a lads' mag under the desk.

'Sorry nurse, it's the bang on my head. I'm not feeling myself.'

'Or anyone else come to that. Now, do you know how long you've been in here?'

I explained that I didn't have a clue. The last thing I remember was keeling over at home. Apparently I was brought in at one o'clock in the morning and it was now twelve hours later. It was the best sleep I've had for weeks and not entirely alcohol-induced this time.

'The doctors have cleaned and stitched your head and you've had a thorough examination. Apart from the bumps, bruises and sprained knee everything looks OK, but they're a bit worried about your head, so now you're awake, they'll do a few more tests to check everything's all right. We have to be very careful with head wounds. It's the things on the inside, which we can't see, that can be of most concern to us. However, on the face of it, you don't look in bad shape considering what you've been through.'

That was good news.

'How long do you think I'll be in for, nurse?'

'Hard to say, Richard. It largely depends on the tests on your head, but hopefully you can go home tomorrow.'

This would mean another day in hospital. That'll look good for the Sharples'.

'The doctor will visit you later on this afternoon. In the meantime, are you up for a couple of visitors?'

I supposed I was. I might as well get some grapes and chocolates and really enjoy my sick bed. I nodded.

'Good. There are two police officers who want to have a talk with you about last night. They'll be along in a minute.'

With that, she checked my blood pressure, filled in a couple more lines on my chart and drew the curtain back.

I didn't have to wait long for the police, but I was a little surprised that it wasn't Martin. It was two youngish lads who I hadn't seen before. They introduced themselves and asked how I was and if I was up to answering a few questions. I nearly asked if tortoises were involved, but this time I was on the other side of the fence, or garden wall.

222

They left about half an hour later, a little frustrated. I hadn't given them much as I was very careful how I answered their questions. They were young and keen and had expected a full description of my attackers and a subsequent swift arrest and charge.

They had no chance. I told them I'd been walking through the park after a few drinks at the pub. I chucked in Martin's name for good measure and halved the number of beers we'd had in case it got back to the station. They said Martin knew I'd been admitted and would visit me after his shift.

I explained that I was near the exit from the park when I was jumped from behind by what I thought were two or maybe three blokes, and knocked to the ground. They shouted at me to give them my money and phone, but I kicked back and started yelling as loudly as I could. I said one of them managed to get his hand into my pocket and get my money and that they gave me a savage kicking for good measure. I added that one of them slashed me on the head with a knife as they were leaving, as I'd put up a bit of a fight.

No, I didn't recognise any of them and I couldn't remember any distinguishing marks, such as tattoos. They were just average blokes dressed in average clothes.

They left with nothing much to fill their notebooks. This would be another unsolved mugging for the county's crime statistics. The inspector wasn't going to be happy.

I was on my own again and felt surprisingly tired following the interview. I'd had to concentrate to maintain my story. They say liars have to have very good memories and I think mine held up, despite the bangs to my head. Sleep was upon me very quickly. I'd had too many painkillers and there was still a touch of exhaustion from my exertions of the previous night.

I was woken up by an Indian doctor and what I assumed to be a newly-qualified female doctor. They were the head-doctors. After lots of torches shining into my eyes and questions as to my vision, memory and general condition, they were satisfied, and they left with the proviso that if I didn't have any adverse symptoms by morning, I could go home for a bit of R&R.

A cup of tea and a light lunch was quickly followed by a deluge of visitors.

To my surprise, the first visitors through the door were Carol and Tina. The curtains were now back and I saw them entering the ward. Carol had my grapes, bless her, and Tina had a small bunch of flowers which was immediately taken off her by the Health & Safety Gestapo as they can spread awful germs! Greenfly were the least of my problems. It was a nice touch but I would have preferred something I could eat. It's the thought that counts, I suppose.

They were both very concerned. Carol assured me that I didn't have to come back until I felt completely up to it. I told her that I'd probably come back on Monday, but she insisted that it was far too soon. Tina asked more questions about my attack. She'd probably been briefed by Clint as to what questions she should ask.

'Did you see who did it, Richie? Do you know who they were? Are the police involved?'

I spun the same yarn to her as I had to the police. All the answers were negative and I hoped Clint would be satisfied. I just said that it could have been worse and I was just glad to be alive. I thought Carol was going to cry. Forget Wanker of the Year; I was now going for a BAFTA.

Mum and Sis walked in and my colleagues left, wishing me a speedy recovery. Sis looked a bit dolled up for a visit to the hospital and Mum had big red puffy eyes. She'd obviously been crying a lot. They had more grapes and biscuits. At this rate, I'd be gagging for a bacon sandwich. Mum rushed to the side of the bed and gave me a big kiss. I winced a bit as she pressed against a tender lump.

'My poor baby. What have they done to you?' She burst into tears again.

'I'm OK, Mum. It looks a lot worse than it is and I'll be home by tomorrow, hogging the telly and the kettle.'

She gave me another kiss and squeezed my hand.

'Thanks for coming, Sis. You look nice; you didn't need to dress up.'

She blushed a bit and Mum jumped in.

'It's not for you, Richard. She's off to town to see a young man and go for a meal.'

'Mum, Richard doesn't want to hear about me. He's ill.'

'I'm injured, Sis, not ill. Anyway, you have a nice time and be careful 'cos there's some nasty people out there.' She looked at me in my hospital bed, concentrating on the stitches in my head, and said she'd be careful, and have a good time.

Martin, Dev and Vic trooped in. There were no flowers or grapes this time and I was a bit disappointed that they hadn't brought me anything. Still, it was good to see them. Sis chivvied my Mum up and said she was late, so Mum reluctantly let go of my hand. She burst into tears again. All the lads gave her a hug and a kiss as she left, but stopped short of doing the same to Sis.

They grabbed another chair and gathered around my bed.

'Don't tell me, 'you should have seen the other bloke'', was Devon's opening remark. Despite his quip, there was a look of genuine concern on his face and perhaps a bit of anger. After all, we were the best of mates and we all looked out for each other. I suppose they were feeling guilty after leaving me alone last night. Martin sounded far more serious.

'Who did it, Richie? Or more to the point, who did this to you?'

He knew the answer to the first question. He wanted to know who cut me up and put me in a blood wagon. He didn't wait for my reply.

'A beating's one thing but knives are another. Sharples has crossed the line.'

They all had a grave expression on their faces. It was like looking at a vigilante mob.

'Thanks for coming guys, I appreciate it, but where are my grapes?'

Devon slipped his hand into his jacket and produced a rather large hip flask. He slipped it under my sheets and winked.

'Twelve-year-old single malt. Just don't wet the bed or light a match near the pee bottle or you'll end up like Vic.'

Vic shot Devon a withering look and punched him on the arm. Martin wasn't distracted.

'Who did it, Richie? Was it the brothers?' This time there was a bit of an edge to his voice. I'd have to be very careful here or these three would be stringing Ena up from the big oak in his dad's front garden.

I slid my hand over to the flask and took a big swig of Scotland's finest. It burned down my throat and I felt better almost immediately - alcohol and painkillers.

'This doesn't go further than the three of us, OK? Otherwise, they might try again, and next time I might not be so lucky.'

The three of them huddled around my bed. They must have looked like a bunch of conspirators, heads bowed and cocked to pick up on my whispered tones.

'Yes, it was them and I gave back as good as I got; better in fact. I took down the younger one straightaway and the older one took a bit of a beating.' I failed to mention the fact that I'd been saved by a mysterious stranger.

'Bloody hell, Richie, if they came off worse, then they must be in a right state, looking at the mess they made of you.'

Dev was impressed and Vic let out an appreciative whistle.

'The fact is they won't be coming back. I had a chat with the older one after I'd fucked him over and he's reporting back to Fido, who'll tell Sharples that the job was done as per their orders. The fact I'm here is evidence enough.'

'I'm not happy about this, Richie. We can't have toe-rags like these beating up on one of our mates. It sends out the wrong message.'

Martin wanted retribution for my beating. I could understand. He didn't want the Sharples' and Fido to think that they had won and I could understand where he was coming from. We had a long history with Ena and the thought of him gloating at me in a hospital bed was too much for him to take.

'No Martin, its far better this way, believe me. If we beat up the Milibands, they might change their story and I don't want to risk that.'

Like Martin with his back, I made a subconscious move to rub my stitches. They were sore. Vic and Dev nodded and let out a resigned puff of breath. Martin wasn't so convinced.

'So you're going to leave it at that? Ena gets away with it and is laughing in his beer. We can't let him get away with it, Richie. He's gone too far this time.'

'Please Martin, let it go. I've got a few things up my sleeve for Sharples and his old man and I don't want the thought of them coming after me again. Besides, if you lot do anything, they'll be after all four of us and not just me. Just give me a few weeks and you'll see. If you go off on one, you could ruin everything I've been planning.'

I had their interest now and they were all looking at me in anticipation. The mood was quickly dispelled with the approach of the fit blonde nurse. She walked over to the bed with a look of interest on her face.

'Looks like the Bonfire Night Plot over here. All you lads need are hooded cloaks, a lantern and a keg of gunpowder.'

She was actually very close to the truth, as I was planning to piss on Ena's fireworks good and proper. Martin was the first to get into chat-up mode.

'Hello my dear. Can I call you Margaret?' There was an element of lounge lizard to his voice.

'You boys must have the same scriptwriter, and by the way, he sucks. I'd need a lot of white wine and a considerable amount of desperation to fall for that one.'

Martin shot me a quizzical glance and I burst out laughing. Martin had been put down in front of his best mates. At least I didn't have any witnesses to my ignominy.

'I tried and failed miserably too, Mart; join the club.'

She was at the end of the bed and sniffed the air slightly.

'Are you OK, Richard? That stuff is better on the outside of your wound than it is on the inside. No more, understand?'

They're all bloody witches, I thought. Devon in particular looked guilty. With that, she was off down the ward and I handed the flask back to Devon, taking another sip before I did so. Fortified, I carried on.

'I've got a little plan I'm working on but it's best you don't know any details. You'll have to read about it in the papers. Besides, there's nothing any of you can do to help me at the moment.'

Nurse Margaret came over and tapped her watch. Visiting time was over.

'Don't suppose we'll be seeing you on Saturday then, mate? Shame, you'll miss my hat-trick.'

I'd forgotten about Saturday and our day on the lash.

'I'll be there mate, bandages, stitches and limp. The girls love a bloke who needs a bit of TLC. I'll be fighting them off with a big stick.'

'You haven't got a big stick, Richie,' was Devon's retort.

'Fuck off, tripod.'

They all laughed. The mood had changed from retribution to recreation. Even Martin seemed to have come round to my way of thinking.

They trooped out of the ward but not before Martin had one last attempt at wooing Nurse Margaret. There was a brief encounter and I could see his shoulders visibly droop as she put her verbal pin into his balloon. He left with his tail well and truly between his legs.

After dinner I slipped into a deep sleep. I woke up feeling a lot better than I had the previous evening, which wasn't that difficult. The head-doctors came around again and gave me a clean bill of health with a proviso to take it very easy over the next few days. I took that to mean that I'd have to sit down whilst I poured copious amounts of fermented barley and hops down my throat.

I went home in a taxi. My knee was still playing up and the bruises were sore, but overall, I wasn't too bad. I had my battle scar on my forehead which I kept admiring in any mirror or window I could get near.

I reckoned it made me look hard, but then I thought it's those who don't pick up battle scars who are the cleverest. It was too late now.

I eased myself out of the taxi outside the house. Rodney Pratt was mowing his bloody lawn again. He stopped to watch me limp to the door and had a little smile on his face. This time, I didn't acknowledge him as I didn't want to give him the satisfaction of ignoring me. Maureen came out and asked how I was, much to the displeasure of her husband. I was overly nice to her, just to wind him up.

The house was quiet when I got inside. Mum would be at work and Sis at school. Time for a strong cup of tea, switch the TV on, put my brain on the coffee table and chill out. I was feeling a bit tired.

After an hour or so, I had to give in to my fatigue and wandered up to my bedroom. As I passed Sis' bedroom, I thought I heard something. I stopped and listened at her door. I could hear something; it sounded like sobbing. I knocked at the closed door.

'Sis, is that you?' No answer. I tried again and waited.

'Go away, Richie. I'm alright, so just leave me alone.'

She didn't sound alright to me and her voice sounded very strained and croaky.

I couldn't leave it; after all, she was my sister. I tried the door and pushed it open a bit and peeked inside. She was lying on the bed on her front with her head buried amongst her pillows. Her head turned towards me as she told me in no uncertain terms to 'fuck off'. The slight glimpse I got of her face was enough to tell me why she was crying. There was a deep purple bruise around her left eye and her top lip was slightly swollen. She quickly buried her head again and shouted for me to get out.

I shut the door behind me and sat on the edge of her bed. She'd been knocked about by someone and I wanted to know who. Now I know how Martin had felt the previous night. Nobody does this to my mates, let alone my own flesh and blood.

'Sorry Sis, but I can't. You need to talk to me. Can I get you anything?'

She started to sob uncontrollably and her feet started to kick against the bottom of the bed. I put my hand on her shoulder and tried to comfort her. After a minute or so, she started to calm down.

'What happened, Sis? You'll feel better getting it off your chest. Was it the bloke you saw last night?'

Her head started to nod amongst the pillows and she eventually turned over and sat beside me on the side of the bed.

'What happened?'

Amid the sobs, she told me about the previous night. She'd met her bloke in a pub and they'd had a couple of drinks and went on for a cheap Italian. Things seemed to be going well and she accepted a lift from him. Then it all went wrong. Instead of taking her home, he took her to a deserted lane and started getting a bit heavy. He wouldn't take no for answer and started getting a bit physical.

'Did he make you, well, you know, Sis?' I couldn't bring myself to say the words. She smiled.

'No Richie, I protected my honour in true family tradition. But I got thumped in the process though.'

It seems that he gave up in the end and dumped her at a taxi rank in town. When I get my hands on this bastard, I'm going to rip him apart.

'You know, the strange thing Richie, is that his car stank of curry; absolutely reeked.'

I felt like I'd been punched in the stomach. Curry, no, it couldn't be.

I asked her about the car and the name of the bloke. I knew the answer even before she told me.

'Tim, I don't know his surname and it was an old white car. German I think. Should've been Indian I suppose.'

She gave a little laugh, but not me. I'd underestimated Ena and his desire for payback.

'I'm sorry Sis, this is totally my fault.' She flashed her bruised face at me with a look of bewilderment.

'Your fault? Don't be stupid, it's mine for trusting an older bloke and jumping into a car with someone I didn't know well enough.'

'No Sis, it's my fault. The bloke was Timothy Sharples and he's responsible for the state I'm in as well. I'm so sorry.'

She looked at me aghast, not knowing what was going on. How could her situation be connected with my current poor state of health? I explained about the longstanding feud and my recent run-ins with Ena and his father; also that my

232

ending-up in hospital was probably arranged by them. The last thing I expected was that they would target my sister in an attempt to get back at me.

'Have you told the police?'

'No, what's the point? It's his word against mine and the bloke always gets away with it anyway. He said no one would believe me over him and that I should keep my mouth shut, or else. To be honest Richie, I don't think I could face the police or the courts. It's not something I want to be made public, or known by my mates. How could I be so bloody stupid?'

My sister was growing up. She sounded like an adult and was being very pragmatic. I had to agree with her point of view.

'I got away lightly, I suppose. Better than you, by the look of it. I'll put it down to experience, I suppose, but I'll get him back one day. One way or another, I will get him back.'

She was being like a chip off the old block and was showing me a side of her that I had never seen or known before.

'Well, I might just beat you to it, Sis.' She looked at me, intrigued, and I let her know about my plans for the Sharples', but without details.

'I'd suggest a cold towel on your bruises and a bit of make-up. I don't think Mum's heart could stand another shock.'

For the first time ever, we gave each other a hug. We had something in common at long last and I suddenly felt very close to her and a bit proud. I also felt very guilty and angry. My guilt was because she'd been dragged into my feud and my anger was at Sharples for using her to get at me.

I needed to sleep. My physical and emotional batteries were in the red and I needed a clear head to decide what to do next. I left Sis in a much better state than when I found her.

I woke up some time later and wondered where the white curtains were. I was disorientated for a second, and then heard Mum downstairs talking to Sis. What got me out of bed was the smell of food wafting up the stairs.

'How's my wounded soldier today? You look a lot better than you did yesterday. Now, sit down and I'll get you some food.'

It was steamed steak and kidney pudding. Babies' heads, as I called it; it was my favourite. I didn't realise how hungry I was, as I wolfed it down in seconds. Mum fussed around me like a mother hen and Sis was also quite talkative and helped Mum in the kitchen which was unusual for her. After a while, she left and went up to her room.

'Your sister seems different all of a sudden, Richard; all grown up. She even had a bit of make-up on. Do you know something that I don't?'

'How would I know, Mum? Brothers and sisters don't talk to one another, let alone share secrets. She's just growing up. Maybe she's pregnant.'

She twirled around with a look of shock on her face similar to the other night. When she saw my broad grin, she threw the soggy dish-cloth at my head. It whizzed past my ear and splattered against the fridge.

'I can tell you're feeling better, you cheeky little monkey. Now sod off back to bed and get some rest.'

I made a couple of calls to my mates from bed and arranged to meet up at the ground the following day. I was beginning to look forward to a blowout and I was determined not to do anything stupid this time. There'd be no curry powder or chillies to be seen anywhere. However, as soon as I get a drink inside me, all the best-laid plans tend to go out of the window and tomorrow would probably be no exception.

We met at a pub just outside the ground. Well, the three of us did. Devon was probably going through his pre-match exercises by now. It was a top-of-the-table clash and the pub was full of both sets of supporters. I was always surprised how well the sets of supporters got on in this lower level of football. If this was league football, there would be bottles and glasses flying about by now and the police would be putting their restraint techniques into practice. It was more like a rugby crowd, which suited me. I'd had enough of violence for a while.

'How's your head, Richie?' Vic was well into his first pint and raring to go. He seemed up for a good day as his wounds had healed nicely.

'A lot better, thanks mate. Probably a bloody sight better than it'll be tomorrow morning.' And with that, I set about catching him up.

We bought a round each and then set off for the game. We were in good spirits and looking forward to seeing Dev knock a couple in and so boost his prospects of a big trial. I wouldn't say the fans were streaming into the ground, but there were quite a few for an early season game. Everyone was full of optimism for their team and the season to come.

We took our seats and the players were soon out on the pitch to cheers from the couple of thousand supporters. Dev had a good start and soon drew the attention of a couple of opposition supporters who started giving him a few racist chants. After one particularly nasty observation, I'd had enough. I couldn't help myself. Standing up, I shouted down to Dev's abusers;

'Oi, you racist bastards; shut the fuck up and watch the football.'

They both turned around and started to get up. Seeing me with a head full of stitches, they stopped midway. I still looked a bit of a sight and had obviously been in a recent fight. If you know that someone's a fighter, it tends to focus the mind a bit. Shall I or shan't I? In this case, they didn't and sat down muttering obscenities at me under their breath.

'You're getting into this confrontation lark aren't you, Richie?' There was a touch of concern in Vic's statement.

'Sorry Vic, I just can't let idiots like them get away with stupid racist comments like that, and it's my mate they're shouting about. If no one stands up to people like that, they won't know they're doing anything wrong.'

'Looks like we've got ourselves a crusader here, Vic. A proper knight in shining armour, rushing to the aid of Prince Devon. Save some for a damsel in distress, Richie, the rewards are much more interesting.' Martin had a point and I immediately thought of Nicola. That was strange.

I wasn't sure if Devon had been stung by the racist calling but he upped his game and knocked in the game's first goal. He made a point of making for the two fans and celebrated his goal with a cupped hand to his ear.

Half time arrived shortly afterwards and we indulged in the great football institution of a pie and hot drink during the break. Martin enjoyed his so much that he went back for another.

Devon had a couple of chances in the second half but didn't improve on his goal tally. His was the only goal of the game and full-time came with numerous slaps on his back from appreciative team mates.

'To the bar, chaps. There's a few pints of beer with my name on them.' Victor was off like a shot with us trailing through the crowd after him.

'Bloody hell, he's keen, Mart. What's got into him?

'I think it's his accident last weekend. He needs a good blowout to put it behind him.'

'Unfortunate choice of words but I know what you mean.'

I was in a similar situation and I thought that a long consultation with Doctor Beer would sort me out too. It might dull the pain and fuzz up the memory a bit.

Vic already had three beers lined up when we arrived. We grabbed a seat and waited for Devon. He arrived a pint and a half later and, as he entered the bar, he came face-to-face with his two antagonists. He towered above them and just stood menacingly over them for a couple of seconds as if willing them to repeat their prejudices. The two just stared at their feet, not wanting any eye contact, or any other contact come to that.

Dev walked past them towards us but clipped the shoulder of one of them, spilling beer all down the guy's front. Dev didn't acknowledge his action and strolled over with a slight grin on his face.

'Fuckin' thickos. It's the twenty-first century, for Christ's sake. Why can't people grow up and live in the real world?' Martin followed up Dev's anguished question.

'Unfortunately Dev, for people like them, it is the real world. I see them every day on the council estates around town. It gets so fuckin' depressing. To be totally honest, there's little hope for people like that and, more worryingly, they are a large part of our society today.'

Devon was obviously upset, and so were we, at Martin's cutting observation on society, but he soon got over it after his first pint. Various team mates and management came over and congratulated him on a good game. There was no free beer though; I thought we might get a couple, but this was non-league football, I suppose. There was not a single pound of the millions from TV or sponsors at this level. There wasn't even a beer. I wondered just how these professional footballers managed to spend their money. After a few years on a couple of hundred thousand pounds per week, I don't suppose money had any meaning anymore yet they still bitched and behaved like spoilt kids. It was completely beyond my comprehension. I suppose if I was lucky enough to be in the same situation, I'd be the same as them. Unfortunately, I'd never know.

'Any scouts here, Dev?' Martin was looking around the room for any likely candidates.

'A couple I think, but not from any big clubs. Still, at least there were some, which shows there could be a few players they're looking at.'

'Never mind mate, there's always the lottery.'

'Vic, there's as much chance of me winning the lottery as there is of you taking a gorgeous young lady home to your parents and telling them of your impending marriage and her planned pregnancy.'

'Ouch, that's below the belt, Dev. You never know mate, I might surprise you all one day. I might see the error of my ways and give up my pursuit of brown love.'

That was a bit too personal for me. It was time to change the subject before any of us regretted what we said.

'Right guys, what's the plan of action for tonight?' Martin was our planner-in-chief. He picked up on the gossip during the week and knew where everyone would be heading and where we could expect to meet the most girls on a fun night out.

'My spies tell me that town will be heaving with hot totty tonight and, if we fail to pull, then it's off to the nearest monastery for a life of celibacy, stale bread and water. That should suit you, Richie, after your diet of hospital food over the last few days.'

'Thank you, Brother Martin. Monastic life should suit you as well after your work in the community, especially amongst the needy and desperate housewives.' He scratched his back again.

'Point taken, but I enjoy my missionary work. In fact, I enjoy it in any position.'

The banter was starting to flow as the beers went down. It was time to move off and hit the bright lights of town.

It was late summer and a beautiful evening. I liked this time of year as all the girls were still wearing very little and you didn't need a very good imagination to see what was underneath. In most cases, it was nothing at all.

We started off in the big pub just around the corner from the disco where we'd had our last Rhino Hunt, and where I had met Nicola. It faced out on to the big wall across the road. It was in a good position as it was the first big pub on the way into the centre and most people's first port of call on route to a night of debauchery. Well, let's hope anyway. There was a constant stream of girls heading down the road towards us, and the pub was starting to fill up.

'You weren't wrong, Martin. Where do you get your info from?'

'Can't reveal my sources, Richie. It's the first rule of informant handling; if I tell you, I'd have to kill you.'

We were starting to eye up potential conquests as more and more girls squeezed passed us to and from the bar. I have to admit, we could have moved a bit more out of their way but it was a cheap thrill to have an attractive, well-endowed girl rubbing up against you. Both sides knew what they were doing and you watched out for those who went just that bit further than the rest. They went towards the top of the list for later on in the evening. I think the technical term is frotteurism and it is regarded as a fetish. I'd diagnosed myself as a pervert, but I wasn't complaining as a girl with huge shirt potatoes brushed against my back. I turned my head to get a good view of her silicone valley.

'Easy tiger. If your blood pressure rises any more, those stitches are going to pop.'

Martin watched admiringly as the girl slid past my back, carrying a round of drinks for her mates.

'It's starting to look a bit like the slaves' market, mate. I'll start my bidding at one Bacardi Breezer.'

Dev jumped in with his bid.

'One Bacardi Breezer, one gin and tonic and one bag of crisps. Have her stripped, washed and sent to my tent.'

It was a generous offer but he'd have to wait for any takers. There certainly were some sights in the pub now. It was going to be a good night; I just hoped that I could last, as I was starting to flag a bit. My head was aching, as was my knee along with my assortment of other bruises. Perhaps this wasn't such a good idea but I decided to make the most of what time I had.

'Let's pop outside for a minute and I'll arrange a fashion show for us.' The other three looked puzzled but followed me out to the pavement anyway.

There were still a few groups walking into town. It wasn't long before I saw a likely group of girls which fitted the bill. I handed my beer to Martin.

'Here, hold this a minute, mate,' and I walked across the road to the big wall.

The wall curved slightly so as I got to it, I was out of sight of the group of girls. There were about eight of them. All dressed in miniskirts, high heels and skimpy tops and, from the sound of them, they'd had a couple of drinks already. I could almost smell their perfume from here.

I put both hands out in front of me and leaned against the wall. My right leg was extended behind me, so it looked like I was pushing against it. It didn't take long before the girls rounded the slight bend in the wall. The other three were looking over, wondering what the hell I was up to. The girls approached a bit cautiously. Their laughs and loud voices dropped as they saw me and as they got closer, I spoke to them as a group,

'Hi girls, could you help me a minute? I don't think I can do this on my own.'

They'd stopped now and were looking at me with furrowed brows. Well, those who hadn't had Botox injections were.

'I'm an engineer for the Council and I've noticed that this wall has suddenly buckled a little bit. It's not dangerous, or going to fall down, but it needs a bit of support until the Fire Brigade get here. Can you give me a hand, just for a couple of minutes?'

They all looked at each other to see what they should do. They were a bit uncertain; after all, who would want a wall falling down on them?

'Please girls, it's only for a couple of minutes and it won't fall as long as we can keep pressure on it. Please?'

One brave girl stepped forward and came to my side.

'It's dead easy. Just put your arms out like this and put your weight against the wall. Legs straight and just lean against it. Easy, isn't it?'

The other girls were coming forward to help us out. All of them followed their mate's lead and pushed against the wall.

'Thanks girls. Now, if you can stay here for a couple of minutes, I'll call the Fire Brigade and they can fence it off to stop anyone walking by and getting injured.'

I left the girls by the wall and went back to my pint over the road.

'Well, what do you think of that, boys?'

Across the road from us, the eight girls were leaning against the wall. They were bent at the waist with extended arms on the wall. The position it left them in was nothing short of spectacular. All eight skirts were now halfway up their backs, revealing an array of skimpy knickers and pink buttocks. It was quite a sight. There were a couple of tattoos on show, along with thongs and some black lacy numbers. Unfortunately for one of the girls she wasn't wearing any at all. At least her collar and cuffs matched.

We stood admiring the impromptu exhibition in front of us, quietly sipping our beer with the air of connoisseurs.

'It reminds me of the fruit market. Eight little, pink fluffy peaches all in a line. Thanks mate.'

Devon spoke, never taking his eyes off the girls.

'Looks like a couple of them have been cut in half by those cheese-cutters they're wearing.'

Our show was now attracting attention from inside the pub. Crowds of lads were piling out to see them and a few were hanging out the windows. One or two started to call over to the girls, who were starting to realise that something wasn't right. Anxious looks were being exchanged between them. One finally pushed herself off the wall and looked over at the now-large crowd. She turned to her mates and then realised what was happening when she saw their exposed position. They all left the wall and turned to the crowd with faces as red as beetroots. It was probably a mixture of anger and embarrassment. They straightened their skirts down as far as possible in an attempt to cover their modesty. It was too late girls, as we'd seen your modesty along with about fifty other blokes.

They continued up the road shouting abuse and throwing 'V' signs in our direction. A round of applause whistles and cheers followed after them from everyone who had gathered outside the pub.

'I don't know what goes through your devious, perverted mind, Richie, but I'm glad you're our mate and not an enemy. Best fashion show I've ever seen.' Victor, along with everyone outside the pub, had a big smile on his face.

We returned inside and all the lads were full of themselves talking about the line of girls that had paraded in front of them. Most were trying to work out what they were doing and why.

After another drink, I finally realised that my night would be a short one. The alcohol was catching up with me and my head was thumping. I made my excuses to the disappointment of the lads but they could see that I wasn't going to make it. Now that I felt a lot safer after the spectre of the Milibands had been lifted, I decided to walk home, rather than spend out on a taxi. The walk may clear my head and burn off a bit of alcohol.

The route home was scattered with a few late stragglers on their way into town. A couple of girls were walking towards me and when they drew closer, I realised who they were. It was two of Nicola's friends who were with her when we met for the first time. The taller girl was the one who'd been particularly antagonistic towards me at the disco, the centurion from Nicola's Praetorian Guard. It was unlikely that she'd changed her opinion of me since our last meeting.

We were getting closer to each other now. The tall one - I still couldn't remember her name - swung her little handbag over her shoulder. She'd swung it back-to-front, so it was hanging just over her front-right shoulder. As we converged, she made a quick comment to her friend. She was definitely not pleased to see me; her expression looked like she'd been licking piss off a stinging nettle.

'Hi girls, can I have a minute?'

They kept on walking but the taller one didn't deviate out of my way; instead she walked straight up to me. I suddenly realised why she'd positioned her bag over the front of her shoulder. I suddenly had two lumps in my throat; unfortunately it felt like they were my bollocks. I swallowed hard. I was on the ground in a crumpled heap, curled up clutching my meat and two veg.

As we met, she'd very deftly swung her bag over her shoulder and into my balls. I don't know what these girls carry in their bag but it felt very heavy - a Louis Vuitton sling-shot right into the pork sword.

'Why the fuck did you do that? I only wanted a word.'

She stood over me menacingly, jumping back when she realised I was looking up her short skirt, as I searched for her face through a sea of excruciating pain. Give me the Milibands any day.

'And I only wanted to break your balls and see you suffer, just like Nicola, the poor girl. How could you do that to her; in her condition?'

She paused for breath. Her eyes were out on stalks and the little veins on the side of her temples had popped out with the effort and anger she was putting into just a few short words.

'Leave her alone and don't try ringing her again. She won't answer anyway. Just fuck off out of her life, you selfish twat.'

I glanced across at her shoes. Big, pointy heel and a sharp, pointed toe. 'I know you're angry but please don't kick me' - this was my initial thought as I tried to gather some breath on the dusty pavement.

'It was all a mistake. She wasn't part of my mates' game and I really need to talk to her.'

I'd managed to squeeze the words out through gritted teeth. She hadn't kicked me yet, so that was a bonus. She glared down at me and her head extended towards me.

'Well, she doesn't want to talk to you. Have a nice day, arsehole.'

The two of them left me on the pavement and walked off into town. I just wanted to be sick as I was in so much pain. This was getting to be a habit, but I'd keep this one quiet. I'd been beaten up by a girl; I'd never live it down. As I struggled to my feet and shuffled painfully home, I consoled myself that at least there'd been two of them. Not a fair fight.

There was something bothering me about the brief conversation we'd had. What the hell did she mean when she said 'in her condition'?

I didn't have a clue but it gnawed at me as I struggled home and I was sure as hell going to find out.

Chapter Ten

I spent the whole of Sunday resting in bed and let Mum, and to a lesser extent, Sis, look after me. To be honest, I wasn't fit to do anything anyway. There was no trip to the pub nor was there a mate's house to go to for a natter and a beer. I settled down in front of the box for the usual diet of omnibus television with plot lines about infidelity, teenage pregnancy, death and despair. You just know that when something good happens to someone, it's going to come back and bite them on the arse.

I finished the day wondering if this type of programme is in some way encouraging stereotypes of antisocial behaviour amongst some of the people that watched them. What worried me most of all was that a lot of people believed that what they were seeing on television was actually true-to-life, and then they'd mirror this on-screen behaviour in their day-to-day lives. People's moral compasses were being adjusted by a quest for improved TV ratings on the back of ever more outrageous scripts.

I cleared my disturbed mind with a dose of *Time Team* and the *Antiques Roadshow*. Bloody-hell, I must be getting old.

I walked to work on Monday morning, despite the rain and a few aches and pains. My love spuds were still aching from the unprovoked and dastardly attack on Saturday night; the walk would do me good. The slightly musty smell of the rain on hot pavements was all-pervading as I walked past the virtually stationary traffic. There was almost a sense of a new beginning, the rain somehow cleansing the last couple of weeks and washing the past away. But, as I got close to Ena's office, some of the dark thoughts started to re-emerge. Our feud was exactly that, between the TWO of us, and nothing to do with my sister, you bastard. My resolve built as I walked the last few hundred yards to the office. I was going to bury Ena and his cronies once and for all, but I'd need far more than a pot of curry powder or extra hot chillies to do it.

'Richard, I certainly didn't expect to see you today, or any time this week, in fact.' Carol got up and gave me a little hug. It was a bit motherly, but I appreciated it all the same.

'I might as well be here than sat at home feeling sorry for myself. I can still answer the phone and do the usual things around the office. The only problem might be meeting the clients.'

I ran my finger over the stitches in my forehead.

'I might frighten a few away, looking like Frankenstein's monster.'

'I don't think that'll be a problem. There's not much on the books this week, so we'll take it as it comes. But you must take it easy; you've had a bad experience and you don't want to rush things. Now, are you sure you're up to our hectic pace?' She laughed sarcastically as she said it. Things were as slow as usual and I could tell she'd received another pep-talk from head office.

I explained that I was OK as I picked up the post. I'd only do what I felt comfortable with and pace myself accordingly. Of course, I had an ulterior motive for being here, but I wasn't letting on to that.

With my bundle of post under my arm, I limped over to my desk. I didn't sit down straightaway, but stood at the window, looking directly across the road towards Ena's office. He was sat at his desk and it wasn't long before he noticed me.

He stared at me and I could see his smiling face through the rain drops running down the window. Normally, I'd just get on with my work, but today, I just met his smirking face with a stony gaze. I wanted him to know that I knew and that I was here to stay.

It was him who backed down first as he started to fiddle about with a few papers on his desk. He still had his smug little smile, but he wasn't challenging me anymore.

I'd learnt something though. He was happy and that was good for me. The Milibands had probably told the Sharples' that they'd earned their money with a savage beating and my couple of days in hospital was a testament to their actions. Well, you little shit, you just sit there in your little bubble of complacency, but you'd better be careful because I've got a very sharp pin.

It was the usual post, the same as I'd seen for the last few months and it was totally uninspiring, until I got to a particular plain brown envelope. There was something about it which screamed anonymity. It was addressed to me, but it had been printed, not handwritten. There were none of the identifying marks on the envelope that you'd usually see on a letter from a company or institution. There was a local postmark and Royal Mail stamps, not franked through a company's postal system. It felt like there were a few sheets of A4 inside, but it wasn't at all bulky. I hoped that it was what I thought it was.

I slit the top of the envelope and pulled out its contents. The envelope did indeed contain a few sheets of A4. Each sheet was typed with an address and description of a property. There were scant details on each but it did show a rough date of sale or exchange. There were no values, photographs or estate agent details shown but there was enough there to carry out some research. That said, there was nothing at all in the details which could be traced back to the originator of the information. It was exactly what Mrs Edgar was looking for. A few of the properties were actually on my list, but there were significantly more which weren't; some very expensive properties, in fact. Good old Terence, he'd actually followed through, so to speak. I suppose he wanted to stay on my good side after what had happened between himself and Vic.

I tucked the property details away in a drawer and started to sort out the rest of my work. Tina rolled in about an hour late. It was Monday and I suppose she'd had a wild weekend. Carol wasn't so sympathetic.

'Good afternoon Tina, nice of you to drop in. Must be a terrible inconvenience having to come to work every now and again. Must play havoc with your social life. Never mind, head office are looking to cut staff numbers in light of the current down-turn in the market and you never know, you might be lucky and they might choose you to be one of the staff made redundant. I'm sure you'll get enough in benefits to pay for your nights out. Fingers crossed, hey?'

Ouch. That was as subtle as a brick. Despite her fragile state, the sarcasm, and not so thinly veiled threat, weren't lost on Tina.

'I'm ever so sorry, Carol. Me and Clint, well we just......' Carol finished it for her.

'Tina, I don't really want to know, but I've got a good imagination and I think I can work out what you and Clint just.... In fact, it's the same idea that I've had for the last few Mondays. Just don't be late again or head office will get a copy of your written warning. Do I make myself clear?'

Tina was making a good impression of a goldfish, with her mouth wide-open, and big staring eyes. I hadn't heard Carol tell Tina off like that before. Normally, it was a gentle little word which Tina completely ignored. This was different. I think head office must be putting a lot more pressure onto

250

the branch managers like Carol to either improve their results, or cut overheads. At this moment, I'm sure she was looking at Tina, not as a person, but as an overhead that costs X amount of pounds sterling per year. It was a good job that I came in today.

Tina took in the significance of Carol's dressing down. She knew that she was in trouble and that she was also very vulnerable. If it was a male boss, I'd bet she'd have given him a blow job on the spot. As far as I was aware, Carol only drove on one side of the road.

'I'm ever so sorry, Carol. It won't happen again, I'm sorry.'

She scurried to her desk, picking up her work as she went, and the next hour or so passed by in an uncomfortable silence. I began to wonder if my job was also under threat. After all, they paid me a bit more than they did Tina and I didn't exactly rake in that much money for the firm.

Lunch time came around slowly and, after grabbing the office car, I dashed around to Mrs Edgar's, clutching my envelope from Terence. When I got there, I wasn't allowed to jump straight in and tell her about the last few days; I was made to wait until I had a cup of tea and a slice of cake in front of me first. 'All in good time', she liked to say.

'It's carrot cake, my favourite. I think you'll like it, Richard. Now tell me how you came by those nasty stitches in your head.'

She nestled down in her chair and listened to my adventures from Wednesday night onwards. She said very little; just the odd prompt here and there, a few nods and words of encouragement. Finally, she spoke.

'You've done very well, Richard, very well indeed. I was tempted to say that you've been very lucky, but I don't think it was luck at all. You've been very resourceful and brave. It takes a lot to stand up to two thugs who want your blood. Most people would have run away, you know. Now, the thing you mustn't do is seek revenge for your sister's predicament immediately. If you do, we'll lose all the advantages you've won over the last few days. You and Elizabeth will have your revenge, but it may take a little while.' I was being taught well. She changed the subject deftly.

'What's in that envelope you've been clutching ever since you walked in? I'm dying to know.'

I showed her the printed sheets from Terence and her face lit up.

'There's far more here than I thought there would be. Of course they might not all be part of Mr Sharples' little scheme, but they certainly fit the bill.'

She thumbed through the sheets. A thought suddenly crossed my mind.

'Mrs Edgar - Lyn - now that you've got some properties to investigate, what exactly are you going to do?'

To be honest, I didn't have a clue how this little old lady would proceed from here.

'That's the easy part, Richard. You're the estate agent; you know how the process works. All we have to do is follow the audit trail. See who bought the property and paid the relevant fees and expenses, which companies are involved, and then see exactly what they've been up to. Simple.' She sounded very confident in her appraisal.

I thought about it for a moment and started to see what she meant. I had assumed, incorrectly, that what she intended to do would be very difficult, if not impossible. I had reckoned that she was going down a blind-alley, where information was difficult to get hold of and, when you did, it turned out to be worthless. But the more I thought about it, the more I could see that the vast majority of what we needed was, in fact, in the public domain and easily accessible via the Internet or visits to the council, library or Land Registry.

'I'm presuming that you intend to get what you're looking for over the Internet. I don't want to put you off, but is it possible to get that sort of information in enough detail to help us?'

I could tell this was going to get a bit surreal. An old lady, who grew up in an age when children rushed out into the street to see a car go by, and when radio was the main form of entertainment, was about to lecture me on the information super-highway.

'Of course it is, Richard. Surely you know the capabilities of the Internet? A lad of your age, you must be a whiz with this stuff. Far better than the likes of me, surely?'

It was a genuine question, but I didn't think she'd believe the answer.

'Well, not exactly Lyn. I'm afraid a lot of this stuff has passed me by. I use it at work, but I only know what I need to; just enough to get by. I don't even have a computer at home, although Sis has a laptop, which I borrow from time to time. To be honest, I can't afford one.'

There was more than a bit of scepticism on her face. I'm sure she thought that lads of my age spent most of their waking day glued to a computer screen, either sending messages or watching porn.

'I'm afraid I'm one of the odd-balls of my generation. If I want to speak to someone, I'll either arrange to see them face-to-face or ring them up to actually have a conversation with them. It's a bit unusual in this day and age, but I suppose I'm a bit old-fashioned. If I want to play a game, I'll get a football and go up the park with my mates, rather than shoot

253

each other to bits online in an electronic orgy of blood and guts. You can't drink online and you don't meet nice young girls or enjoy someone else's company. Little Miss Gagging-For-It in the Internet chat room is probably a sixty-year-old fat knacker who gets his rocks off sweet-talking little boys. So, as far as what we can actually get off the net, you've probably got a big advantage. If you've got a computer, then you definitely have.'

As soon as I'd finished, I knew I'd said a bit too much and been a bit too graphic. It was just that I had a bit of a phobia about computers. To me, it seemed that everything we did in work, and, increasingly in our leisure time, revolved around a computer. I'd seen people completely fall apart when their computer packed up. They were totally incapable of functioning as a normal human being without their plastic brain. Well, I didn't want to be one of those sad fuckers, so I dragged my heels and used old-fashioned methods of communicating, like talking.

'You are indeed a turn up for the books, Richard. I think you'd have been happier in my time, rather than in yours. Mind you, your colourful language would have got you into a spot of bother though.'

She had adopted a cheeky grin and motherly look.

'In answer to your question, yes, we can get the majority of what we need off the Internet. If we can't get certain information, then I shall call in a favour or two from some old friends to fill in the gaps. When we've finished, I'm sure we'll have enough facts to provide the police with a very powerful case against the Sharples' and their associates. Now, I'm sure it's about time you got back to work. We don't want to make a bad impression on your first day back, do we, Richard?'

I'd been dismissed from the headmistress's office. I felt like a little schoolboy who'd been given a bit of a lesson. The old may look and smell a bit funny but don't discount a lifetime of knowledge and experience.

'And do remain vigilant. I wouldn't put it past those thugs to try something again. Your sister will also need a lot of help too. She's a lot younger and more vulnerable than you, and I'm sure she could do with a bit of brotherly love. There's no knowing how she may react once the initial shock of her ordeal subsides.'

She settled down and started to read through Terence's papers. With her glasses perched on the end of her nose, she furrowed her brow and pursed her lips, concentrating on the task at hand. She was lost in thought as I let myself out.

I parked the car at the back of the office and exaggerated my limp as I walked around to the office. I didn't look over at Ena, but I was sure he was watching and smirking.

After an hour or so of catching up, Carol sent me home. She said I'd had enough for one day and, to be honest, I had. I was still tired, battered and bruised, so the thought of a couple of hours' kip was quite appealing.

Mum was at work when I got home, but Sis was in her bedroom. I guess she didn't want to go to school with her bruised face and fat lip. I didn't blame her. Kids can be cruel; I should know as I used to do that sort of thing.

She came down to the kitchen as I was making myself a cuppa. It was unusual for her to come out of her room, but it was even more unusual when she actually started to talk to me. I made the most of it and we sat down over tea and biscuits to discuss how she felt about things and where to go from here. I explained that plans were under way to get Ena and she seemed happy with that. I got the impression that she wanted to do something herself, but at the moment, neither of us could come up with anything constructive, or destructive.

We both headed off to our rooms in a happier frame of mind after our chat. Like a lot of brothers and sisters, we'd grown apart as we grew up. It just wasn't cool to be mates. It was a shame that it took something like an attempted rape and a beating to bring us closer together.

The next few days drifted by. Nothing of any note happened. I kept expecting a call from Mrs Edgar, but my mobile was especially quiet. All the lads were working and, to compound matters, there were no drinks during the week. I was actually starting to feel a bit like Billy No-Mates. A chat with Martin might cheer me up. He usually made me laugh with his stories about the local criminality he'd encountered in the course of protecting Joe Public and their possessions.

Martin picked up almost immediately and sounded a bit tense. I could tell that something wasn't right.

'Hello, mate, sorry but I shouldn't have my phone on. I'm at the hospital.' In slightly hushed and concerned tones, he explained that his mum and dad were in hospital after a break-in at their house. They'd both taken a bit of a hiding, especially his dad who'd tried to take the two burglars on. Unfortunately, a lifetime of cigarettes and alcohol had made him easy prey for two young lads high on drink and drugs. Apparently, things would have been a lot worse if it hadn't been for the next-door-neighbours coming to their rescue. Martin explained that the neighbours were also in hospital, having been battered by the burglars as well.

As soon as we finished the call, I jumped into my old banger and headed for the hospital. It was only a few days since I'd come out myself. I knew there was little, or nothing, that I could do, but I might be able to give a bit of moral support to Martin and a hip flask of rum to his dad.

The traffic was bloody awful getting to the hospital. Even I could remember the old hospital in the centre of town. It was easy for everyone to get to, not like the new one on the outskirts of town. It was especially difficult for the old, sick and the injured - just the people who need the hospital the most.

I soon met up with Martin on the ward where his parents were. His parents were actually side-by-side and he was sat between their beds with a concerned look on his face. No doubt he was rehearsing in his mind what he was going to do to the two lads when he caught them; I wouldn't want to be in their shoes. There were two others with him, sat down between the beds as well. They had their backs to me, but they looked vaguely familiar. As I approached, I could see that the male had his arm in a sling and the girl had a dressing over her left eye. It was the Indian husband and wife I'd seen the weekend before. I suddenly felt guilty about letching at her in those tight spray-on denim jeans.

Martin must have announced my arrival because everyone looked over as I walked up to the beds. They all looked to be in a terrible state. Mum and Dad were battered and bruised. Mr B's eyes were almost closed and he had a few missing teeth; the burglar had probably done him a big favour. The young Indian girl had a livid bruise around her eye and possibly had a few stitches under her dressing. The couple made to get up as I arrived, but Martin soon arrested their motions with a hand on their respective shoulders.

'You don't have to get up; he's not bleedin' royalty.'

I could tell he was pleased to see me.

'Richie, this is Virinder and his sister, Mira.'

He emphasised the sister bit and, as I looked back at him. There was a sly smile on his face that I'd seen on many an occasion, invariably after eight pints and with a pretty girl on his arm. It seemed a bit out of place in the context of the situation, but I wouldn't put anything past Martin.

257

'If it hadn't been for this brave couple, my Mum and Dad would be in a lot worse condition than they are now.'

I shook hands with the two of them. Mira was even prettier close up. She had typical Indian features with wide brown eyes and raven black hair. Less typical were the injuries she'd suffered, trying to protect her neighbours and their property. Her brother looked in a similarly battered state. I suddenly became a bit overwhelmed with emotion. My eyes welled up and they went a bit misty.

'Thank you both so much. I, we, can't thank you enough.'

A tear actually ran down my cheek. Mira saved a bit of my embarrassment as she leant forward and gave me a big hug and a peck on the cheek; the dry one. As I glanced over her shoulder, I could see Martin glaring at me. Fuck off, you racist bastard, I'm enjoying myself and so is she, I hope.

Martin's dad cut the moment short.

'Mira, Virindar, I'm sure you'd like to get home rather than be worrying about us old farts. But, seriously, I'd like to say a big thank you. Without you two, I think we might be dead on the kitchen floor. Thanks very much.'

It was the first sensible thing I'd ever heard him say. There was no swearing or sarcasm. It was straight from the heart and he meant every word. Mira had let me go and Martin had quickly replaced me, giving both of them a big hug. I noticed that he was nuzzling into her neck as he thanked the two of them.

Mira and Virinder said their goodbyes and limped towards the door. They could go home tonight, but Mr and Mrs Bormann would be in for a few days. I grabbed a chair and sat between the beds. I suddenly wished I'd brought some grapes. It was a tradition in British hospitals to bring grapes, even on the haemorrhoid ward where there were already quite a few bunches of them.

As I sat, Martin brushed past me and caught up with Mira at the door. They had a brief conversation in which the brother wasn't involved. It ended with a brief, but what seemed to be an affectionate kiss. He sauntered back to the beds with a bit of a swagger. As he did so, he was shot down in flames by a familiar voice from across the ward.

'Got yourself a new scriptwriter or hasn't she heard any of your cheesy old chat-up lines before?'

We all looked around to see that Margaret, the blonde nurse who'd put us both in our place the previous weekend, had arrived on the ward. She wandered over to us.

'Back here so soon, Richard? Looks like you can't stay away from the place. Let's hope Mr and Mrs Bormann recover as quickly as you have.'

She gave an admiring glance towards my head and the much-improved cut. With a deft flick of the hand, she started to draw the curtains around the beds, and Martin and I were ushered away from Margaret's work.

'Sorry, boys, but I won't be long. Just need to do a few checks.' She turned to Martin.

'Your parents have taken a bit of a beating and we need to monitor them very carefully. Just try not to wear them out by staying too long. Sleep is sometimes one of the best remedies in a situation like this.' The curtain swished again and she was gone.

We stood in the middle of the ward feeling a little exposed. It wasn't polite to stare at the other patients if you weren't sat next to one of your own.

'Bloody hell, Richie, I need a drink, but I'll have to settle for a coffee. Want one?'

I didn't bother to acknowledge the question; I just set off towards the coffee shop, fumbling in my pocket for some change. I felt the same as Martin did; sad, frustrated and angry. How could people do this to old folk in their own homes?

We grabbed a coffee and headed out towards the main exit for a bit of fresh air. Instead of fresh air, we were hit by a wall of cheap cigarette smoke and a scene which would make even the most ardent smoker consider quitting on the spot. It must be one of the saddest sights you could wish to see. There were people, mostly patients in the hospital with smoking-related diseases, desperately puffing on a gasper and coughing their lungs up. Some were even in their dressing-gowns and a couple were in wheelchairs. I began to get a bit angry, thinking that it was all self-inflicted, but then I thought back to the few occasions that I'd been brought to the hospital after drinking way too much on a piss-up in town. Pot, kettle, kettle, pot. It was sad though. I remember talking to a couple of elderly friends who smoked. They said that you could just as easily get run-over by a bus tomorrow, so why worry about the damage that smoking does to you? That's all well and good if you stand in a bus lane all day, but why take the chance of an almost certain painful death? Just bring the primary school kids by the busload and park them outside the main hospital entrance for half an hour and you'll save the NHS billions of pounds in about fifty years' time.

We found a low wall away from the smokers. I didn't want to be too close to them in case one of their oxygen bottles went up. We sipped on our coffee in an uneasy silence. I knew what the likely outcome was going to be in this scenario and it wasn't going to be all hearts and flowers.

'Martin, promise me you're not going to do anything stupid. You've got a career and a future ahead of you, which is more than most of us.'

I tried to sound persuasive, but in my heart-of-hearts, I knew my seeds of conscience had fallen on very stony ground.

'Don't fuckin' preach to me, Richie, especially after all the shit you've stirred up over the last couple of weeks. You're the last fucker to have any morals when it comes to a bit of payback. Just remember where you were a few days ago and the back-up you were offered at the time, so don't be getting all righteous with me, old buddy. My Mum and Dad are there upstairs in a hospital bed, all fucked up because I haven't been doing my job. Just try to imagine how that feels.'

He was taking this very personally. His parents had been rescued by his Indian neighbours and he thought that, as a policeman, he had a responsibility for keeping the scum off his immediate streets. An attack on his parents would be the ultimate humiliation, both personally and professionally. Bollocks, it would take some wordmansmith skills to get out of this one.

'Firstly, Martin, you don't know the half of what has been going on between me, Ena, his dad and associates. It is best that you don't know and it is best you don't ask, for your own benefit. If you end up stood in the dock and you don't know anything, then you're not tempted to lie.'

I had his attention now.

'One thing you certainly don't know is that Ena tried to rape Liz the other night.' I paused for a bit of effect, although I didn't really need to. Martin sat bolt upright and stared at me straight in the eyes, to see if I was bullshitting him. I met his gaze and he must have picked up on the emotion in my face.

'You're not kidding, are you? He actually tried? What the fuck are you going to do?'

I took a sip of coffee and wished at that moment that I smoked after all. I was aching for a hit of nicotine to give me a bit of a buzz. Coffee would have to do.

'That's exactly it, Martin, I'm going to do nothing, at least nothing in the short term. Yes, I admit I've been a bit stupid over the past few weeks, but all I've done are a few practical jokes and bruised some jumped-up fuckers' egos. That doesn't condone attempted rape and a contract beating. It was only sheer luck and bloody-mindedness that both Sis and I have got away so lightly.'

I took a large swig of coffee and stared into the gathering darkness. The main entrance was still busy with the steady stream of smokers. The moths mingled amongst the clouds of smoke which shrouded around the neon lights. I wondered if insects could get cancer from cigarette smoke. They probably wouldn't. When we've wiped each other out, probably in the name of religion, years down the line, there will still be moths, flies and cockroaches doing much the same as they're doing today.

'I'll get Ena back, but it won't be with short-term violence or an exaggerated practical joke. I intend to hurt both him and his dad, and hit them where it hurts, in their pockets. That's all I can say at the moment but please don't repeat it. If you do, you could fuck-up what we've already set in motion.'

Martin was hooked.

'What the hell are you up to now, Richie? And what's with this 'we' business. You're not ganging up against the Sharples', are you?'

It was too late. I had to tell him something, if only to stop him from doing what I fully expected him to do next.

'As a matter-of-fact, that's exactly what's happening at the moment. I'm working with another party looking into the criminal activities of the Sharples' property business. This is a

262

medium to long-term project but, in the end, it will damage Ena and his dad far more than a quick kick in the bollocks or a nipple-wrench.'

He looked at me and tried to work out if I was bullshitting or just diverting the subject away from his parents who were sat upstairs in their hospital beds.

'Straight-up, Martin, just don't ask any more questions. What I'm trying to say is that I know what your next move will be and whoever it's against, it won't be very subtle. If you get caught, you will probably lose your job and the hope of any decent job in the future. Please mate, just stand back for a couple of days and start to think about it clearly, rather than with the image of your Olds laid out in bed in the forefront of your mind, clouding your judgement.'

If I didn't know him so well, I probably would have missed it; it was the almost imperceptible sagging of the shoulders and a deflation of the chest. He seemed to be coming down off his testosterone and adrenaline-high of the last few hours. Perhaps my little speech and revelation about Ena had brought a little bit of perspective into his plans for a swift and savage retribution.

'I know you're right, Richie, but just at this moment, all I want to do is beat some fucker senseless, actually, two fuckers senseless. I'm out there day after day protecting society and on the day that my parents get beaten up and burgled, I'm not there for them. They had to be rescued by the next-door-neighbours, for Christ's sake.'

'Is that what's really beating you up? That someone else helped out your mum and dad and not you? You're not fuckin' Superman, Martin. You're not His Great Omnipotence that can be in all places at all times. For Christ's sake, stop beating yourself up and try and accept that what's happened is no fault of yours.'

He actually started to nod. I was beginning to get through. Perhaps I'd saved his job and a couple of blokes from a good kicking.

'Come on, mate, let's go and say good-night to your Olds, go home, and get some sleep. I think we all need some.' By now, his head was like a nodding dog in the rear window of a car on a very bumpy road.

'You're right, mate. Thanks for coming, and for those wise words. It's good to have a bit of perspective, rather than the thoughts of knee-jerk brutality. Anyway, Ena had to go after your sister as well as you.' He looked at me, waiting for my reaction and a reply. I was confused as to where he was coming from.

'Why? Why would he go after Sis as well?' He just smiled and laughed.

'Because two Heads are better than one, Richie. He had no choice.' I had to laugh as well. With friends like Martin, who needed enemies?

We wandered back towards the entrance. An old guy was puffing frantically on a bent roll-up. He was in his pyjamas and slippers. He started to cough so much that I thought he was going to peg out there in front of us.

'Take care, old timer. If it's brown and hairy, swallow it down hard 'cos it'll be your arsehole.'

Not much compassion from a supposed protector of society. But I wasn't surprised that Martin was a bit low on compassion at this very moment. The old geezer started to swear at us but was overwhelmed by another series of hacking coughs.

We arrived back on the ward to find them both asleep. Martin wanted to wait a few minutes on the off-chance that they woke up. Before I left, Martin had actually promised to wind his neck in a bit and not do anything stupid. I wasn't sure if I believed him, but it was a starter-for-ten. We also started to make plans for a night out on Saturday. I was recovering well and needed a bit of blowout. My fun batteries were seriously depleted and needed recharging.

With a promissory note for a wild time on Saturday, I retraced my steps down to the main entrance and braced myself for the toxic clouds of Chinese counterfeit cigarette smoke. Instead, I was greeted with a sight I didn't expect to see. It was Nicola's Praetorian Guard with the Louis Vuitton nutcracker sweetie in the lead.

They were just coming in through the main doors. In fact, it was all the girls who'd been with Nicola on the night we first met. I quickly ducked into the charity shop and hid amongst the yellowing second-hand books about bodice rippers and ex special-forces mercenaries. To be honest, if I had to read a book or a magazine in a hospital or doctor's waiting room, I'd bring my own. The diseases that must be spread by them probably fill up a couple of wards a year. I can't imagine the book pile in the Clap Clinic to be especially well-thumbed. *The Chlamydia Chronicle* and the *Pustulating Pimple Gazette* would be left on the table to gather dust.

'Can I help you, dear?'

It was a little old lady who was behind the desk of the shop. I must have looked a bit odd hiding amongst her books.

'Sorry, my love, I was just trying to avoid some rather nasty people who are looking for me. Things have got so bad on the transplant wards that the doctors are now sending out people looking for suitable donors for the organs they need. They call them Harvest Squads and they look for homeless lads like me with no relatives. It just takes a quick bang on the head and, before you know it, I'm living, breathing and walking in about ten different bodies in ten different areas of

265

the country in a week's time. I blame it on the Government cuts. Wouldn't have happened in your day, would it, love?'

She was standing behind her desk with her mouth open. I didn't think she'd believed me, but I wasn't going to hang around to find out.

'Anyway, must dash. Nice to meet you and you never know, I may see you again. Or someone else might if they get my corneas. Either way, have a good day.'

I slipped out of the shop and slid in behind the girls at a relatively safe distance. They all had an air of gravitas around them. You could sense their sombre mood as they headed for the stairs to the upper levels.

As soon as they walked in, I had a fair idea why they were here. The nutcracker sweetie's words suddenly flashed into my mind; 'Poor girl, how could you do that to her in her condition?' If what I thought was correct, then I wasn't surprised at the level of protection and animosity they'd shown me. I hoped I was wrong but there was only one way to find out. I had to follow the girls without being noticed.

Standing outside the door to the stairwell, I could hear their footfall on the concrete as they climbed. I guessed they were at least one level up by now. I opened the door and slipped inside. Glancing up the vertical gap in the stairs, I could see their hands on the rails approaching the second level. I started to follow and listened intently for any conversation I could hear. There was no talking as they went passed the second level. I kept to the outside of the stairs and stayed about one and a half levels below them. They were getting close to the third level by now. Suddenly they stopped.

'Well, here we are girls. Remember, happy faces and be positive.'

With that, a door opened and they all went through. They'd gone into the third level and what I'd heard hit me like a punch in the stomach.

I rushed up the stairs and pushed my head around the door to see them disappearing down the corridor on the right and on to the far ward. I didn't have to peek because I knew exactly where they were going. The sign on the wall in front of me said it all. **CHEMOTHERAPY WARD**, followed by a big arrow pointing to the right. My grandfather had been here for a long time a couple of years ago and I knew it quite well.

It was all falling into place. I'd known something wasn't quite right when I first looked into those big eyes of hers. There was a pain, a secret or maybe a bit of both. She hadn't been drinking alcohol and seemed very tired all the time. And as for that raven black hair of hers, well it wasn't hers; it was a bloody wig.

No wonder her friends had been so protective. They were protecting her from herself, as well as from me. How could I have been so bloody stupid? To be honest, it would have been difficult for me to know. After all, I wasn't a doctor and there was no reason why I should have been in the least bit suspicious, but just like Martin's feelings of guilt earlier, I thought there was always something that I could have done.

Well, maybe there was something I could do. I didn't have a bloody clue what that could be, but there was only one way to find out. I had to discover what was wrong with Nicola and work something out from there.

Listening at the door, everything seemed quiet. No chatting or footfall. I pushed it open and went to my right. If any of them came around the corner now I'd be clocked and totally screwed. I'd just look like a stalker and never live it down. Reaching the end of the corridor, it was still quiet. I peeped around the corner to see the door to the main ward shut. Like a lot of wards these days, the door was locked and people were only admitted by way of voice identification by the nurse on duty. I suppose it was good for security and helped stop disease transmission in that the number of visitors could be strictly limited. That's all well and good but it didn't help me.

Luckily, there was a small window in one of the doors to the ward. I couldn't get in but at least I could have a shufty. Peeping through the window, I could see three of her friends outside a door which I assumed would lead onto a private room. The tall girl wasn't there; she was probably inside. Why hadn't the others gone in? Straining to listen, I didn't hear the footsteps behind me.

'Can I help you, young man?' It was a middle-aged nurse. She was a bit officious looking and had probably seen it all and done most of it too. I would have to think very quickly.

'Not really, thanks, nurse. I've had to wait outside as there's already too many inside to see Nicola. Best wait out here for my turn.'

I waited to see if it had worked, trying to look relaxed in the process. She gave me a cursory smile and went to enter the ward on the door key-pad. As she opened the door I took a bit of a gamble.

'Nurse, sorry to trouble you but I might have to go shortly. Is there any chance you could give me an update on Nicola's progress and if there's anything I could do?'

She stopped halfway and seemed a bit miffed. A tut came from her lips but she didn't shut the door.

'If you must know, it's much the same as before. She's had another session of chemo and, as usual, she's a bit knocked about. As for helping her, well, if you're a match for a blood transfusion or bone marrow then I'm sure her doctors would love to see you. Now, I must be getting on.'

As the door closed behind her, I could hear footsteps coming closer. Having come this far, I didn't want to get caught now. I was up on my toes and down the corridor to the stairs before I heard the ward door open behind me. I was close, but I'd have to be a lot closer to get what I wanted. I'd also have to do it soon. Maybe I could do a bit of planning tomorrow, which was a welcome Friday and maybe a bit more over the weekend. Then I'd pay another visit to the hospital but in a different guise.

I did a lot in work on Friday but absolutely sod all to do with estate agencies. The first thing I did was rummage around out the back of the office for some props for next week's visit. I needed a name-tag with a particular coloured neckband. We had a large box of the name-tags that go around your neck which we'd accrued over the years from various conferences and meetings. If there was nothing meaningful to do, then you could arrange a conference about any old bollocks and dish out name-tags by the dozen with free pens and clipboards – that would guarantee promotion.

I found what I was looking for near the bottom of the box. It was a perfect match for what I wanted. As an added bonus, I found a particularly nice black diary and a fancy clipboard. The diary was three years old but I'd colour over the date and no-one would notice. The next thing I needed was an expensive-looking pen which I found in one of Carol's drawers. I didn't think she'd miss it for a couple of days.

Then it was off to the charity shops and the opticians. I found what I wanted in the first Chazza Shop just up the High Street - a pair of tweedy trousers and a pair of smart comfortable shoes. The opticians came up with a pair of dark-rimmed reading-glasses with the lowest prescription I could find. It was very Michael Caine, or maybe even Clark Kent and pretty-much perfect for what I wanted. All I needed now was a smart, plain shirt and most importantly, a plan and a lot of luck. I spent the rest of the day on the phone to the lads making arrangements for the following night.

I was really looking forward to our night out. The previous Saturday had been a bit of a let-down, apart from the girls flashing their orange buns at us, of course. I winced as I recalled the pound and a half of designer bag, make-up and probably a small bottle of vodka smashing into my wedding tackle. This weekend would be different.

About once every six months, the biggest pub in the town centre had a fun night. It was basically a wild fancy-dress night where anything goes. You could wear whatever you wanted and come as whoever you wanted. On the last fun night we went to, I must admit that we didn't really enter into the spirit of the event. I think we dressed up as a boy band but just looked like we did on any other Saturday night out in town with gelled spiky hair and stupid shirts. This time, Vic had promised to spice things up a little for us but he wasn't letting on what he had planned. All he said was that we could wear what we wanted and he'd bring the rest.

I didn't have a bloody clue what he was up to.

Our Vic was a bit of an enigma sometimes. To be honest, none of us really knew what he did for a living. He was always a bit vague; graphic this, design technology that. All we knew was his firm paid him a fair old whack at the end of the month.

There was one more phone-call to make before I left the office for the weekend. It was to Devon's mum, Mrs Ambrose.

I rang her on my mobile on the way home as it wasn't a call I wanted to make from the office. If it was overheard, I'm sure a few ears would be twitching and a few awkward questions would come afterwards. I rang Devon's home number and it was picked up almost immediately. Unfortunately it wasn't Mrs Ambrose, it was Mr Ambrose.

'Hello, who's that?' The Caribbean lilt came over the phone like he was singing.

'It's Richard, Mr Ambrose. Could I possibly speak to your wife if she's there, please?' There was a pause at the end of the phone.

'I'm sorry, caller. It's a very bad line; you'll have to speak up.' It seemed OK my end, but I cranked it up an octave or two anyway.

'Mr Ambrose, this is Richard. Could I speak to your wife, please?'

'I'm sorry, caller, but you're very faint. Why don't you try shouting at the top of your voice and, at the same time, apologise for making me look a complete tool in front of my neighbours.'

I didn't think he'd forget that quickly, but at least there was a hint of mischievousness in his voice.

'I'm sorry, Mr Ambrose; it just seemed a funny thing to do at the time. I promise it won't happen again. I'll make it up to you because if I don't, I won't be able to visit and try your wife's wonderful cooking again, will I?'

I knew that would placate him a little because he was so proud of his wife's food.

'I know what, the next time I'm over I'll bring you a bottle of spiced rum and some ginger beer and we'll have a couple of *dark-and-stormy's* together.'

He loved *dark-and-stormy's* and so did I, for that matter. It's basically rum and ginger beer poured over ice with a slice and squeeze of lime and it's bloody gorgeous.

'OK son, you're forgiven, but don't forget about the rum. Now, it was my wife you wanted, was it? You're not going to ask her out are you son, because she's spoken for? Ha, only joking, here she is!'

Mrs Ambrose came on the line. She had the same lilt but was a bit more trill than her husband.

'What can I do for you Richard? Is it by any chance a recipe for one of my famous Caribbean dishes?'

'Sorry, Mrs Ambrose, but it's something entirely different.'

There was more than a hint of disappointment in her 'Oh' after my opening line.

'I'd like to pick your brains on some symptoms and medical procedures, if I may.'

Mrs Ambrose had been a nurse for many years in the local hospital and had worked on several wards. I hoped that if I bounced what I knew off her, perhaps she might be able to give me an idea of what was wrong with Nicola. I explained her symptoms as best as I could remember them. Then I recounted what the nurse had said about a transfusion or bone marrow transplant. It didn't take her long to come to a considered judgement.

'I take it this is concerning a friend of yours. Well, what I can say is that your friend is a very sick person indeed. Chemotherapy, combined with possible transfusions or marrow transplants, suggests a form of leukaemia. There are different types, and not all require the same procedures, but the bottom line is that it doesn't sound very good.'

Shit, leukaemia, cancer of the blood cells. I didn't know much about it, but what I did know was enough to tell me that Nicola was in some considerable trouble. I suddenly felt sick in the pit of my stomach and could see the hurt in her face as she confronted me in the pub.

'Thanks very much, Mrs Ambrose. It's not really what I wanted to hear but it just confirms what I'd initially thought. Thanks again.'

'If there's anything I can do, Richie, just ask, and if you need another opinion, well, you know where we are. Good luck.'

That was the confirmation I had dreaded. If I could help her in any way, then I'd have to act very quickly. However, to be honest, I wasn't sure if there was anything I could do. I needed to help her and assuage my guilt, but I didn't have a clue how to do it.

Chapter Eleven

I woke up on Saturday morning feeling like a five-year-old on Christmas day. For the first time in quite a while, I felt as if I actually had some degree of control over my future. Destiny is too big a word, too long a time span, so let's just say control over the next few days or weeks. That was enough for me.

After breakfast, I laid out my new clothes on the bed, together with the other kit I'd assembled. For the next couple of hours, I worked on my new appearance. I had to look the part if my plan was going to succeed. I paid a lot of attention to my hairstyle. Once I was satisfied with that, I started to look through my props. The diary was easy; I just got a black marker-pen and wrote over the embossed year on the front cover. It would pass all but the closest scrutiny. Next, it was the turn for the clipboard. I'd taken a few sheets of technical stuff from work which would fit the bill: just loads of figures and graphs; sales plans and projections for the coming year. Again, it was just for show and should get me by.

After a morning's work, I stood in front of the mirror and looked at my new persona with a critical eye. To be honest, I was impressed. I didn't look like me at all. I looked very much like the laid-back academic, which was exactly the impression I wanted to make. I would stand or fall on those first impressions I made on Monday lunchtime. If I fell, then it would be from a bloody great height, but it was something I had to do.

With that job done, I still had a few hours to kill. The thought of killing immediately rekindled the sight of Rodney smirking at me as I struggled up to the front door. Bastard. As it was a nice day, I could do some gardening for Mum and take the opportunity to wind up dear old Rodney at the same time.

As if on cue, I could hear him berating Mo in the front garden over what would probably be a small misdemeanour, like stepping on the front lawn or walking past a weed.

One thing for sure was that he was a creature of habit. Once he'd done his morning's work, he'd always have a bite to eat and a cup of tea in the front room whilst watching the television. The more predictable you are, the easier it is to be wound up. I've always found that creatures of habit tend to get into a bit of a flap if their routine is messed up in any way.

I had a quick glance out of the front window to find him pruning his roses. It wouldn't be long now before he settled down in front of the television. There was one thing I had to do before I went out into the front garden and that was to check the *Freeview* box for a couple of channels. With all those channels now available, I should be able to find a couple I wanted. I found two, stuck the remote control in my back pocket, grabbed a few gardening tools and made like Alan Titchmarsh.

Rodney was still in his garden.

'Good afternoon, Mr Pratt, are your aphids giving you a spot of bother? I'm sure you can get a cream or a spray for that. I've heard that if you don't treat them quickly, they can play havoc with your begonias.'

I didn't wait for an answer, as I wouldn't get one as per usual. True to form, all I got was an irritated humph and a few mutterings under his breath.

I settled down on my hands and knees in front of one of our rather sad-looking borders. I immediately wondered if this was such a good idea. It probably wasn't, but my vantage point gave me a really good view into Rodney's front room and a full view of his television. The thought of sharing the front garden with me was too much for him and he scurried indoors to shout his lunch order to Mo. I don't know why she put up with him. I knew she played around, but why stay with him?

I bet she gave him a few extra bubbles on top of his tea. If I was her, I'd do a lot more than spit in his cuppa; I think I'd get a good mushroom book and pick a few Death Caps for him. Frying them up with a bit of butter and garlic on a nice piece of toast would mean certain death and no murder charge - just a show of absolute remorse and then a big insurance pay-out. I'd get her the mushroom book for Christmas.

Rodney had demanded cheese-on-toast and a cup of tea with not too much milk. What a shame; no mushrooms.

I settled down by the border and started to trowel out the weeds, trying to resurrect the division between lawn and dirt. It was a bit hit-and-miss. I looked up every now and again to see what he was watching. He was flicking through the channels, trying to find something which took his fancy. As it was a late summer's afternoon, still a bit hot, and fine and dry, he had most of the windows open. I could hear the television quite clearly from our front garden. Now, with a bit of luck, he'd wander out to the kitchen for some sauce or another cup of tea.

I didn't have to wait very long before he got up and left the room. I gave it a couple of seconds, whipped the remote out from my back pocket and tapped in a channel's number I'd seen a few minutes before on my telly.

A few months previously, I'd met an old mate from school down the pub. He was always wheeling and dealing at school and it would appear that he'd carried on his budding career after failing all his exams with some considerable style. While we were chatting over a pint, he opened his coat to reveal a row of flashy-looking TV remotes. He explained that they were top of the range and could operate almost any

277

television. It seemed too good to be true at the time, but I bought one anyway. On the way home, I realised that we already had remotes and didn't need another. It was too late to do anything about it, but it was good to catch up with him.

After tapping the numbers in, I pressed the *Select* button on the remote and up flashed a huge middle-aged 'crocodilapig' of a munter, dressed as a WPC on Rodney's television. You got a full side-view of all her ample delights, which were on offer to anyone who would like to ring up for about two pounds per minute for the pleasure of talking dirty to her. She had a face like Helen of Troy and, judging by the look of her, she'd launched the thousand ships with it. The lads at the shipyard must have run out of big hammers. You couldn't hear what she was saying but you did get some loud banging music to accompany her gyrations over what was supposed to be her desk. The little hat was perched on her dyed-blonde hair which hung down on to her unbuttoned shirt. Hanging down underneath her shirt were the biggest and saggyest pair of tits you've ever seen. They were held loosely in-check by a black bra which could easily have held a football in each cup. Her pale boobs looked like a motorway map of the United Kingdom as there were so many blue veins on show. The further you went down, the worse it got. The huge amount of flesh on show between her knickers and the top of her straining stockings was just a subcutaneous sea of cellulite. As she moved back and forth over the desk, the waves of fat rolled up and down her thighs. Her cellulite was so bad that her milky, white flesh looked like the aerial view of an Arctic bombing range. Basically, it was all on show, not only to the viewers, but also to everyone walking up our street.

I increased the volume for good measure, stashed the remote away and went back to my gardening. It didn't take long for a strangled scream to come from Rodney's front room. I guess WPC Bingo-wings wasn't to Rodney's taste.

The volume soon disappeared, as did the apparition on the television screen. I could hear him chunter to himself as he settled down to another sandwich and a cuppa. The Accountancy Channel would soon be selected for some racy double-entry book-keeping or a tax return filled in by Brad Pitt's stunt double whilst wing-walking over an active volcano.

After finishing his lunch, Rodney turned his attention to the back garden. I heard him calling for Fang. Maybe Fang was deaf because he didn't seem to be running up the garden to meet him.

Behind me, I could hear the local vicar's wife coming out of her door and starting to get the car out. It was too good an opportunity to resist, especially after my lawn penis. She already thought that Rodney was a bit of a pervert after discussing his front lawn phallus with the councillor's wife.

I got the remote ready hoping that he had set his television on standby rather than fully switching it off. The vicar's wife had reversed her car out on to the drive and was climbing out of it to shut the garage door.

I pressed the *ON* button and Rodney's television flashed into life. My plan worked perfectly. I turned the sound down and tapped in another three numbers, selecting another channel. By pressing *Select,* a perfect arse, barely covered by a pair of the skimpiest black-lace knickers, filled the entire screen. The girl was on her hands and knees looking over her shoulder pouting towards the lens. She had a mobile in her hand and was giving the viewer a seductive *'Come here'* gesture with her middle finger.

Mrs Vicar had shut her door and was starting to turn towards her car, and Rodney's front room. I turned the volume up to full volume; it had the desired effect. She glanced up towards the noise and got a full bay-window of bottylicious babe. She stopped in her tracks and focused on the television across the road. Her hand then went up to her mouth and she let out a little cry of shock. At that moment, Rodney burst into the front room. The first thing he saw was the look of shock on the vicar's wife's face. Next, he turned to the telly and a similar look of shock appeared on his. He turned back to the window. I couldn't hear what he was saying above the banging music, but he was waving his hands and appeared to be mouthing 'No, No, No!'

Next, he searched for his remote and switched off the television. He came back to the window and was still shouting. 'No, No, It's not what it seems. I didn't do it. I don't know how this happened.'

He carried on his protestations as the vicar's wife headed for her front door. Poor love, she must have had an attack of the vapours.

It was all too much for me, as I was struggling to stop myself from laughing. Rodney watched her go indoors and he caught sight of me in the garden, struggling to restrain myself.

'You!' he bellowed out of the window. 'You did this, you little shit. I'll fuckin' kill you. I'm sick to death of you, you fuckin' arse-wipe. I hate you and your fuckin' single parent parasitic brood. I hope you all rot in fuckin' hell.'

The spittle was flying out of his mouth, all over the windows and curtains. He was crimson with rage.

It certainly impressed me, but I think the vicar was even more impressed. He was stood at his front door, trying to see what had upset his wife. Rodney caught sight of him and I thought he was going to cry. His whole world as a pillar of society had crashed around his big hairy ears in a couple of seconds. I just carried on weeding my border whilst my belly tightened up with spasms of near uncontrollable laughter. That was the best twenty pounds I'd ever spent in the pub.

Rodney slammed all the front room windows shut as the vicar slammed his front door behind him. My fun batteries were out of the red and on their way to getting charged. Maybe a good night out on the town would see them become fully recharged. I carried on the weeding whilst wondering what Vic had in store for us tonight. I was intrigued, as were the other lads. We'd chatted over the phone and came up with all sorts of ideas but, in the end, we'd just have to wait and see, as Vic was giving nothing away.

Dev was playing away in the afternoon and so the chances were that he was going to be a bit late for our few beers before the fun night. We'd arranged to meet in a pub just off the town centre. It was a busy place where people met up before heading off to the late night places in the centre around the corner. We were transient pissheads en route to a good night out or oblivion. For me, it was usually a combination of both. I would certainly be punishing my evil liver over the next few hours.

I had a quick bite to eat and a brief chat with Mum and Sis. I hadn't had much of a chance to catch up with them over the last few days, but they both seemed to be OK. I'd been particularly worried about Sis but she seemed none the worse from her ordeal inside Ena's curry-house on wheels.

I got ready in double-quick time, throwing on my usual party gear combined with a big splash of smellies and an artistic comb of the hair. I must have been irresistible to the opposite sex; how could any girl resist me? Obviously quite easily, as the evidence of my lack of attraction to females over last few weeks had shown!

I walked into town quite slowly. It was a bit hot and sticky and I didn't want to stink of sweat before I'd paraded my funky stuff on the dance-floor, so it was a steady stroll. It's surprising how much more you notice by walking slower and also taking the time to look around, especially upwards.

As I got closer to the Centre, I was noticing things I'd never seen before like the beautiful stone carvings over the windows on some of the old Victorian houses and buildings. These were places that I'd walked past for years and never even glanced at. Was I getting old or, even worse, was I going through a premature menopause? A few beers would put me right.

Martin and Vic were already there and I joined in their round. I didn't have much catching up to do. Martin was the first to crack.

'Come on Vic, what have you got lined up for us for fun night then?'

A wry smile crossed Vic's lips and he took a big swig of beer to draw out the tension.

'You boys will just have to wait and see, but I'm not sure if you're going to like it. I'm having second thoughts that what I've managed to get hold of might be a bit over-the-top, even for us.'

I was starting to get a bit worried about this now. Anticipation was starting to give way to apprehension. For Vic to say that he was having second thoughts was not good.

'Well, on that sobering note, I think I'll have another beer. Do you want the same again?'

Vic and I polished off our pints and thrust the glasses to Martin, who was at the bar. It was still early evening, but the place was filling up fairly quickly. There was some top-totty hitting the town tonight. A few were obviously going to the fun night. One group of girls were all dressed up as Wonder Woman. It was quite a sight. Golden whips, tiaras and very tight costumes.

'Why do Superheroes always wear their pants on the outside?'

I'd often wondered why my boyhood heroes could look so bloody stupid, but with Wonder Woman it was entirely different.

'Maybe their superpowers don't extend to having a huge knob and balls the size of lemons.'

Martin had followed up the conversation without taking his eyes off one particularly stunning super heroine who was flashing a few suggestive glances back in his direction. If she fluttered her false eyelashes any harder, I swear she was going to take off.

'Balls like lemons? What is Lemon Jiz? Sounds like a fuckin' cleaning product, Martin. Or should it be Lemon Jiz Man, here to save the day and clean up the filthy underbelly of our fair town from its rampant criminal classes?' Vic was joining in the fun and ribbing Martin at the same time.

'A quick one off the wrist and the local criminal mastermind cops for it full in the face, 'No more Lemon Jiz Man, I know when I'm beat. It's a fair cop and society is to blame. Oh, and by the way that citrus really stings'.'

'Alright, smart arse, so I'm not the fuckin' adjective-king of 2014, but you know what I mean. It was all a bit weird when I was young. But with these honeys in blue panties, it's a different kettle of fish.'

Martin's gaze had gone back to his Wonder Woman.

'If you ask me, Mart' fancies a night in thick tights with nylon knickers over the top, so a kettle of fish is an apt description.' Vic was pulling Martin apart.

'Vic, if you don't stop being a smart arse, I swear I'll rip you another arsehole.'

Martin was beginning to get a bit wound up. He hated having his intellectual credentials examined. He'd struggled to get into the police, due to a lack of academic skills, but he

283

was great with his hands and had a great rapport with people. He could talk to anyone; rich; poor; upper or lower class, and always come away as friends. This is a gift not many have, especially academics, yet Martin hated to be the butt of any jokes about his perceived lack of intellect. Vic had just crossed the line, but he hadn't realised it.

'So Martin, you've finally come over to the dark side. Perhaps you won't have to be so rough with me. I can be very submissive when the occasion arises'

Unfortunately for Vic, Martin was wound up tighter than a piano string because of what had happened to his mum and dad. He turned towards Vic, tearing his eyes away from a few square inches of straining blue nylon. I didn't want any falling out this early in the evening. It was time to join the Diplomatic Corps.

'Come on guys, it's been a heavy few days for us all. Victor, you've overstepped the mark. Martin, your stress and testosterone levels are off the scale. I declare the verbal sparring a draw. Basically, you two should wind your necks in or our night out will go for a ball of chalk.'

I tapped my pint glass against a tall wine glass on the bar. Two sharp taps; ding, ding.

'Now, come out of your corners and come out hugging.'

Luckily, they took on board what I was trying to do. They were both a bit wound up and a couple of pints had brought down their defences, but they took a brief step towards each other and had a very brief man hug.

'Sorry mate, bit stressed.' Martin sounded genuinely remorseful.

'Back at you, big guy.' Vic had a smile on his face but not of smugness. These two, as we all did, had a genuine affection for each other, in a brotherly sort of way.

'But I did like the hug.'

Martin bridled for a second then relaxed. Danger averted.

'Just don't push it, Vic. I'm not your bitch; you can't afford me.'

'You mean, you won't stretch that far, Martin?'

It was a joke and Martin took it as such.

'Dream on, Vic, dream on. Anyway, what pants have you got on tonight?'

'Actually Mart', I don't wear pants when I'm out on the town. Spoils the cut of my trousers. It's all about image with us guys but it chafes like hell. What pants have you got on, Richie?'

I thought of a suitable riposte for a second. All I had on were my bog-standard nylon shreddies. They weren't as tight as Wonder Woman's over there, but not far off, if the truth be told.

'I've got my drinking pants on.' Both of them answered at the same time,

'Drinking pants, what the hell are they?'

'Well, I've designed these pants for lads like us who go out every now and again and get so bladdered that they may lose control of their bodily functions. As a result, I've designed my patented two-tone grundies. Your mum, wife or live-in-lover won't notice your indiscretions of the previous night because they're yellow at the front and brown at the back. Your alcoholic evacuations are completely undetectable and go straight into the wash without a single cross word or detention for the following weekend.'

I was quite pleased with my off-the-cuff pants design. As I thought about it, it occurred to me that it was a plausible idea. Maybe I was on to something. It was time to put Martin on the spot.

'What pants have you got on, Mart'?'

'I've got my *Meatloaf* pants on.'

He was looking at Vic as he said it. It was directed at him and I was definitely excluded from his reply. Vic picked up,

'What the hell are *Meatloaf* pants?' Martin smiled, not taking his eyes off Vic.

'Well, on the front they've got, 'I'll do anything for love'. And on the back they've got, 'But I won't do that!''

He just walked forward and gave Vic a big hug. The hot Wonder Woman had picked up on Martin's X-ray gaze over the last few minutes and shouted in his direction.

'Ere, are you gay? I didn't think you were, 'cos you shagged my mate a few weeks ago 'n I was 'opin' for the same treatment a bit later on, if you know what I mean.'

Martin quickly disengaged from Vic's embrace,

'Sorry love, but it's a man thing.'

He was trying to sound a bit butch and his voice had dropped a couple of octaves.

'Well, so are penile warts and I'm not interested in them either, you up-hill gardener.'

In an attempt to restore his honour and reputation amongst the heterosexual males in the vicinity, he immediately made a bee-line for his accuser. A manly arm went around her shoulder and very quickly went south until his thumb was hitched into those tight blue pants.

'You've got to hand it to him; he's a bit of a lad.' Vic was impressed with Martin's charms.

Right on cue, Dev walked in and headed straight for Martin as a good wing-man should. A couple of the girls vied for Dev's immediate attention. I waved a pint-pot at him and he gave a thumbs-up. I didn't think Vic or I would be seeing those two for a while.

'Looks like it's going to be just the two of us for a few pints or so, mate. Now we're alone, why don't you let me in on our get-up for tonight?'

'Better still Richie, why don't I show you, and we can set things up; it might save a few minutes later on. Come on out the back to Uncle Bill's playroom.'

Vic's Uncle Bill ran the pub and Vic had almost a full run of the facilities. He led me out to what was called Bill's playroom. I'd been there a few times before for after-hour sessions and games of pool. Bill's lad, Marcus, was playing a game with one of the barmaids as we entered. The room smelt of cigarettes and stale beer, just like pubs used to smell before the cigarette ban. It took me back to my underage drinking days, when you used to hide at the back of the pub in the clouds of smoke and fag ash. I sucked up the nostalgia.

'Hello Vic, come for your packages? And what's with all the girls' clothes? You're not turning into a tranny, are you? I thought you were a straight gay-bloke?'

Marcus had a way with words and most of them were questions. However, he did have a point. The question of women's clothes had got me a bit worried though.

Four boxes lined the back wall, about eighteen inches square. Alongside them was a black plastic bag which was brimming with skirts and skimpy tops.

'Vic, there's a lot of things I'll do for a good night out, but dressing up as a girl isn't one of them. There's some pretty weird and wonderful characters going to the fun night and I don't fancy having my arse tweaked all night or getting deflowered over a wheelie-bin out the back of the pub.'

Vic smiled and walked over to the boxes.

'The clothes are for the girls, Richie, not for us.'

'What, you've lined up four naked girls who are going to roll up and select their ensemble for a night of wild debauchery?'

'In a manner of speaking, yes. That's exactly what I've got planned.'

I was really intrigued, as were Marcus and the barmaid. We were all gathering around Vic, who was beginning to open the first of the boxes. He cut the tape on the box and lifted the lid. As one, the three of us jumped back with a fright. A head stared back at us from inside the box with blank, lifeless eyes. A box with an accountant in it? There was a shock of shiny blonde hair on top of the head but it was the mouth which was the most alarming. It was wide open. I suppose on the advert it was described as a receptive oral cavity. She, or it, would give you a blowjob in other words. Personally, I wasn't into latex skull-fucking, but I suppose there were people out there who were. Needs must, I suppose; if you can't get the real thing, then maybe this was the next best option. If it kept a few blokes from pestering little girls up the park for a quick fumble, then Latex Laura has a place in society, or on a grubby mattress in a small bedsit.

'Behold; our escorts for the night's festivities.'

Vic pulled Laura from the box. She looked as if a vampire had been sucking on her all night. The husk of a cheap hooker.

'And what the bloody hell are we going to do with Nitrile Nora, Rubber Roxy, Latex Laura and Plastic Pammy, apart from the bleedin' obvious?'

288

I was starting to get very worried about Vic's idea of a fun night out.

'Well, the first thing we do is pump them up, in a manner of speaking.'

Marcus stepped forward for a closer examination.

'Well I hope you've got a foot-pump, mate, because I'm not putting my mouth anywhere near that. You don't know where she's been.'

'I can assure you that they're not shop-soiled. They're still virgins. I got them from one of our clients for services rendered a while back and have been saving them up for tonight. So, let's get pumping, shall we?'

I still wasn't sure what was happening.

'Just how are we going to use them, Vic?'

'As I said, Richie, they're our escorts. After we've pumped them up we dress them in these clothes, simply strap them to our backs and we have an instant girlfriend draped over our shoulders. A very affectionate and clingy girlfriend who is constantly hugging you. And the best thing is, they don't need any expensive drinks and they don't talk back.'

I was beginning to see his plan and was getting quite excited. An instant dancing partner for the disco floor. It would make quite a sight and would get everyone laughing.

We eagerly set about pumping up the girls. When we got to the last box, I got quite a shock. It was a coloured girl.

'Bloody hell, I think I've got her CD back in my bedroom.'

She looked just like an eighties' soul singer, complete with a shock of nylon black frizzy hair. Vic laughed.

'She's not necessarily for Dev. You can't stereotype, not in these days of equal opportunities. We'll take our pick of the girls when the other two turn up and dress them up to our own tastes.'

We laid all the clothes out on the pool-table. There was quite a choice from hot-pants, short skirts and sparkly boob-tubes. There was even a selection of bras and pants. I was impressed.

We went back to the bar to look for Dev and Martin. They were still chatting to the group of flirty superheroes. Well Dev was, at least. Martin was swapping spit with his accuser and engaged in what looked like a very vigorous game of tonsil-tennis.

Dev noticed us first and made his excuses to the girls and wandered over. The bar was packed with the night's revellers. It was a good atmosphere and everyone seemed to be enjoying themselves.

'Where have you two been? I've been looking for you for ages and I've run out of beer.'

I started slapping the top of my trousers.

'Liar, liar, pants on fire. You've been otherwise engaged while we've been working. Anyway, we've lined you up with another girl for the night so you can forget about Wonder Woman over there. Vic's found you the perfect girl.'

Dev's eyes lit up and widened in anticipation.

'Can't wait. Where is she?'

Wonder Woman was suddenly forgotten. Martin came wandering over, wiping his lips. I think he won on the tie-break.

'Jesus, that girl can sure kiss. I think she's sucked out all my fillings.'

Bright red lipstick was still smeared over his lips and cheek. He looked like he was suffering from high blood-pressure. Vic was eager to get the party started.

'Right, if you guys are ready, let's go and pick up our girlfriends for the night and start to have some fun. After all, that's what we came for, wasn't it?'

Martin and Dev exchanged quizzical glances. Vic headed off to the back room, closely followed by Martin and Dev. I brought up the rear, because I knew what was coming and wanted to see their reactions. When we got to the room, the pumped-up girls were lined up against the back wall. They looked quite a sight. Dev was the first to react.

'Fuck my old boots. It's the naked Nineties girl group. Only these are probably better singers. Looks like they're trying all to reach a high C'

'No mate, it's a set of nocturnal golfers. They're for some dirty old geezer who wants three holes-in-one over the course of the night.'

The two of them stood for a moment staring at the quartet of dolls. Dev then cast his eye over the clothes. Vic didn't wait for any more questions and explained his plan. He had strips of beige Velcro with which we were to attach the girls to our backs. The first thing we did was choose our respective partners. Martin chose the coloured girl, much to Dev's amusement.

'Once you've had black, there's no going back, Martin!'

'I agree mate. You're not a man until you've had a bit of tan. Vic, do these girls come with slip-in dentures for that authentic feel?'

We eagerly set about dressing them up and strapping them to our backs and ankles. Once we'd finished, we looked around at ourselves and all cracked up laughing. I had to admit we looked stunning. I had Laura, Dev had Nora, and Martin and Vic had Roxy and Pammy respectively. It was time to show off our new 'dolls' to the world.

We walked into the packed bar to a howl of cat-calls, whistles and shouts of appreciation. We each gave Vic a relieved smile. His idea looked to be a winner. We grabbed a beer and mingled amongst the crowd. I slipped outside to see the smokers and bought a ciggie for a quid off one of the girls then blue-tacked it into Laura's mouth. She looked every inch the tart in her sequinned red boob-tube and white rah-rah skirt, fag hanging out of her mouth at a jaunty angle. We were the focus of the pub. Lads were coming up and lifting up the girls' skirts. We'd all put knickers on the girls to protect their modesty and avert a charge of public indecency.

'My round, I think lads. What's Roxy having, Martin?'

We were getting into the banter with our strap-ons.

'Not sure Richie, she's the strong, silent type. Actually, I think she's got a bit of an inflated ego but, taking everything on-board, she hasn't been a let-down yet. I'll have a beer and a helium for the young lady.'

I made my way to the bar and waited to get served. I glanced up and down the bar at the party-goers. The beer and spirits were flowing and everyone was getting tanked-up very quickly.

I was suddenly aware of a very large presence behind me. I sniffed the air and knew instantly what it was. If I was a munter hunter, I would be chambering a round in my gun and getting ready for action. I couldn't tell one wine from another, but I was an expert on munters. My nose could pick up the bouquet at ten paces - the lingering odour of cheap perfume, stale cigarettes, alcopops and sweat. This was a big munter. I could hear the wheezing over my shoulder from too many Chinese counterfeit cigarettes and hours and hours spent moulding her settee into the shape of her enormous arse. I just hoped she wasn't smoking at the time and put a hole in Laura.

I gathered up the pints and edged around, which was difficult with Laura on my back. It was indeed a prime specimen of Muntera Maxima, complete with hairy chin and bingo wings that would double as sails on a large yacht. As I squeezed by, I wondered where I'd seen her before. Then it struck me. I'd seen her on the night I met Nicola, on The Rhino Hunt, when this munter and her mate had caused a partial eclipse of the glittery disco-ball. This made me panic a little; I hoped they wouldn't recognise Martin and Dev. I squeezed back to the lads, keeping an eye on the calorific-challenged girl at the bar.

She left with a couple of pints of euro fizz and a pudgy fist full of alcopops. She was carrying two pints; that meant they were with blokes. I followed her with my eyes through the crowd and back to a table where she joined her mate and two savage-looking blokes. These must be the blokes Martin was telling us about. They must have been let out of prison and were on a bit of a bender. Thinking about it, I didn't think that the munters would tell their husbands that they had tried to seduce two blokes while they were doing time. I was about to find out differently.

The other munter stood up and scanned the bar. Her eyes settled on Martin and Dev who were chatting to a couple of girls. She sat down and started nodding her head, getting quite animated. The bigger of the two husbands suddenly slammed his glass down on the table, spilling most of his lager. This wasn't looking good. He shouted over to a group of similar-looking blokes. There were four of them, all muscle and tattoos. He was gathering the troops. If I didn't move now, we were in serious trouble.

I moved over to the other three. Martin was the closest.

'Martin, do you remember our last Rhino Hunt when you and Dev picked up those two munters?'

Martin thought for a second.

'Yeah, the two who followed us to the kebab shop and wanted carnal knowledge along with chilli sauce and all the trimmings.'

'That's them. Well, they're over in the corner with their husbands and a group of Neanderthals. I think it best that we leave ASAP, before the brown stuff hits the whirly thing.'

Martin glanced over my shoulder to scan the crowd. He was about to say something, but was beaten to it by a loud shout over the drinkers.

'You, you fucker. Try to shag my missus while I'm inside? You're fuckin' dead.'

Vic and Dev heard the shout and recognised our frightened looks, as well as the munters and their husbands at the same time. There was no time for diplomacy, we just turned and ran, closely followed by the shouts of irate husbands and protesting drinkers as they were barged out of the way in the husbands' attempt to reach us.

We burst out of the pub with Martin in the lead.

'Follow me,' he shouted as he and Roxy turned left and headed towards the centre of town. We were there a few seconds later. There were eight of us, running for our lives, closely followed by the pack of tattooed bruisers.

Unlike most town and city centres, ours still held on to its Victorian heritage. It was laid-out in a series of small grass strips surrounded by low rosebushes. It looked lovely but, with today's austerity measures, you wondered how long the council would maintain the expensive up-keep before it turned into a large expanse of concrete and paving slabs.

Martin headed directly for the middle of the first set of rosebushes. It looked like a low fence.

Normally, we could all outrun our pursuers, but we had the latex lovelies strapped to our backs and they were seriously slowing us down. I could feel the lactic acid starting to build up in my legs. We hurdled the first rosebush fence and ran across the grass to the next, trying to keep up with Martin. The three of us were more or less in a line abreast. The faster we ran, the more the girls' heads jerked up and down and side-to-side. I could hear our pursuers behind us as they jumped the roses. A scream rang out across the centre as it sounded like one of them had fallen at the first. One down, five to go. I wasn't sure where Martin was going, but I just followed in blind panic. The baying pack was close behind. All I needed was a fox's tail shoved up Laura's arse.

People all around the Centre were starting to notice us. We must have looked like the strangest horse race in history. The rose fences lay out in front of us like the Grand National and us with our jockeys on our backs. Shouts of encouragement echoed around us, along with a few starting to lay bets. If we got caught, it was the knacker's yard for all of us.

We cleared the second fence, and then the third, with no mishaps. We were holding our ground, but at the fourth, Vic and Pammy hit it hard. There was a sudden hiss and Pammy started to deflate. The effect was disastrous for Vic, as Pammy started to wrap herself around his legs. Dev could see the funny side, despite our impending doom.

'Fuck me Vic, that's the first time you've had a girl go down on you for a long time.' Martin didn't see the joke.

'Shut up and keep running. We're nearly there. Just keep going for a couple more fences and we're safe.'

I could see what he meant. Ahead of us, at the end of the bushes, were three police cars. They were there every Friday and Saturday night to sort out any over-exuberant revellers. The sight gave us hope and that last bit of energy we needed. The police had seen us too and were getting out of their cars. Vic was really struggling, but he'd got over the second-last. Everyone was cheering now and willing us on. The last was coming up fast. As we got there, I went behind Vic and pushed him as hard as I could. He didn't go over, more like straight through, with a Colin Jackson-like dip at the line. We were at the police cars.

Martin rushed up to the sergeant. He stood wide-eyed as he recognised Martin.

'What the hell are you up to, Martin?'

Martin stopped in front of his sergeant, gasping for breath. Roxy's head was bobbing up and down in unison with his gulps for air.

'Sorry Sarge. We need your help to keep these nutters from breaking our heads.'

His hands rested on his knees as the three of us came up alongside him, coughing and spluttering and gulping down the air to refill our lungs.

'Stole their girlfriends, have you lads? Better than your usual standard, Martin, I must say. Use a bit of lube though; I don't want you off sick with a blistered knob!'

With that, our pursuers crashed over the last fence and stopped in front of the police, who were by this time between us and the munters' husbands and remaining mates. They stood there, not knowing what to do. The bigger of the two husbands broke the uneasy stand-off. He pointed at Martin.

'You're fuckin' dead, you and your mates. We'll get you sooner or later.'

He was breathing heavily and his big belly was wobbling up and down as his diaphragm pumped his nicotine-filled lungs. The sergeant moved forward.

'Right you lot, I would strongly suggest that you stop using threatening language and behaviour or you'll all end up down at the nick instead of enjoying a nice cold pint somewhere. The choice is yours.' He stood there supported by his fellow officers.

'All right, we'll fuck off, but this isn't the end of it.'

He was pointing at Martin as he spat out his threats. I glanced over at Martin who had his work-face on.

'Right, I've had enough of this shit. You and I need a word in private to set things straight. You're not ruining my night, or anyone else's.'

He walked up in front of the bloke and stared straight into his eyes. It was confrontational. Martin was calling his bluff. I wasn't sure if he wanted to talk to him or entice the bloke to take a swing at him in front of his fellow officers.

'We need a chat to set things straight. You've been sold a crock of shit by your missus and her mate. If you take a swing at me or my mates, you've violated your parole and it'll be straight back inside. Now, what's it going to be?'

Roxy stared over Martin's shoulder at the bloke, who was looking at her rather than Martin. It seemed to take the edge off him.

'Let's talk.'

The three of them stepped a few paces away from us and had a couple of minutes of animated chat. Roxy was leaning over Martin's shoulder, listening intently to the conversation. The bloke started swearing and shaking his head. Then, to all our surprise, he shook Martin's hand and wandered off back to his mates and across the Centre back towards the pub. The sergeant stepped forward,

'Well done, son. It looks like he's seen the error of his ways and saved us a lot of work. Now, I suggest you get off my streets and find yourself a room for you and your new girlfriend.'

With the tension dying away, Martin's colleagues started to rip the piss out of him. All sorts of comments were passed about him and his soul-singing jockey.

'We'll be off, Sarge, but just one more favour. Have you got a puncture repair kit or a roll of gaffer tape in the car for my mate and his friend? She seems a bit out of breath after all her exertions.'

We patched up Pammy whilst sat on a couple of benches in the Centre. Martin ran over what he'd said to the bloke. Basically he'd explained what had happened and put it to him that it wasn't plausible that two very good looking blokes like him and Dev would be trying to drag his missus and her mate into bed. The bloke had a sudden attack of reality and saw that his missus was a fat, lying bitch that was playing away from home whilst he was inside, dreaming of her feminine charms. I don't think that those two munters would be terrorising the male population of our town for some considerable time to come.

It was a close call. We'd got away by the skin of our teeth, and a bit of skin off our shins, but it had also been quite exhilarating. The adrenalin was staring to wear off and we were starting to feel a bit washed out. I looked us over and we were a bit tattered and torn. Pammy had a big wrap of gaffer tape around her ankle and the girls' clothes were all over the place. Laura had lost her cigarette over the fences and her hair was a mess. After a couple of minutes of contemplation, Dev was the first to try and stir us into some action.

298

'Come on guys, this is fun night. Let's get ourselves together and wander over to the pub and sort the girls out.'

We dragged ourselves up and headed across the road.

'Just one thing, do we use the Ladies or the Gents toilets when we need a piss? Nora Bone here is a bit sensitive.'

'Just leave her outside if you're worried she might peep over your shoulder, Dev. Me and Roxy here are just about to get engaged, I think.'

Martin had rearranged Roxy's hands and arms. Her left arm was around his shoulder and he'd tucked her right down the front of his trousers.

'Tell you what Vic, if this one can cook and clean, I think I'm in love.'

We joined the queue amongst the other bizarrely dressed clientele. There were all sorts there but, I have to admit, we all looked a bit bedraggled and dishevelled. As we hit the front, I noticed that Clint was at the door. He greeted me like a long-lost friend.

'Do you lot count as four or eight? This might turn out costly for you boys, if you're paying for them as well.'

I shook hands with Clint. It was good to see him.

'Sorry, Clint, but they're royalty. They don't carry cash but they can offer favours in kind. I'll just leave her round the back and you can help yourself. They don't smell, they don't tell and they're always grateful.'

'So when are you getting married then, Richie? Anyway, your head looks fine. You were a lucky lad.'

'Let's just say I had a bit of help from some very good mates, for which I will always be grateful.'

A little knowing smile passed over both of our faces and we shook hands again. It went unnoticed by the others, but

Clint and I had a bit of a bond. I really liked this guy. A few heckles started to come from behind us.

'Get a move on baldy, we haven't got all night.' Clint glanced down the line, picking out the heckler. The bloke had just pissed on his own fireworks and would be looking for another venue for his evening's entertainment. Clint looked back at us,

'OK, lads and lasses, in you go and this one's on the house. Just buy me a beer later.'

We funnelled into the club and grabbed a beer at the already-crowded bar. The Wonder Women were there along with a load of other gangs of girls. This was going to be a good night. We mingled amongst the crowd with our strap-ons, to a lot of favourable comments and banter. It was time to hit the dance floor. I gathered the lads together and we rearranged the girls from our backs to our fronts. They were the perfect dancing partners.

As we hit the floor, most of the other dancers moved aside and we put on a bit of a show for a couple of records. The girls were bouncing around all over the place and Pammy was still holding up. Unusually for this early in the night, the DJ put on a slow record and we duly obliged with a seductive smooch with our Hindenburg hotties. There was a lot of squeezing of the girls' buns and the occasional lifting of skirts for the voyeuristic crowd. The record finished to the sound of clapping and whistles. Fun night was certainly living up to its name.

Dev and Martin were soon in the superhuman clutches of the Wonder Women. Martin had found a quiet corner and propped Roxy up alongside him whilst he continued his tennis match. Dev didn't bother. He had his Wonder Woman pinned against the wall, trying to suck her fillings out whilst Nora watched with interest over his shoulder. It was a bizarre sight.

He looked a bit like a marmite sandwich with two slices of white bread.

Vic and I just drank and enjoyed the company of everyone who came up and chatted to us. That was until we were interrupted by the last person in the world I wanted to see tonight.

'Well, if it isn't Al Pacino, or shall I call you Scarface?'

Ena and his mates had sidled up behind us. He stood there with a gloating smile on his face as if to say, 'I did that'.

'Take a look in the mirror Ena. Pot, kettle, kettle, pot.'

His face flushed with anger, highlighting his own scars. He touched his face subconsciously.

'Maybe next time, they'll take a Stanley knife to the sides of your mouth and wipe that fuckin' smile off your face.'

The smirk was still there, despite the mounting anger in his voice and posture.

'What do you mean, next time, Ena? What makes you think there'll be a next time? And who are 'they'?'

He'd said a bit too much and he knew it. It only intensified his anger and frustration with himself.

I remembered a joke about two lads in a pub. A football referee and a group of footballers walked in. One lad turned to the other and said, 'Fuck me, I'm off. It's all going to kick off in a minute.'

And it was here too. We had no back-up to take on Ena and his mates.

Help came in the nick of time in the shape of Clint and a couple of his lads. He must have noticed what was happening. He pushed in between Ena and me.

'Sorry to break it up, lads, but it would be a shame to spoil such a good party. This is fun night, not fight night. Why don't you all move along and enjoy yourselves?'

Ena flushed again.

'Just remember who pays your wages, Clint, and gets you all your work.' Clint was unmoved.

'I'm just doing my job, Mr Sharples.'

He stood between us in an uneasy stand-off between all parties. Eventually, Ena and his cronies moved off and were soon lost in the crowd.

'Thanks again, mate; this is becoming a bit of a habit.' The irony wasn't lost on him. This was the third time that he'd saved my arse.

'He's not going to let it go, Richie, despite the other night. I'd suggest you leg it before closing or he might be outside in the shadows.'

He was right. It was a good time to leave while the streets were still a bit busy. It was a shame, because I was enjoying myself, but an early night was better than another hospital bed. I said my goodbyes to Vic, but I didn't want to interrupt the other two.

'Just one thing, Vic, what do we do with the girls now?' A blank expression crossed his face.

'To be honest, I don't know. I hadn't thought that far ahead.'

I had this vision of mum bringing me a cup of tea in the morning to be confronted by Laura either in bed with me, or sat in my chair alongside the bed. It would traumatise her for life. I glanced over towards Martin and noticed that Roxy was missing, probably stolen by some lads. I could see her strapped to a bus-stop in the morning, with her arm out. I pity the poor old bus driver.

'I'm sure you'll think of something, Richie; you always do.'

And, at that moment I did. All I needed was a roll of wide *Sellotape* and Laura would be off my hands, and my back.

Laura was indeed soon off my back. She was starting to chafe. Maybe I should use a bit more *KY Jelly* next time. I took her off as soon as I got out of the club and tucked her under my arm. I got some very strange looks from passers-by; I was just hoping that I didn't get lifted by the police as a suspected murderer.

I stuck to the main roads on the way home. It wasn't ideal because of Laura, but it was better than a taxi. When I got to my road, everything was pretty quiet. Most of the bedroom lights were out and there was no one about. It was time to get rid of Laura.

I'd already had one go at Rodney today. The last thing he would be expecting was another strike at his veneer of respectability so soon. I got a few houses away from Rodney's and got the *Sellotape* out which Clint had sourced from the pub's office on my way out. I pulled off a few strips, each about five foot long and stuck them all over my front, taking care not to overlap them. I didn't want to do it outside Rodney's front door, as the rip of the tape coming off the roll might alert him. With the strips done, I crept to his door. It was a sort of porch arrangement with two posts supporting the roof. I stuck the strips from post to post and then arranged Laura on the path in front of the door. I placed two flat stones from his garden on her feet to hold her upright. I banged on Rodney's front door and quickly jumped over the wall, opened our door and screamed at the top of my voice, like a girl being attacked.

'Help me, help me, arghhhh!'

The light came on in his bedroom, closely followed by the opening of the window. All he would see would be the shock of blonde hair on top of Laura's head. I could faintly hear the thump of his feet on the stairs. Luckily, he didn't put his light on. The next thing was his front door bursting open. I watched from our window as Rodney raced towards Laura who was standing just outside the porch.

Rodney hit the cobweb of *Sellotape* I'd strung across the posts. It totally enveloped him from his chest down and he fell into Laura, propelled by his momentum. He hit her with his chest directly on hers and stuck fast. I'd double-sided the tape so they'd stick together. Rodney landed on top of her on the path.

The whole neighbourhood was coming to life now at the sound of Laura's screams and what were now Rodney's howls of anguish. The first to get up and investigate were the vicar and his wife, who came out of their front door. Just as they came out, Mo switched on the hall and outside light, so illuminating Rodney and Laura on the path.

Rodney was on top of Laura, writhing about, trying to get unstuck. But to the untrained eye it looked like something entirely different.

'Oh, my God, the pervert! Call the police; he's gone too far this time. The poor girl.'

The vicar's wife just stood there, with her hand to her mouth, unable to carry out her husband's instructions. He ran over to save Laura from the clutches of the evil sex pervert rolling around on top of her. With impeccable timing, Laura finally gave up her 'resistance' and suddenly exploded. Rodney collapsed on to the path with what was left of my latest girlfriend underneath him. His weight and the sharp stones in the path were probably too much for my evening's companion. Shame, I was going to miss her. The vicar reeled in shock.

'My God, what have you done to her? You need help, Rodney. You're a very sick man.'

He struggled to his feet with Laura hanging off him like a second skin. He looked like a fat bloke who's just lost ten stone. The flabby latex skin was hanging loosely from his front with a large lump of blonde chest-hair.

'Maureen, get this thing off of me,' Rodney demanded.

She was stood in the doorway, trying not to laugh, her hand stuffed into her mouth; good girl. It was time for me to make myself scarce.

As I drifted off to sleep I could hear Rodney's screams as strip after strip of *Sellotape* was pulled off his legs and chest by Maureen.

Back, sack and crack, sir?

Chapter Twelve

There were no knocks at my door on Sunday morning. Neither Rodney nor the vicar had called the police. I suppose that they didn't want their names to be associated with late-night sex-toy wrestling. All of this left me with a free day without much of a hangover.

My preparations were complete for my little fact-finding mission tomorrow, so I was at a bit of a loose end. I'd see how the day panned out. The only thing I would do was stay away from Rodney. Twice in one day was too much, even by my standards, and he'd be hurting, both mentally and physically.

I hadn't annoyed Victor's parents for quite a while, so I arranged to meet up with him at their house later on in the day. It was getting to be a Sunday habit. A visit to a friend's parents for tea. Very civilised indeed.

There was a lot to do around the house and I cracked on with the cleaning and tidying. If only my mates could see me now. The only things missing were a little apron, big yellow gloves and a scarf tied around my head. The next thing would be me on my hands and knees scrubbing the front step.

In reality, I knew that I had a lot of respect from the lads. They'd all grown up within a fully functional family unit and had had it a lot easier than me when we were younger. They always had all the new kit at school, whilst I had to make do with second-hand football boots and a lot of stuff from car boot sales. I didn't mind too much and it also gave me a greater appreciation of material things. Life was what you made of it. At least, that's what a lot of poor people say.

Once the chores had been finished, I checked that the coast was clear before I headed off to Vic's parents. Rodney wasn't out cleaning his car, which was unusual. He was probably in the same situation as me; avoiding the vicar and his wife. He'd be sat indoors, trying to figure out a way of restoring his reputation. That wasn't going to easy. I'd done a good job on him yesterday and, in the eyes of the local clergy, he was a rampant sex-fiend who would surely burn in hell. That served the bastard right for all the years of spite he'd inflicted on my poor mother.

Walking was a lot easier than it had been the previous week. All the aches and pains of the Miliband bruising had faded and I was almost back to normal, apart from the scar on my head. That would stay with me for quite a while.

A little while later, I was in Vic's parents' street. This was middle class heaven. All the lawns were perfect and the uPVC windows and cladding were all gleaming and white, whilst the curtains behind were tasteful and expensive. To me, it was a bit of a reflection of their outlook on life. Most people in this street were probably more worried about what their neighbours thought of them, their social standing, position in society and reputation than about actually getting on and living life to the full. Gossip would be the byword in this area. In my mind, that made them a bit boring and slightly paranoid. They were afraid to live life, in case they upset someone who might gossip about them to the rest of the street; total bollocks in my view.

Despite my prejudices against the middle class and above, I liked Vic's parents and got on well with them.. At least, that was until one of them would start quizzing me on my thoughts about the current political situation or the failings of society and the role of the Government. They'd listen to the radio all the time and get involved with all the phone-ins. I could imagine their idea of a good night-in was a couple of hot chocolates and settling down in front of *Question Time,* shouting at the participants. I found it all a bit odd, because the only thing they could do to change the situation was vote once every four or five years in the General Election. Mind you, that's still more than a lot of people do. Most are in a frenzy of apathy when it comes to the Government.

The road was buzzing with the sound of lawnmowers and hedge-trimmers. They just couldn't have an unkempt lawn or messy shrubs around the garden. What would the neighbours think, or even worse, say?

As I got closer to their house, a familiar sight greeted me in the distance. God does indeed work in mysterious ways, and on his day of rest too. It was the God Botherers on their regular Sunday missionary visits to the lost souls of suburbia. If they saw me again, I'm sure they would think I was some kind of religious stalker.

I quickened my pace to the front door.

Vic's dad answered the door and I ducked in. There was the sound of the radio emanating from the kitchen and I could hear his wife tut-tutting and talking to the presenters, giving her views on their opinionated statements.

'Hello Richard, we haven't seen you for a while. How are you, after your troubles of last weekend? I blame this bloody Government, you know. It's just not safe to walk the streets anymore, is it? They're just not tough enough on crime and these feral youths can just roam our streets harming whoever or whatever the wish. It's an absolute disgrace.'

It didn't take long, did it? I hadn't even had time to wipe my feet on the mat.

'I'm fine thanks, Mr Smith. I just popped over to see how everyone is and catch up with Vic.'

I was trying to be polite. I'd seen Vic less than twelve hours earlier.

'Oh, by the way, you might get a knock on the door in a while. I've just seen some canvassers for the local MP working the street, trying to drum up a bit of support for him for the forthcoming local elections, I suppose. I don't know why they have to come out on a Sunday. The bloke's brought out his entire family for moral support. He's even got his children with him. In view of the total mismanagement of this current Government, I can see why he's hiding behind his family. It stops people from saying what they really think. Don't you agree, Mr Smith?'

With the pin pulled from the hand grenade, I retired to the front room with Vic to await the explosion. At this rate, I was going to meet up with Rodney in a very hot and unpleasant place, and I don't mean Benidorm.

'Edith, Edith, did you hear that? They're canvassing on a Sunday, with their children. I've never heard anything like it. If they come knocking at our door, I'll give them an earful. Just you wait and see if I don't.'

Mum joined in the tirade, saying it was symptomatic of the lack of morals associated with the incumbent regime. That was too many syllables for me.

Vic was sat in the front room. The television was on, but he wasn't watching it. He was giving a good impression of someone suffering from severe concussion. His eyes were rolling around his head like a couple of marbles.

'You've really done it now, haven't you? Light the blue touch paper and retired to somewhere safe before it blows up. You just don't get any better, do you?'

I explained to Vic that it wasn't canvassers and that it was in fact the God Botherers that I'd met over the previous weeks. Why should his parents get away with it after Martin's and Dev's had copped for it?

'It's me that's got to live with it, mate. Well, that is before I go back to my flat anyway. It's just such bloody hard work. You know they blame the Government for me being gay. It's got nothing to do with me or my sexuality. No, it's the Government's policies and the teaching in the schools. Genetics don't come into it as far as they're concerned.'

He had a point. It must be hard living in a debating chamber for most of your life. Vic's mum brought us in a couple of beef sandwiches and a cup of tea.

'You two can just call if you need anything else. There's a good programme on *BBC Three* in a minute with that nice Jeremy Paxman interviewing the Health Secretary. It should be absolutely fascinating. Perhaps he'll ask him about all those quangos and why they haven't got enough nurses, despite all the money they throw at it. They've got enough managers though. And another thing……'

Vic raised his hand to cut her off.

'Mum, that's enough. We're watching a film about a group of gays and their journeys through a mythical world. It's called *The Fellowship of the Ring.*'

It went completely over her head like a giraffe's fart. We tucked into the sandwiches and caught the tail-end of a bit of rugby. It wasn't long before there was a knock at the front door and Vic's dad was like a greyhound out of the traps. He didn't mince his words.

'You've got a cheek coming around on a Sunday. Typical of you lot. Orders from upon high, I suppose?'

The family was a bit taken aback at first, but the father soon got his composure back.

'Well, in fact, that's correct. We find Sunday is a very good day for getting out in the community and spreading his word.'

'Spreading his word, door to door? Isn't there enough of it on the television and radio, rather than banging on doors on the day of rest?

'It's a day of rest for some, Sir, but there are others like us who prefer to get out and meet people in the community and show them that there is another way, a better way, don't you agree?

'No, I bloody don't. It's because of your boss and his policies, that this country, and the world for that matter, are in the state they're in today.'

The father was taken aback by Vic's dad's sweeping criticisms.

'Sir, you surely can't blame him for all the world's ills? That's why we're here; to show people that there is an alternative - a better way of life and a better way of living. That is by living by his example and following the holy written word.'

'I don't care what his manifesto says. It's all lies and rubbish as far as I can see. Say one thing and do another. You're all the same.'

'I can assure you, Sir, that we live our lives according to his words and teachings, even the children. We read the book to them every night before bed and they too are following in his pious footsteps.'

Both parties were beginning to get a bit excitable by now.

'Oh my God, it's worse than I thought. This is total and utter indoctrination. Surely, you could spare the children at their tender age?'

'I'm sorry, Sir, but the younger they believe, the stronger the faith will be in later life. That's what we believe, isn't it children?'

He looked down at them with pride.

'Well it's beyond me. Your big boss, sat there in his ivory tower surrounding himself with his disciples and sycophants, spouting his ideas for a better world. I bet they're all fiddling their expenses and travelling the world at our expense. It makes me sick to the pit of my stomach. Well, I've seen a better future. You see my wife and I have gone over to the other side. We've seen through your policies and have gone over to his adversary.'

The whole family looked shocked and shook their heads in disbelief.

'Y-you mean, you've gone over to the dark side? You've turned to Satan?'

'I wouldn't call him that. He can be a bit radical, and has a bit of a chequered past, but we believe that his policies are basically sound. He's even improving his Green policies; like cutting down on fossil fuels. He's advocating burning refuse and using other, more ethical fuels in a bid to reduce his carbon footprint. Now, what do you say to that then?'

It was the first time that I'd seen the Botherers lost for words. It was the thought of the devil burning lost souls with garden refuse.

'Sir, it's not too late to change. We can help you to find another path. It's never too late.'

Vic's dad was in full flow.

'Yes it is. I've already signed up and I'm going to the next meeting. He's going to be there in person you know, to give us new recruits a talk. There's even talk of a slide-show presentation of his new policies on social unrest.'

'But can't you see that the social unrest is mostly his doing? He's the cause of the evil in our society. If you came back to us, you would see that.'

'I'll show you the result of your society. It's the society that you've created and obviously whole-heartedly support. Come with me.'

Before I could react or hide behind the sofa, they were all filing into the sitting room. They recognised me immediately.

'Look at this poor lad. He was the victim of a random attack. They were no doubt after his money and mobile phone to support their drug habit. This was your fault and we need to do something about it.'

I just sat there under the increasingly angry stare of Mr Botherer. Even the kids were giving me the evils. There wasn't anything I could say or do other than wither under their gaze. I swear he was shaking with anger. He took a deep breath and pulled himself together.

'I've got the impression that we've both been at cross-purposes here, Sir. Now, if you'll excuse us, we'll be on our way.'

They trooped out of the door and disappeared down the road. Vic's dad seemed pleased with himself.

'That showed them. They couldn't stand to see the error of their ways and couldn't admit that they were wrong.'

He headed to the kitchen and began to tell Edith how he'd put a flea in the canvassers' ears.

I felt pretty bad for the Botherers. This was the third time I'd played a trick on them and I was feeling a bit guilty. I'd certainly get a good tan from the fires of hell in the afterlife. Vic sat there shaking his head.

'I can understand you taking on the Sharples', but to take on God? That's a bit far even for you, Richie.'

'It won't happen again, mate. Besides, I've run out of parents to stitch up. Next week, I'm off to church and the confessional.'

'You should take a few days leave then, because it's going to take a long time.'

More sandwiches and tea arrived. We scoffed them down and went our separate ways after saying goodbye to Vic's parents. They were still discussing the merits of his dad's debating skills as we left.

I was off home to finalise my preparations for the forthcoming day. I'd already gone over my plan a dozen times but perfect planning prevented piss poor performance. On the walk, I ran over everything and made as many contingency plans as possible for anything that might go wrong. However, if I knew what was going to go wrong, I just wouldn't do it, would I?

Monday morning soon came around and I packed my guise into a rucksack and set off for work. I'd have to ask for a couple of hours off over lunchtime, but Carol wouldn't mind. She hadn't expected me in last week, so a little time off today shouldn't be a problem.

Autumn would soon be upon us, as there was a bit of a chill in the air and the leaves were starting to turn brown. Still, summer might be rapidly slipping away, but that meant the start of the rugby and football seasons proper, and that meant more beer down the pub or at Dev's or Martin's clubs. That was a little silver lining, but I swear I got a twinge of complaint from my kidneys as soon as I thought about more beer.

The traffic was its usual shit state as I walked up the High Street, and passed the traffic-jam. I noticed Ena's Audi a few cars ahead of me and I could smell the mix of pungent curry powder and air freshener wafting from his open window as I approached from behind. He was on his mobile with his arm resting on the door frame. I drew level.

'Taxi to the Taj Mahal, please mate, and don't spare the elephants.'

His head turned to meet me as I walked on past. He must have been riding the clutch because the car shot forward as his foot slipped off. He stopped it inches from the back of the car in front. As I walked on, I could hear his curses. I didn't turn around to give him any satisfaction. I walked the rest of the way to the office with a grin and a warm glow. I hoped that the rest of the day would be as good.

I busied myself throughout the morning, trying to keep my mind occupied. If I got caught this afternoon, this might be my last morning at work. The sack would be my employer's only option.

Twelve o'clock soon came around. I'd planned on arriving at the hospital around lunchtime. Carol had agreed for me to borrow the car for a couple of hours. Thankfully, she didn't ask any awkward questions.

The drive didn't take too long. I parked up in a secluded part of one of the hospital's many car parks, grabbed my rucksack and took a deep breath. There was still time to turn back and forget about it, to just turn around and walk away, but the memory of Nicola's face at the pub spurred me on. If there was anything I could do to help her, I had to try, but was this the right way to do it? I still wasn't sure. If things started to unravel, I'd just walk away. I'd already found out she had cancer, or more likely, leukaemia. Knowing was one thing, but I had to try and find out if there was anything else I could do.

The view from my moral high-ground was pretty good, but morals were one thing, breaking the law was an entirely different kettle of fish. The problem was that it was a long way down from my lofty perch and a fall would cause me a lot of damage.

I arrived at the main doors and headed straight for the toilets. I selected a vacant trap and locked the door. I was already wearing the trousers and shoes that I'd bought from the charity shop and changed into my new shirt. Out came the clipboard and diary, along with my new glasses. I waited until the toilets were empty and slipped out to rearrange my hairstyle. After a quick restyle, I looked at Doctor Head in the mirror. I looked quite the academic with smart black glasses, slightly unruly hair with casual lived-in clothes. My newly-acquired scar was slightly covered by my hair in the hope that it didn't attract any attraction. The clipboard and diary gave me a professional-looking air of authority and belonging. It was time to head for the stairwell. My name tag was tucked into my top pocket but the ribbon on show was the same colour as all the other NHS ribbons I'd seen so far. I just hoped no-one asked for my ID, as I hadn't got that far. All it said was *Richard*. If I got caught with a false NHS ID, I would really be in trouble. As it was, I was just a confident-looking visitor who just looked like a Houseman. Confidence was the key.

I took the stairs at a jaunty clip, passing a couple of nurses who were discussing a problematic catheterisation. They didn't even give me a second glance, but the thought of a tube shoved up your luncheon meat lance sent my already queasy stomach into a rapid spin-cycle. There was still time to turn back. I had faint sheen of sweat on my brow and my armpits were starting to get sticky.

Before I knew it, I was in front of the exit doors from the stairwell. I stared at them for a moment. If I went through, there would be no turning back. The decision was made for me. Suddenly, one door opened and an auxiliary nurse appeared in the aperture. He immediately moved back into the corridor and held it open for me.

'After you, Doctor,' and motioned for me to come through.

I stood for a split second with my mouth moving, but nothing coming out. I felt like a goldfish that had just jumped out of his tank and was flapping around on the floor, completely outside its natural environment. Then the word 'Doctor' hit me. I got a sudden rush of confidence and my balls felt as big as footballs.

'Why, thank you very much.'

I walked into the arena, armed only with my clipboard and corduroy trousers, ready to do battle with the crusty old matrons. 'I'm Spartacus', I thought.

I headed down towards Nicola's ward, stopping just short of the locked doors. This was my first big obstacle. I thought back to last week, when I'd run down this very corridor. I hoped that I wouldn't have to do it again.

Voices and footfalls were coming from the stairwell behind me. I stood near a window and started to examine my clipboard with a studious expression on my face. The doors opened and another auxiliary came through and walked down the stairs towards me. He nodded as he passed, keyed in the pad on Nicola's ward and opened the door and went in. As it was closing, I called out to him,

'Hold it, please.'

He stuck an arm out and stopped it from closing a couple of inches before it shut. I skipped to the door and opened it up.

'I do apologise, I was miles away trying to make some sense of this latest set of results. Thanks very much.' If he'd asked, I would have told him they were Saturday's football results.

He nodded and headed off to the ward proper and leaving me by the door. I felt completely naked.

There was the murmur of voices and machinery from the ward beyond the short corridor. I stood for a second and pondered my next move. Again, it was decided for me as a young nurse came from a side room. She was very pretty and filled her uniform really well, with a lovely pair of top bollocks and a great arse. Stop it, Richie. This was no time for ogling.

'Excuse me Nurse, please could you help me?' She stopped and turned towards me, looking me up and down as she did so.

'Yes Doctor, how can I help you?' She was a stunner.

'Hi there, my name's Richard. I'm a new Houseman down at A&E. I just started a couple of days ago and am still finding my feet in the hospital. I was on a break and thought it'd be a good opportunity to familiarise myself with the other wards. You never know when you might be working on another one, do you?'

She smiled and nodded. So far, so good.

'Are you busy on the ward at the moment?'

She explained that they were almost full and things were a bit hectic. I agreed with her and said that I found A&E totally manic and that I wasn't looking forward to the weekend, when all the drunks and domestics came in. We chatted for a little while and, to be honest, got on really well. I was beginning to feel like a real doctor.

'Well, I'd better dash, nurse. There's still a lot of the hospital to get around before I get back to broken wrists and little Jonny with a saucepan stuck on his head.'

We both laughed and said our farewells. Just as she turned away, I made my move.

'Sorry nurse, but could you possibly help me with one more thing? I believe a friend of a friend might be one of your patients here on the ward. Her name is Nicola, suffering from leukaemia, I think.'

'Nicola Williams?

I nodded in the hope there was only one Nicola on the ward.

'She's in one of the side rooms, just there.'

She pointed to a room twenty feet further down the corridor and walked towards it. I followed her and stopped at the door. I couldn't go in for obvious reasons.

'Sorry nurse, I don't want to disturb her, but how are things looking for her?'

As the nurse explained, I glanced in through the small eye-line window and was shocked by what I saw. There was a drip up and a few machines around her bed. A woman in her late forties was sat next to her, holding her hand, presumably her mum. The nurse explained that Nicola was on chemo, which was something I already knew.

'We've finished our tests and thankfully, she doesn't need a bone marrow transplant. She needs a blood transfusion though. Unfortunately she's got an uncommon blood type and we're finding it difficult to find a compatible donor. Still, its early days but we need a donor ASAP, if you know what I mean?'

To be honest, I didn't. I'd only watched *Casualty* a couple of times and the storylines hadn't included leukaemia or blood transfusions in those episodes.

'What blood group is she, nurse?'

'O Negative off the top of my head. The hospital is calling for her relatives to come in and be tested for compatibility at the moment, but no joy so far.'

I took a bit of a step back. I was O Negative. A few years ago, when I had an attack of civic responsibility, I'd been a blood donor for a few months. It didn't last long because I changed jobs and didn't need the time off work, but the end result was that I knew my blood group, unlike most of the general public.

'Let's hope they find someone quickly for her, nurse.'

As I was looking through the window, she looked up at the door. I just managed to turn my head but the back of it was framed in the window. I just hoped she didn't recognise me. I was beginning to think that I was pushing it a bit, and I was. I saw the older nurse I'd talked to outside the ward last week coming towards us. Bollocks.

'Thank you so much nurse, and I look forward to working with you in the future.'

I turned and walked hurriedly to the door and buzzed myself out. Double bollocks. The nutcracker sweetie was walking down the corridor. I buried my head in my clipboard, hoping my disguise would see me through. We passed in the corridor. I heaved a sigh of relief a bit too soon. Her footfalls stopped behind me and I could feel her eyes drilling into my back. There was no shout behind me, so I kept on going. After a few seconds, I heard her set off down the corridor towards the ward. I heaved another sigh of relief.

I didn't want to go back the way I came, for fear of meeting her again, so I set off around the hospital, looking for another way down. I'd got what I'd come for and it was time to make my escape. The problem was, for all intents and purposes, I was still a doctor in a very busy hospital. I needed to get to my rucksack, which was hanging on the back of the trap door, and change back to mild-mannered Richard Head, without the Superman glasses. I just hoped that my little post-it on the rucksack saying, 'Back in a minute' would stop a bomb scare.

The problem with hospitals is that everywhere looks and smells the same and the signs would test an arctic explorer. I felt a bit lost. I'd ended up at the Maternity Ward. If I kept going, I was sure to find a stairwell which would take me back to the loos and my rucksack.

As I confidently walked passed Maternity, I saw a sign for the stairs and, to my relief, the exit. There were just a few yards to go. I focused on the stairs and the sign, feeling like a prisoner-of-war heading for the barbed wire gate and an escape. A feeling of relief welled up inside me as all the tension of the last half-an-hour began to fade away. I was having an adrenalin dump and started to feel a bit sick. It was then that my luck ran out, within a few yards of my escape. There were no wailing sirens or searchlights catching me in their beams, no Dobermans tugging at my trouser legs; just a heavy hand on my shoulder. I very nearly shat my pants on the spot.

'Doctor, thank God. Please come with me; I need your help urgently.'

It was a female voice. To the best of my knowledge, they didn't have female security guards in the hospital. I turned around to see a rather rotund lady in a blue uniform. She looked flustered. By her name-tag, I saw that her name was Joan, but it was the other wording on her tag that frightened me - *Midwife*. What title do you call a Midwife? Midwife just sounded wrong.

'Joan. Sorry Joan, but I'm on my way back to A&E and I'm running late; I've got to get back as quickly as I can'

I tried to turn and walk away but she grabbed my arm and dragged me into the adjacent room.

'Sorry, Doctor, but this is an emergency. You'll have to explain when you get back. I need help now and there's no time. She's going to sprog at any second.'

As she dragged me through the door, I was met with a sight that I'd seen many a time on television before. The young girl was half-sat-up on a bed with her knees up in the air. Her long, black hair was plastered across her forehead, soaked in sweat and she was as red as a beetroot. Her face was a paroxysm of agony. My gaze automatically shifted from her face to between her legs. It wasn't a pretty sight. I'd never eat liver again.

'Joan, I can't do this. I'm from A&E and I haven't got a clue what I'm doing. Can't you get someone else?'

Panic was welling up inside me. What the fuck had I got myself into?

'With all due respect, Doctor, just shut the fuck up and help. There's no time to get anyone else and I need another pair of hands, NOW.'

Her emphasis meant that she wasn't going to get anyone else or that we didn't have time; probably both. I dragged my gaze from the gaping crotch and surveyed the array of air tubes, bottles and masks around the bed. The girl started to scream,

'For fuck's sake, just get it out of me! I can't stand anymore of this.' Her hand grabbed my forearm and I thought her nails would go straight through the skin. Her strength was

322

incredible. I remembered a girl I used to go out with describing her kid's birth in graphic detail. She said for me to get any idea of what it was like to give birth, I should imagine I was trying to crap out a melon, and a fuckin' big one at that. After I'd wiped the tears from my eyes, I was thankful that I'd been born with meat and two veg, rather than fallopian tubes.

'Now, now Beverley, it'll soon be over. Just try to do what we ask you and it'll be a lot easier.' Beverley nodded through a grimace of pain and clenched teeth. It was time for me to get into character, or face a lengthy jail sentence.

'Just tell me what to do, Joan and I'll do the best I can. I'm just out of College, so please be gentle with me. What painkillers has she had?'

I was desperately trying to play to her compassionate side and hoped she'd be a bit motherly towards me. She was between the girl's legs examining what was happening. To my relief, she had a bit of a smile on her face as she looked up.

'Just go with the flow and give her a bit more gas and air when she needs it.' Then it was back to the workface for her. I grew a bit more confident.

'How much is she dilated, Joan?'

Fuck me, I sounded like a professional. I'd watch a bit more of *Holby City* in future. Perhaps I could sell her a house as well, while I'm at it.

'About eight or nine centimetres. It won't be long now. Wait, I can see the head now. Give her a bit of a puff and we'll go for it.'

Bollocks; arrogance comes before a fall and I was tumbling down the side of Everest as I looked at all the gizmos at the back of the bed.

'Help me out, Joan. It's a bit different to A&E. Which one is it?' She looked at me quizzically for a moment.

'That one there to the right, Doctor.'

I didn't like the way she said, 'Doctor'. It was almost sarcastic but, as a real doctor, I should know where the gas and air mask was. I unhooked the mask and put it on Beverley's face. Luckily, it was on-demand and I didn't have to worry about any valves.

'That's it Beverley, take a few deep breaths and it'll feel a lot better. Is it a boy or a girl?'

The gas and air seemed to take effect and she looked in slightly less pain. She still looked a state though. Joan answered for her.

'It's a boy and he's very nearly entering the big, wide world. And, speaking of big wide things, you're fully dilated now Beverley, so when you're ready, and when I say, I'm going to ask you to give me a few pushes. Are you up for that?'

Beverley nodded vigorously. Her teeth were still clenched.

'Doctor, could you clean her face up a bit for her please, and then we'll give it a go, shall we?'

I made some doctor-like grunts of affirmation as I mopped Beverley's brow in the best doctor-like way I could. I gave her a few reassuring words as I did so, they were as much for me as they were for her.

'OK, Beverley, when you're ready, give it a push for me.' She nodded and took hold of my arm again. I could feel the strain through her hand. Joan was giving her some words of encouragement and the head started to appear. Well, according to Joan. I was staying where I was. No way was I going down to the business end. I was talking to Beverley, telling her to pant at the appropriate moment and generally telling her she was doing fine. I even gave her a few more puffs of gas and air. Before long, the head was out and we were nearly there. Then, just as it was getting close, her husband came through the door.

'Bloody hell, have I missed it?'

He rushed over to the bed. Business end first, then up to my end. He introduced himself to me and he was advised to get scrubbed up by Joan. He rushed back from the sink in time to see his baby son being born. Beverley was screaming her head off but he didn't seem to notice. He was a proud father. By this time, my arm looked like it'd been worked on by an epileptic tattooist. It was all the shades of red and purple under the sun. Joan had clamped the umbilical and baby was with his mum. She was delivering the afterbirth when she began talking to me again.

'Give her some entonox please, Doctor.' I looked at the array again and was stuffed.

'Remind me Joan, which one is entonox?'

Her look wasn't quizzical this time; it was very different. It was a look of alarm. She looked at me for a long time.

'Doctor, as you should know, entonox is gas and air. Surely, they taught you that at College?'

She looked down at my name tag for just a bit too long. I'd been rumbled and we both knew it. It was time to leg it or I'd be sharing a cell with big Dave, the predatory homosexual with a penchant for tight little estate agents. And I didn't mean thrifty with money.

'Joan, I really have to go. Sorry I wasn't much help, but its early days, you know.'

I made for the door and was stopped by the new father. He thanked me profusely for delivering their new son and wanted to call him Richard, after me. All the time, I could see Joan hurrying to get finished and call security. I had to act fast.

I shook his hand and made for the door. As I went, I turned to Joan.

'Sorry Joan, I could have been a lot more help. Sorry.'

And with that, I was out of the door and running down the stairs. I just hoped my rucksack was still there with my bits and pieces still in it. Knowing my luck, some bastard had crapped in it or stolen my other clothes.

I reached the loos and ran in. I was in luck. The toilets and my trap were empty. I went in and found my rucksack exactly where I'd left it. God bless honesty. I quickly changed. Thankfully, I'd planned for a quick exit under the noses of security. I'd packed a T-shirt, shorts and trainers which I quickly put on. I slipped my doctor's clothes, shoes and clipboard into the rucksack and zipped it up. I hurried out to the sinks and got a handful of water, throwing it over my face and hair which I slicked back over my head, exposing my scar. It was quite livid; probably due to my heart beating furiously away in my chest. I knew how Ena felt now. It was just in time. A security guard came in just after I'd finished my hair. He stood in the middle of the toilets looking around. All the traps were empty and no-one was taking a piss. His gaze finally settled on me. Confidence was the key.

'Hello mate, can I help you or are you going to arrest me for blocking the U-bend with last night's chicken tikka masala?

He looked at me for a second, his eyes settling on my scar. He grunted and turned on his heels and left. I was nearly sick with relief. It was time to go.

When I got to the front door, there were security all over the place and also a couple of coppers. Martin wasn't one of them or I'd have a bit of explaining to do. He could get me off crapping on a tortoise, but impersonating a doctor and delivering a baby, was beyond the bounds of friendship.

I made it to the car and threw the rucksack in the boot. By the time I got onto the main road, I was in a pool of sweat. That was probably the most stupid thing I'd ever done. Maybe I'd see the God Botherers and change my ways, because this time I had surely sinned.

How I managed to get the car back to the office without a prang, I don't know. I badly needed a shower and was suffering from a bad case of Betty Swollocks. I smelled like a moose on heat.

I crashed into the office with my casuals on; completely forgetting these weren't the clothes I'd worn when I'd left. Carol raised an eyebrow.

'Been to the beach, have we? Hope we don't get any prospective clients other than surfers in this afternoon!'

It was a bollocking, albeit mild, but a bollocking all the same.

'Sorry Carol, I'll get changed but I didn't have time earlier.'

She looked at my dishevelled state and must have taken a bit of pity on me. I must have looked like I was suffering from Post-Traumatic Shock, which wasn't far from the truth.

'Want to talk about it?

Christ, I must have looked a right mess. Tina was looking anxious as well. She didn't ask any questions. I got the impression that she knew more than she was letting on. I'd take a bet that Clint had whispered a few truths into her ear whilst taking a break from trying to attain his Duke of Edinburgh gold shagging award.

'No, I'm fine thanks, Carol, but I nearly had an accident on the way back. Shook me up a bit. I'll be fine.' Liar, liar, pants on fire. I could feel my shorts self-combust as the words came out of my mouth.

I took my rucksack out the back and got changed. I had a quick wash in the sink and started to feel human again. I'd had a bad case of adrenalin dump. Still, I'd come away with a good idea of how Nicola was. She needed a transfusion and beyond all my hopes and expectations, I might be able to help. I was O Negative. The problem was that I wasn't a donor anymore, but perhaps there was a way around it. Also, how would she feel about receiving blood from an arsehole like me? If I was her, I wouldn't be totally enamoured with the idea, but in her position, I guess I wouldn't have much choice. It was time to put on my shiny armour again and mount my trusty steed. But I'd have to run it by someone first and that wasn't going to easy.

Suitably groomed, I went back into the office with coffees all round. I was very appreciative of their discretion in the face of my obvious trauma, which was a feminine trait I suppose. If it was my mates, it would be on *Facebook* by now.

'By the way Richard, Mrs Edgar rang for you. She wondered if you could pop over when you had a minute.'

She said it so matter-of-factly, but I knew she was wondering what the fuck I was up to. Carol would soon be running out of patience. I had subconsciously put Mrs Edgar on the back-burner over the last few days but her call, or summons as it was in reality, brought the other pressing matter I had in my life to the fore. I'd see her tomorrow. I wasn't in a fit state for a visit today. I needed a beer.

'Thanks Carol, but not today. I think I've pushed my luck a bit too much.' That was so true, both with Carol and the NHS security.

I worked like a beaver for the rest of the day trying to catch up a bit. It was a welcome diversion. It was getting late in the afternoon when Carol sent Tina home early, which was very unusual. I gathered that I was in line for a one-to-one pep talk from Carol and I didn't have to wait long.

'What's going on, Richard? Your mind, and body for that matter, just isn't on the job at the moment. I need you to be focused, because I'm getting a lot of flak from Head Office and I need results. I don't need you borrowing the car all the time, not knowing what you're up to, coming back like a stressed-out beach bum. Now, what the hell's going on?'

She had a point. I wasn't feeling myself. Well, that's not technically true. I hadn't had a shag for ages and I was getting a bit too well-acquainted with Madam Palm and her five lovely daughters.

I had to give her something or she'd chain me to the desk.

'I'm sorry Carol. I know exactly what you mean but I've got a couple of major things happening in my life at the moment and they've just escalated, not out of hand, but just a bit bigger than I expected.'

'A problem shared Richard. You know what they say.'

She was inviting me to unload. To be honest, I didn't have any option. I took a deep breath and explained about Nicola and her battle with leukaemia. I just said that she was a very close friend, leaving out the bits about the Rhino Hunt and my exploits as a newly-qualified Houseman at the local hospital. I didn't think she'd appreciate my breaking umpteen laws on the firm's time. I told her about our blood groups and that I could possibly be the answer to the hospital's search for a donor. Unfortunately, that would mean a bit more of the firm's time, but I'd make it up.

When I'd finished explaining about Nicola, I got the impression that I'd touched her compassionate side as she said she'd help me as much as she could, but not to the detriment of my job. I thankfully agreed.

'You said there were two things at the moment; what's the other one? If I don't know, I can't help you.'

Fuck, she had me now. I couldn't go there, for all our sakes.

'I'm sorry Carol, but I'm asking you to trust me on this one. I just can't tell you anything about it at the moment. For your own sake, you're best off not knowing anything. If there's a fall, then I'm the one who takes it. Please trust me; it's for your own good.'

She sat there across the room at her desk, shaking her head.

'So you think I can't be trusted and you're making decisions about 'it' on your own. If your decisions involve me in any way, I want to know, and know now, Richard. I'll be the judge of what affects me, not you, Richard Head.'

She had a point. I'd have said the same if I was in her position and she was pressing me very hard. I had to be very careful how I put this.

'With all due respect Carol, as my boss and as a friend, I'm afraid I can't tell you any more than I already have. For your own protection, it is better that you don't know anything. Things may get a bit messy and possibly dangerous.'

Bollocks, I should have left out the dangerous bit. She went off on one.

'Dangerous? Fuckin' dangerous! You're telling me that I could be involved in something dangerous?'

She was standing up now, obviously concerned.

'No, Carol, not for you, but possibly for me. I'm trying to protect you, professionally. You're not in any physical danger, but I may be.'

She was walking around the office now, shaking her head.

'Just what the hell have you got yourself into, Richard?' She thought for a second, then turned and faced me.

'Is Mrs Edgar involved in this too?'

It was rhetorical because she knew that she was. Suddenly all the calls from her and our subsequent meetings were making a bit of sense.

'And please tell me that your little escapade in the park hasn't got anything to do with this as well?'

She was looking at me again, hoping that I wasn't going to say 'yes'. Unfortunately my 'tell' of unconsciously touching my scarred forehead gave her an affirmation.

'Christ, what the fuck have you got yourself into?' She sat back down, obviously worried. I wasn't sure if it was for me or for her.

'I'm sorry, Carol but I really can't tell you anything else. Please trust me.'

She was rocking backward and forward in her chair, trying to piece together our conversation over the last few minutes. Things obviously hadn't turned out the way she'd imagined. A mild bollocking had turned into revelations of contract beatings and Machiavellian intrigue.

'Richard, I don't know what to do. I can't just ignore what you've said, not if it involves threats to me or the business. What am I going to do?' She needed a bit of help. She was worried.

'It won't affect the business, not in a negative way. It could have some very beneficial effects, but I'll just need a bit more time and some trust, please.'

'How can I trust you if I don't know what the fuck's going on; right under my bloody nose, Richard? OK, I'll trust you and won't ask any more questions, but the minute you step out of line or the business is affected, by whatever means, then you're history. And you can trust me on that one, Richard. Now, bugger off home and let me think for a minute, and take a valium. Go on, piss off.'

I left in a hurry, in case she had any more questions that I couldn't, or more likely wouldn't, answer.

The blast of fresh air on my face was a welcome relief from the rigours of a very stressful day. I decided to stop in at the corner shop on the way home and grab a bottle of Shiraz and a DVD to take my mind off things. I needed a bit of escapism, but not mindless violence; I wasn't in the mood for that.

Just before I set off on my walk home, I glanced across at Ena's window. He was sat there as usual and had the same smug, self-satisfied grin on his face as he looked over at me. He's such a bastard. I'd have to do something to ensure that he took his eye off the ball; a little diversion from the things that would, hopefully, soon be unfolding around him. I set off for home, hatching a plan.

Chapter Thirteen

The girls were home when I eventually arrived from my contemplative walk via the shop. My bottle of wine and DVD didn't go unnoticed; Mum was the first to react.

'Was it a hard day at work, Richard? You don't often come home with offerings, especially on a work night.'

Sis didn't say anything, but her look was one of concern. She knew a bit about what was going on and my coming home with a bottle of piss showed her that I was under a lot of stress.

'Sorry Mum, I just need a bit of 'Me' time, and yes, it's been an extremely hard day. I sat down and joined them at the table for dinner. It was nice; the three of us, sharing a meal together as a family. It didn't happen often, probably like most families these days, when we all sat down and actually talked over a meal at the dinner table. I felt a lot better afterwards, like I belonged somewhere. I had a sudden thought as to what my dad might be doing at that same moment. Perhaps he was sat down with his new family? I'd probably never get to know or even see him again. Or maybe he'd turn up at our door having just won the lottery and seek our forgiveness for running out on us. Another pig flew by the window.

Sis got up and excused herself as she left the table. As she did so, she gave me a glance and a nod to go upstairs. She wanted to talk, which is something that would never have happened a few days ago. I quickly cleared the table and did the washing-up before heading upstairs to her room.

'What's wrong, Richard? Are you in trouble again?'

Bloody hell, I hoped that this wasn't my second inquisition within an hour. As it turned out, it wasn't. She was just a bit worried. She knew that I was onto Sharples and just wanted to know if I was OK. I explained that hopefully Ena would be toast, sooner rather than later, and that she would have some element of revenge, albeit at my hand, for what he'd tried to do to her. I also let her in on a little jolly jape I had lined up for him in the meantime. She seemed content with how things were going, but she was my flesh and blood and we were similar in many ways. In that respect, I knew that she might not be satisfied with me doing all this retribution stuff.

We actually hugged before I left for my room and a night of comedy; Ninja Warriors were saving the planet from an evil wizard. Oh, and a bottle of Australia's finest would help me get to sleep later. If I was really lucky, then I might find a lump of out-of-date Stilton in the fridge, which Mum had grabbed from the supermarket bin, to go with the wine.

Before I settled down, there were a few calls that I needed to make; these were a social call to both Dev and Martin, and a business call to Vic. I needed to draw on his computer skills and some of the technology at his work. I decide to ring Vic first.

'Victor, how's your love life? Or, is Terence suing you for grievous lower-bodily harm?' He chuckled.

'No mate, I got away scot-free on that one but Terence is looking at some pretty serious reconstructive surgery. The word on the street is that he has to use a butt-plug the size of a World War One artillery shell. Poor old bugger. Sorry, that was an unfortunate turn of phrase.'

We both cracked up at the expense of poor old Terence.

With the formalities over, I explained what I needed from Vic and his computer wizardry. I say wizardry, but it was pretty simple really. I just needed to scan an NHS letterhead I had from a letter concerning my head wound onto a new sheet, add another address and phone number, and insert some new text. 'That's easy–peasy', said Vic. He'd have it ready for me in a day. We also tentatively booked a Saturday night out. Game on.

Next, it was on to Martin and Dev. This was general chit-chat with both of them and a booking for a Saturday on the town. I needed a night out already and it was only Monday. Dev said he was tied up on Saturday morning with a fire and evacuation scenario at the local council buildings. It was a regular drill as they had the biggest office in the town by far. A light suddenly came on in my head, and hopefully in the council buildings on Saturday night, for a possible joke. That meant another call to Vic.

Martin was not working on Saturday and was getting excited already. His parents were both out of hospital and recovering well, despite being banged about and still in shock. He sounded relieved. Just before hanging up, I asked him if he'd had a case across his desk referring to a bogus doctor delivering a baby at the local hospital today. I added that if he had, then please don't look too hard.

'That was you? That was you, you fuckin' idiot. I should come round and arrest you on the spot. Delivering a baby? Christ, do you know how many years you'd get inside for that? Impersonating a doctor, and delivering a baby. What the fuck were you thinking of?' He went on swearing and ranting in questions.

'Anyway, how the hell did you get to deliver a baby? I know there's a lot of Government cuts at the moment, but I doubt if you were there putting up a *For Sale* sign outside the Maternity Ward.'

I explained that it was all about Nicola and that I needed to know what was happening with her. Then things got a bit out of hand.

'Out of hand? They couldn't get any worse. 'I did it for love' isn't going to wash with the bloke in the grey woolly wig, mate. I don't suppose you did a brain transplant while you were in there, did you? If so, the first person you should perform one on is yourself, you fuckin' brainless halfwit.'

'If you sit on the fence any longer, Martin, you'll give yourself a hernia and an arse full of splinters. Like I said, it all got out of hand, but I got away. Now, let's leave it at that, shall we? See you Saturday.'

I'd been given yet another bollocking. I was getting used to it, unfortunately. I'd ring Vic tomorrow.

With my ears still ringing, and my arse stinging from a metaphorical spanking, I headed down to the fridge. There was no Stilton. I'd have to make do with some cheese slices that were turning up at the edges. They summed up my mood; they were very tired and wilted. Perhaps I should have got some porn and seen if Madam Palm had any energy.

I felt a bit woolly when I woke up in the morning, but there was something I had to do before I got into work. I hoped that it wouldn't take too long as I wasn't sure if Carol's patience would last, especially after last night's revelations.

I set off early and grabbed a seat by the window of a small coffee shop a couple of streets away from the office. It was up at the traffic lights where I'd caught sight of Nicola's mate some weeks before, when was I driving to Mrs Edgar's for one of our meetings.

The coffee tasted good and it began to clear my head from the 'fourteen percent intake of an intense berry fruits with a spicy after-taste' concoction from last night.

I'd never make a spy. I felt very exposed and thought that everyone in the café was looking at me.

I didn't have to wait long for my quarry to appear. She was carrying her Louis Vuitton bag and was walking with a bit of purpose. She must like her job. I'd already paid for my coffee and left half of it in the mug with the rest on my top lip. I now had a comedy fake moustache for my disguise.

I slipped out on to the road and quickly crossed over and took up my position about forty yards behind her. I wouldn't get too close, but I needed to see where she went. Luckily, there were loads of people making their way to work and I mingled with the pedestrians. I just hoped that I didn't bump into anyone I knew.

After about one hundred yards, she made a quick right and disappeared. She'd gone into the bank. It was too early for it to be open so she must work there; success. Next came the hard part; I needed to talk to her. I'd thought about confronting her in the street, but I knew it would just get ugly. If I could catch her at work, where she'd have to behave, perhaps I could make her see a bit of sense and persuade her that I may be able to help. I'd pay her a visit at lunchtime.

I got to my office about five minutes late. Carol and Tina were already in. Tina gave me a cheery good morning, but all I got from Carol was a very gruff, 'You're late,' which made Tina look at the two of us in turn with some confusion.

The atmosphere remained a bit tense all morning, but to give Tina her due, she tried to make conversation, even though she didn't get much response, especially from Carol.

Lunchtime soon came around and I steeled myself for the new task at hand. I wasn't looking forward to this, but at least I'd have a counter and bulletproof glass to protect my bollocks this time.

The bank was busy with workers sorting out their financials. That suited me fine; the more people the better. I scanned the tills and I spotted her working near the end. I just had to time my spot in the queue to get to her till. I stood in the line and pretended to fill in a deposit slip, trying to get the timing right. I got to the front in a bit of a sweat. She was *number six*. A few seconds later, the old lady she was serving walked away clutching her bingo money.

'Cashier number six, please,' announced the automated voice over the speaker. I stepped forward clutching my deposit slip and placed it on the counter in front of me. Her name badge said 'Cynthia.'

In a flash, I remembered her. I was at Primary School with her. She was in the year below and I remembered how we used to tease her in the playground for her posh name and the long pigtails. We teased her and tugged at them, unmercifully. No wonder she didn't like me. I'd probably scarred her for life.

She looked up, then down again to her desk top. She was finalising the previous transaction. Her head jerked back up and her expression had changed to pure malevolence.

'What the fuck do you want?'

I guess it wasn't service with a smile. Her voice came through the electronic speaker on the counter. It was louder than it should have been and one or two of her colleagues had looked up from their desk.

'It's about Nicola. We need to talk.'

'No we don't. Just stay away from her, and me, come to that. You're a shit. You can polish a turd as much as you like, but in the end, it's still a turd. Now, fuck off.'

All the office staff were looking now, including the manager. He was looking at us over his half-moon glasses.

'Cynthia, I've got something she needs.'

'There's nothing in this world that you've got that she either needs or wants.'

'Yes there is; my blood.'

I let the words sink in and she shot up in her chair.

'I know what trouble she's in and I might be able to help. I'm O Negative, the same as Nicola. There might be a chance I can help.'

She sat in her chair, shaking her head. All the staff were looking at us now, along with a few customers.

'It was you. It was you yesterday at the hospital, wasn't it? I should ring the police right now. Give one good reason why I shouldn't.'

That was easy to answer.

'Because if I'm sent inside, she doesn't get the blood she needs. I did what I did for her, no other reason. Now, can we talk in less conspicuous surroundings?'

The manager had got up from his desk and was walking over towards us.

'Do we have a problem here, Miss Blenkinsopp?' Oh yes, we also teased her about her surname.

'No sir, Mr Head was just leaving. We were just discussing a forthcoming deposit.' That was pretty close to the truth. The manager returned to his desk.

'Half-seven tonight at the wine bar on Castle Street, and you'd better not be lying or the police will get a phone call one minute after I've finished my glass of wine.'

Phew. A result of sorts but she'd recognised me, and if she did ring the Old Bill, I was totally fucked.

'Thank you Cynthia. See you tonight.'

Too much stress was tiring me out. When this was all over, I promised myself a holiday. There was still Mrs Edgar to visit and no doubt my stress levels would shoot up again. Still, things were starting to come together and I could see some light at the end of what was becoming a very long tunnel.

I walked around to Mrs Edgar's after work. A request for the car and more time off work in the afternoon would have fallen on very deaf ears.

Mrs Edgar was her usual self, meeting me at the door with a promise of tea and cake.

'We can have it in the front room. You'll have to excuse me; I've got guests at the moment, but go on in and make yourself at home.'

I walked into the room to see a family drinking tea and eating cake. The children were immaculately dressed and the parents looked formal and a bit staid. It was my worst nightmare; it was the God Botherers.

As I walked in, they all looked at me. I wished the ground would open up and swallow me whole. Mrs Edgar came in behind me.

'Richard, this is the Pearson family on one of their regular visits. They're spreading the word of the Lord you know. We have our regular chats about life and God, but I haven't succumbed to Mr Pearson's persuasions yet, have I, Mr Pearson?'

Mr Pearson was still looking at me.

'No, Mrs Edgar, but there is still time for you. While there's still breath, you know.' He took some tea.

'Now Richard, do sit down. Are you by any chance religious?'

Having stitched up my present company on three occasions over the last few weeks, I guess the answer to that one was a resounding, 'no'.

'No, Mrs Edgar, I'm not. I did R.E. at school and couldn't get my head around why people followed or dedicated their lives to someone who lives somewhere out there in the sky. I'm afraid I'm with Darwin on this one, and go with evolution over billions of years, not the premise that we were created a few thousand years ago in the Garden of Eden. Sorry, but that's just the way it is.'

I didn't want to offend the Pearson family, but I felt quite strongly about it. I hoped they took it as such.

Mr Pearson took a sip of tea and placed the cup and saucer on the table in front of him. He was obviously preparing to say something.

'We've met Richard on several occasions over the last few weeks, Mrs Edgar, and let's just say he has tested our resolve and perseverance to such an extent that I believe we are better people for the stern examination he has given us. That being said, I just hope that Richard doesn't plan any further examinations for us in the future or someone down below will be welcoming him with open arms and increasing his carbon footprint. Don't you agree?'

I felt the hand of God on my shoulder, showing me the way to a more righteous path, or was it a warning from Mr Pearson not to piss on his fireworks again. Anyway, he was right. I'd been a bit on the mean side to them. They had their beliefs and I had mine. The bottoms of my feet started to feel warm. Either Lyn had under floor heating or it was the fires of hell licking around my ankles.

'I can safely say, Mr Pearson that your resolve, and that of your family, will not be tested in any way in the future.

And can I apologise for any distress I've caused both you and your family by my actions over the last few weeks?'

He stood up and walked over to me. Christ, he was going to belt me. As his arm extended, I took an involuntary wince backwards. He held his hand out. I stood up and shook it.

'Thank you Richard. I think we've all learnt a little lesson today. Goodbye, Mrs Edgar. Thank you for the tea, and for the cake particularly, which was as delicious as usual. Goodbye Richard; maybe we'll see you at our Church one day?'

'Don't hold your breath on that one, Mr Pearson, or you'll go very blue. I'll stick with Darwin, if that's OK.'

They trooped out of the front door with Mrs Edgar waving goodbye.

'That sounded like a bit of a confessional, young man. Have we been getting up to naughties with God's chosen on earth?'

'Sorry Lyn, but I've been upsetting a lot of people lately and I'm afraid I've taken a few too many liberties with the Pearsons as well.' She laughed.

'I won't ask what you've been up to, but you must remember that they may have a very powerful ally. Now, let's get down to business.' She sat on the sofa, reached down the side of it and pulled out a heavy folder. 'You look very tired. What have you been up to since our last meeting? Visits, I should call them visits. Meeting sounds so formal, don't you agree?' I did.

It took me about half-an-hour, and more tea and cake, to run through my escapades over the last few days. She took particular interest in my foray into a medical career. To my surprise, I didn't get a telling off; quite the opposite in fact.

She was genuinely impressed with my attempt to get information about Nicola and my planned escape from the security guards.

'Oh, I'd love to be young again and feel the thrill of the chase!'

She had that wistful look in her eye again, along with a long loving stare at her husband's photograph on the mantelpiece.

'I'm very impressed with your planning and execution. Of course, you know it was highly illegal, not to mention highly dangerous. I don't mean in a physical manner, but the consequences for you if you were captured. But still, you went ahead with your plan, and all for the love of a girl you hardly know. That is admirable, young Richard. You have hidden talents, as well as a lot of courage.'

I was gobsmacked. I couldn't help but wonder why she used the word captured. It wasn't as if I was being hunted by the KGB. She had more layers than an onion.

'And now, let's move on to the business in hand - the Sharples' family.'

She laid the binder on the small coffee table in front of us. I could see there were a number of different sections within; each labelled with a different address. It looked very professional.

'You have been busy, Mrs Edgar. I mean Lyn, sorry.'

'There's not much else to do at my age, Richard, other than being a bit of a busybody. I actually enjoyed it immensely. It gets the old grey cells working again. Use them or lose them. Don't ever forget that, will you?'

She opened the binder. In the front was a quick breakdown of what she'd brought together. She had started it off with Ena's visit and his gross, and what she'd decided to

343

be a deliberate undervaluation of her property. She'd then listed all the properties she believed had been undervalued, purchased, developed and subsequently sold by the Sharples' companies.

She had company names, lists of directors and secretaries and bank account details, both national and international. She even had disbursements between companies and accounts with dates and amounts cross-referenced to various properties. Basically, it laid out the Sharples' property frauds right in front of you. I was taken aback by the sheer scale of the operation and the professionalism of how it had been dissected and laid bare by this little old lady who had a penchant for baking 'exceedingly good cakes'.

'Bugger me.'

'Mind your language, young man, but I'll take that as a compliment.'

She then brought out a few bundles of paper from the back. They were a complete analysis of each financial transaction she thought had been fraudulent.

'If you look at these, Richard, you'll see the scale of the fraud that these despicable people have been engaged in. What they have also been doing is tax avoidance on a huge scale by way of inter-company transactions. Moving assets between companies; claiming tax back on one side and not paying on the other. A few liquidations here and there and the taxman ends up short of a few hundred thousand. I'm sure the Revenue, as well as the Fraud section in the local constabulary, will be very interested in speaking to our friends. Don't you agree?'

I certainly did. To me, it looked like a conviction on a plate.

A few other pages caught my eye. They were mobile phone call logs, with dates, times, call durations and recipients. Ena's number was there, along with his father's and a few others as well.

'How the hell did you get those, Lyn?'

'Clever boy; I'm afraid this bit is highly illegal and will not be going to the authorities. If they were to know about these, then it could prejudice the entire case. No one must know and neither of us must speak of their existence.'

This was a bit worrying for me.

'Two things: one, how the hell did you get hold of personal mobile phone printouts? The police have a hell of a job getting them themselves since all the fuss about intrusive surveillance over the past few years. It's got to be signed off at a very high level. So, how did you get them? Two, why do you need them anyway, especially as they can't be used in a prosecution case and, if known about, would probably blow it out of the water?'

'I needed a bit of an edge, Richard. The more I looked into this, the more I began to realise just how big a fraud it was. By obtaining itemised billings on the main protagonists, I could see who they were calling and when. It helped me immensely in putting the individual jigsaws together.'

She pulled up one of the lists.

'See here, this is your friend, Ena. On this date, he visited this particular property.' The file on the property was laid on the table.

'Ena visited on this date and time and gave the old gentleman an erroneous valuation. Next, he phoned this person here, who is the Company Secretary. He then called this person here and a cash offer for the property was tabled before the end of the working day. Now, you can also trace the purchase money from this account and all the subsequent transactions through the accounts in relation to that property through the various companies controlled by the Sharples'. There, easy isn't it? However, I needed to know where to start and these call logs were the best way to start.'

It wasn't easy, but I'd got the gist of what she'd laid out in front of me. As long as it made sense to her, and more importantly, an investigating officer, that was all that mattered.

'You've done this before, haven't you, and you're just keeping your hand in? Maybe it was for old times' sake? Anyway, you still haven't answered my question. How the hell did you get the billings?'

She thought for a second then held me in a stare that, to be honest, made me a little scared. It was hard and cold.

'Yes, to both. I have done this before and I am keeping my hand in, as you say. But it's only to keep the little grey cells working. I did things like this for ages, a long time ago, in another era; perhaps another lifetime. As for the billing, well, there are people I worked with many years ago that are now in very senior jobs around the country. They're now pillars of the Establishment, and they owe me a few favours for the work I did for them way-back-when. Now, I hope that satisfies you because, as you so eloquently said to Carol, it's in your own interests that you don't ask any more questions because I can't and won't, tell you anything else. What you don't know can't hurt you.'

She had slammed the door shut on that one. Doctor Spank had taken a trip to botty land and I'd been put over her knee and given a metaphorical six of the best. It was time to change the subject.

'Sorry, I won't pry any more. Just as long as you don't take your cyanide pill before you've explained it all to the police.'

That brought a smile. The steely gaze had gone to be replaced by her rheumy old eyes again.

'You know Richard, I do believe I still have one upstairs somewhere. Now, where on earth did I put it?'

Christ, she even had a death pill tucked away somewhere! This was turning into crossroads where Mata Hari meets Mrs Kipling. Just look out for the cyanide pill in the chocolate brownie.

'That brings us on to our next matter, Richard. The presentation of the findings; namely the documents, hopefully soon to be evidence, contained in the binder.'

That was easy. All she had to do was pop down to the local nick, or get Fraud Squad to bang on her door, and dump the folder in their lap.

'You see, I can't be seen to be directly involved in the case and I certainly can't have my name or face in the papers or the television.

She busied herself in front of me by putting all the papers in order in their correct places in the binder. Once finished, she held it out for me to take.

'That's why you must take it and hand it over to the authorities, Richard. I'm afraid I can't.'

If I was to hand it in, I had the distinct idea that I was going to be on my own from here on in. I also got the distinct impression that she wouldn't, and most likely couldn't, be seen in the public eye. This dear old lady had a dark past on which she'd just firmly shut the door.

'I've left in my name and the details of my initial contact with Mr Sharples as the basis and starting point for 'your' investigation. I will give a witness statement to the police which, if they do their investigation properly, they will undoubtedly require. I will not appear in Court. If summoned,

I will be too ill and there will be no problem in acquiring the necessary documentation. They can go as far as the Home Secretary and they still won't get it. So Richard, I leave this binder in your more than capable hands. I'm sure you know exactly what to do with it.'

I took it from her. It was almost an involuntary movement, but I was partially under her spell.

'Lyn, I wish I'd known you all those years ago. You must have been one hell of an operative.' She beamed and blushed a bit.

'Why Richard, that's the nicest thing anyone has said to me in a long while, thank you. And I do like the word, 'operative'. It sounds so much nicer than spy or, as they're called today, spooks. If you want a window into a long-forgotten world, then read some Le Carre. I'm in there somewhere, I think.'

'I'll give them a read. As for this binder, I know exactly what I'm going to do with it. I just need to speak to a friend firstly. Perhaps Le Carre will write another book after this entitled, *Tinker, Tailor, Soldier, Estate Agent*. I think it's got a certain ring to it, don't you think, Lyn?'

'Yes, Richard, we'll make an estate agent out of you yet. Now, why don't you jump into your Aston Martin and go home for some tea.'

I looked at my watch. It was getting late but I would still make my meeting with Cynthia for seven-thirty. I hurried home, grabbed some nosh, changed and set out for the wine bar on Castle Street. I thought about my visit to Mrs Edgar and tried to put things into a bit of perspective. She clearly wanted no further involvement. Her reasons, though not stated, were pretty evident. She couldn't be brought out into the public glare. So it was down to me to follow it through. I needed to speak with Martin and follow his lead as to how to put it to the Old Bill. I'd ring him tomorrow. Perhaps it would be a bit of a feather in his cap if he could introduce me, and more importantly, the evidence against the Sharples, to the Fraud Squad.

Despite my optimism, I was late at the wine bar; only by five minutes, but late all the same. I went in to find Cynthia already sat at a table near the back. It was a discreet choice. No one would see if she punched me in the gonads again. She didn't have a drink in front of her. To be honest, I didn't blame her; it was my request for a meeting, so why should she pay? She could milk me all she wanted; I would do the same in her position. I walked over expecting a bollocking and I wasn't disappointed.

'You're late. I hate tardiness almost as much as I hate you.'

I nearly rose to her bait but being rude straightaway wouldn't achieve anything. I got the impression my tongue would be bleeding before very long, as I would be spending a lot of time biting it.

'Can I get you a drink, Cynthia?'

Oily charm oozed from my mouth. Perhaps I should have borrowed Lyn's cyanide pill and done the world a favour. Cynthia wouldn't be missed; not by me anyway.

'Brandy and Babycham.' Bloody-hell, she wanted her pound of flesh. I headed towards the bar.

'Make it a double brandy, I'm thirsty.' Two pounds of flesh and a doggy bag for what she doesn't get through tonight.

I brought the drinks back to our table. I'd settled for a large glass of red in the vain hope that I might look a little more sophisticated than if I had a pint in front of me. I jumped straight in.

349

'Look, I'm sorry, Cynthia; we seem to have got off on the wrong foot.'

'Yes, seventeen years ago and I've detested you ever since. Now, say what you've got to say. Someone might walk in and see me talking to you and get the wrong idea.'

'Well, you're not going to get any splinters in your arse from sitting on the fence, are you? Look, I'm sorry for everything. Sorry to you at school all those years ago and, more significantly, I'm sorry for what happened between Nicola and me. It was all a big mistake.'

'The mistake was her talking to an arsehole like you in the first place. Poor girl, how could you?'

'I didn't bloody know, and what happened in the pub, well, it was a mistake. I'm sorry.'

End of round one. We both took a drink. I hoped she didn't spit hers in the bucket because it cost a bloody fortune. She swallowed, much to my relief - as it was with other girls, but I wasn't about to discuss that with her now.

'I can go on saying I'm sorry all night, but it won't change things. What's done is done and I'm sorry for that. That's the last apology you're going to get.'

She nodded slightly which I took as a bit of a result. I'd started to get through to her a little.

'You have to accept that I feel incredibly guilty for what happened to Nicola. It was just very bad timing and she got the wrong end of the stick. She wasn't in the Rhino Hunt. I spoke to her because I thought that she was a genuinely lovely girl and, to be honest, because I wanted to see her again. I know now that's probably not going to happen, but I still want to help her in any way I can. That's why I made my trip to the hospital.'

'So that's it, is it? A fuckin' guilt trip. You're trying to assuage some guilt off your fuck-ups in the past, is that what this is all about? Well, if it is, then go and find another damsel in distress. Nicola's not for you.'

End of round two. More piss.

'You just don't get it, do you, Cynthia? Yes, it is a bit of a guilt trip. I'll never forget her face when she left the pub, or when she tried to run me over.'

I stopped and smiled. So did Cynthia a bit. Perhaps it was the thought of me spread out over the road like a squashed hedgehog.

'But don't tell me Nicola's not for me. I'm not taking that from you. I just want to help her in any way I can. And I might be in a position to.'

'Blood. Is that why you went to the hospital?'

'Sort of. I was wondering if I could help in any way and came up with the crackpot idea of visiting the ward dressed as a doctor. It was absolutely fuckin' stupid, but I came away knowing that I was the same blood group as her. I also know that she needs a transfusion as quickly as possible.'

She didn't come back at me on that one. She just sat staring into her expensive drink, deep in thought.

'She doesn't want your help.'

'Probably not, but I may be able to help her. That's why I wanted to talk to you. If I can help, then I will. What's more to the point is that I don't want anything in return. Nicola doesn't need to know that the blood came from me, not if it will upset her. If I'm compatible, I'll be her donor and she never need know it was me. I just wanted to discuss it with you, her best friend, first. I didn't want to just turn up at the hospital and give a few arms-full for her and then she finds out down the line that it was me. Poor girl's been through enough. How am I doing so far?'

She looked up from her drink, a bit confused. This wasn't going the way she'd expected. Maybe she'd get a free drink and would soon fuck me off with a flea in my ear and perhaps another crack at my crown jewels. She'd enjoy that.

'I'm not sure. I wasn't expecting this; not from you. You hardly know Nicola. Why are you doing this?

Her tone had come down a few notches and she was starting to come around a bit. Her aggression had gone.

'I've already told you that. I like her and want to help. And so can you, by letting me get tested and seeing if she can use my blood. It's that simple. But I'd much prefer your backing and that's why I'm here. What do you say?'

She was torn. I could see it in her face and her body language. Her drink was on the table and she was wringing her hands. It took fully thirty seconds before she came back with a reply.

'OK, I suppose she hasn't got much choice. Tainted blood is better than no blood at all. Just let me know how things go. But she's not to know under any circumstances. If you let on that you've been getting involved in her treatment, then you'll get more than a handbag to the balls. I'll have your ball-sack as a tobacco pouch.'

She wasn't kidding. I'd prefer to go up against the Milibands than cross Cynthia.

She gave me her mobile number and I promised to keep in touch. She'd mellowed a lot and we got chatting over another drink. She had a wine this time, thank goodness. We actually got on really well. Despite saying earlier that I wasn't going to apologise again, I did exactly that as we touched on our time at primary school. We even caught up on what some of our school mates were doing now. Some were inside and a few others had done really well. I felt a bit of a let-down.

'Thanks for meeting up with me, Cynthia. I know it must have been a struggle at first, but hopefully it'll all turn out for the best. I'd better be off.'

She thought for a second.

'Why don't you come round to my place? We can talk some more. I've actually enjoyed it. It's only a couple of minutes around the corner.'

It was my turn to think. I wasn't sure but, in truth, I'd enjoyed our chat. It was nice chatting to a girl without the thump of music in the background, struggling to hear what she was saying, and without the underlying intention of getting into her knickers.

'OK then, but I can't stay long. It is a school night after all.'

She picked up her bag and we headed out into the darkness.

'You know, Richard, you're not half-bad once one gets to know you. But your mates are still complete knobbers.'

'I'll take that as a compliment then. You're not half-bad yourself, Cynthia.'

I glanced down at her bag to check how heavy it was. It wasn't too bad. I didn't think it would do much damage. To my surprise, she slipped her hand around my arm and pulled herself a little closer. This wasn't what I'd expected at all; nothing like it.

Within the minute, we were outside one of the new apartment blocks that had sprung up around town during the boom in the property market.

'Nice place. Nought percent mortgage through the bank?'

'Not quite, but it's the only way I could afford it. Where do you live?'

I thought of all the kids with whom I'd been to school, their good jobs and a pad to themselves. I felt a bit of a failure stood in front of the swanky apartment block.

'Still living at home, I'm afraid, Cynthia. Maybe an extra line on the lottery this weekend will sort me out though.'

She turned and slipped her arms around my waist and kissed me on the neck. It was like an electric shock. This wasn't how I'd expected the night to go. She kissed me on the lips. I could taste her lippie and traces of brandy and Babycham. I'd have to try one myself one day.

'I want you Richard. I want to feel you throbbing and rising up inside me.'

She tried to kiss me again but I pushed her away. I had a bad feeling about this.

'Are you talking about a shag or food poisoning?'

I tried to push her off, but she had her arms around my waist. She pushed up against me again, and then her right hand came around and grabbed my now rampant spam-javelin. What's got two hundred teeth and protects a monster? My zip at the moment. Well, I was always prone to exaggeration. Maybe I was, as my zip only had one hundred and sixty teeth.

'Come on, you'll enjoy it. I won't tell anyone.'

She looked down at my cock and gave it a hard squeeze.

'I can tell you want to.' And with that, not releasing her grip, she started to pull me towards the entrance - of the apartment block, that is.

It must have looked like the last-leg handover on the four-by-one-hundred-metre relay. She had my baton in her hand and she was running for the line. Fuck this. I grabbed her hand and pulled it off my old chap. It hurt a bit because she had a firm grip.

'No, Cynthia, no. I can't, it's not right.'

She stood in front of me; her face lacking any emotion. Then her face split into a sarcastic smile.

'Ha, saving yourself for Nicola, are we? Well, don't waste your time; it's not going to happen.'

It all fell into place. I was being set up. It was my turn for a sarcastic smile.

'Have I passed your little test then, or did my hormones get the better of me?'

Her smile faded and her aggressive pose subsided.

'Yes you've passed. I just had to be sure. I still don't trust you, but yes, you've passed.' Phew. That was the best exam I'd ever had.

'Sorry, Richard, but I had to be certain. I had to know for sure. Shame, I was actually looking forward to it, come the end.'

'I'm afraid there'll be no coming tonight, not unless you've got fresh batteries in your plastic friend.' She smiled.

'It's rubber, if you must know. Anyway, please let me know what's going on every step of the way.'

She turned and went in through her security doors without a second look. Shame, because I was looking forward to it myself. It'd taken a lot of willpower to turn down a shag-on-a-plate. I was quite proud of myself, but very frustrated. Perhaps I should have hung on to Latex Laura.

It'd been quite a day; a day of surprises all round and a very productive one. My thoughts drifted back to Lyn's binder tucked under my bed. It was one of the many things I'd have to sort out tomorrow. It was going to be another busy day.

Chapter Fourteen

I rang Vic on the way into work. It was an easy call as I just needed him to get a floor plan of the Council Offices from the Internet for me. I needed a printout of each office and their telephone numbers. It should be in the public domain and also accessible from the net. Vic said he'd do what he could and that I could pick them up tonight. I'd also try and cobble together the wording of the NHS letter for him. I would make the other calls from the office, or more precisely, from the back room in private.

Carol was still moody. I couldn't blame her, but things were about to get a lot worse. I wasn't about to tell her that though. I'd bought fresh doughnuts as a bit of a peace offering. I put them on my desk and wandered out to make the coffee. It was time for the first call.

'Martin, it's me, Richard.'

'I know mate, it's the twenty-first-century and there's *caller display* on my phone which always tells me who's calling, you technophobe. I'm on duty, mate, so be quick.'

'I know you're working, mate; that's why I've rung.'

'You don't need my help again, do you? What in God's name have you done now?'

'Not over the phone, Mart; I need to meet with you, if you've got a spare half-hour this afternoon. We'll probably need to meet up with the Fraud Squad afterwards. I might have a little something for you.'

'You're joking, right? Why do you need the Fraud Squad? Is this something to do with the bogus doctor thing? If

357

it is, then I can't help you mate. I've got a career to think about.'

'No, Martin, it's got nothing to do with that. It's much more serious. I don't want to discuss it over the phone but it concerns a mutual friend. Can we meet?'

'And what mutual friend would that be to interest me, as a serving constable, and the Fraud Squad?' That was said with more than a hint of sarcasm. I just gave him one word.

'Ena'

The other end of the phone was silent for a second.

'I've got to be in the office at two to clear up some paperwork. I could meet you then. Just come to the front desk and ask for me. How sure are you of the Fraud Squad involvement?'

'Very sure, I'll see you at two.'

I took the coffees into the office and dished out the doughnuts. I waited until the jam was running down Carol's chin before I asked her.

'Carol, sorry if this is short notice, but is there any chance of half-a-day's leave this afternoon? Something important has just come up.'

She wiped the jam off her chin and licked the sugar from her lips, all the while looking at me very suspiciously.

'How important?' She was thinking about our conversation of the other afternoon.

'It's very important; I've got an appointment that I can't put off. I can come back afterwards and make things up if you can't spare me for the whole afternoon.'

She thought about it for a bit.

'OK, you can have the whole afternoon, but don't forget that you've got a viewing at ten and another at eleven-thirty. Does that give you enough time to get to wherever it is you're going?'

Sarcasm was certainly the flavour of the last few hours.

'That'll be more than enough; I'll be as quick as I can.'

I caught her looking at my bulky rucksack which had the binder inside. I suppose she was wondering why I'd taken it with me to make the coffee. By the end of the morning, she was wondering even more, because I'd taken it with me to both viewings. I must have looked a bit strange showing prospective buyers around the two houses with a bloody great rucksack on my back. It was like Ray Mears' Extreme House Viewings.

I grabbed some lunch on the way to the cop-shop. It was exactly two when I arrived outside. I – we - had gone too far to back away now. It felt odd going into a police station knowing that I might be doing some good. Usually, it was on a Sunday morning at about two o'clock, pissed out my mind.

I walked up to the sergeant at the front desk.

'Hello mate, I've got an appointment with Constable Bormann for two o'clock.'

I immediately regretted using the term 'mate'. I wasn't exactly known for my civility in the face of authority, but I suppose I should have shown him a little respect.

The elderly sergeant looked up from his paperwork and slipped his glasses down to the tip of his nose to get a look at me. The fluorescent light shone off the top of his bald head from within its caged diffuser. It was a very disdainful look.

'Name?'

'Richard.'

'Richard what?'

'Richard Watt is my cousin's name. I'm Richard Head.'

Bollocks, I'd done it again.

'Richard Head. What an interesting name. OK, funny guy, what's your real name?'

'It's Richard Head, honest, Sarge.'

'Your mum must have had a really painful time giving birth to saddle you with a name like that, son. I'll give Martin a ring.'

He didn't have to. Martin came out of a side door and called me in. He ushered me into an interview room.

'I thought it'd be best if we had a bit of privacy, especially if Sharples is involved in whatever you're into. His family has got a lot of eyes and ears around this town and this place is no exception. Just remember that. Now, what the fuck is going on?'

I brought the binder out of my rucksack. It looked very impressive.

'Just flick through that and you'll get an idea.'

He dragged the binder over to his side of the desk and opened it up. He didn't say much while he scanned the pages apart from the odd 'fuck' or 'bloody hell'. It took him about ten minutes.

'Don't tell me you did all this on your own. Who put you up to this?'

'It's all me, Mart. All of it is down to little ol' me. What do you think? Are we going down the hall to the Fraud Squad?'

'Firstly cut the 'little me' bollocks. Like I said, technophobe, there's no way you came up with all this.

Secondly, Fraud Squad is upstairs and yes, we're off there now.'

'Martin, please keep your doubts about my technical expertise to yourself. For the purposes of this investigation, it's mine and mine alone. Is that clear?'

'Crystal. I'll get you a job at GCHQ, if you want. Grab the folder and let's move. The guy we're seeing hasn't got a lot of time. Neither have I, come to that.'

We headed upstairs and soon entered the Fraud Squad office. The sight of a civvy and a beat-bobby raised a few eyebrows around the office floor.

'What brings you up here, Bormann? Come to do some real work rather than answer 999 calls from little old ladies who've lost their incontinence pads?'

Martin's accuser was a late forty-something, fat, balding bloke, sat at a desk covered in coffee cups, paperwork and a computer. He had a greasy sheen to his face and his gut was hanging over his belt. He was the sort of person you took an instant dislike to.

'You must tell your wife to stop ringing up, Sloane. The smell of lavender and piss round at your house is playing hell with my sinuses.'

Martin just kept walking through the office with me in tow. Sloan had gone purple and had shot out of his chair, spilling a mug of coffee all over his paperwork.

'Bastard! Bastard!'

I wasn't sure if it was aimed at Martin or the fact that he'd ruined what was probably a whole heap of casework. We kept going.

'Fatty Sloane; pig of a copper. He calls himself the Sloane Ranger and thinks he's Mr Big because he's got

Detective in front of his name. He couldn't detect his arse with both hands in a darkened room.'

I followed him to the back of the office.

'Who are we going to meet, Mart?'

We'd reached the back office. There was a nameplate on the closed door. A youngish, well-dressed man sat at his desk on the phone. We waited.

'Inspector Graeme Lindsay, sharp as a tack, so be on your toes. And treat him with a bit of respect; otherwise you'll see your arse. Oh, and watch out for Sloane; he's dangerous, he's got big ears and an even bigger mouth, if you know what I mean.'

Inspector Lindsay put his phone back into its cradle and beckoned us in. Martin closed the door behind us.

'This had better be good, Constable Bormann. I've got a lot on my plate at the moment. Now, what's so important that you want a private meeting rather than go through the proper channels?'

Martin took a deep breath. He introduced me as a friend and explained where I worked.

'I've only had time to have a brief scan through Richard's findings, Sir, but I think you'll find them interesting.'

'It had better be a bit more than interesting, Constable.'

'I think it is, Sir. It involves the Sharples' and, in particular, their property dealings for some considerable time.'

Everyone in town knew the Sharples' and Inspector Lindsay was no exception.

'The Sharples'? Now I know why you wanted this in private.' His eyes went out to the office floor and settled on the fat detective.

'Right then, what have you got for me, young man?'

Young? I was only a few years younger than him. Cheeky fucker.

'It's probably best that you read this, rather than me explaining it all to you, Inspector.'

I retrieved the binder from my rucksack and slid it across the desk towards him. He opened it up and started reading. He took longer than Martin.

'So, you're an estate agent, Richard?' I just nodded.

'And you've come up with all of this on your own?'

There was a big echo in this building. He didn't believe me either.

'Yes sir, over a number of months. It's all in the public domain. It's just a case of knowing where to look. Unfortunately, some of the financials aren't up to date as the company records haven't been submitted yet.'

He looked back at the binder.

'Ordinarily, that is our job but, I must say, this is a very professional and comprehensive file that you've put together. How many people know of its existence?'

'Just myself, Constable Bormann and now you, Inspector. So, it's just the three of us.'

He thought for a moment, looking at the précis of the fraud put together by Mrs Edgar. We'd been in his office close on thirty minutes.

'I have to make a phone-call.' He picked up his phone and rang an internal number.

'Hello, Sir, it's Inspector Lindsay from Fraud. Could you please come down to my office for a moment? I've got something that will interest you.'

There was a slight pause then a thank you. He'd been speaking to a bigger boss.

'Constable Bormann, thank you for bringing this to my attention, especially in the manner you have. Now, it's vitally important that neither of you breathe a word of the contents of this binder to anyone. I repeat, not to anyone, including police officers. Do I make myself clear?'

We both nodded. The door opened behind us and a suit walked in. He had an air of authority about him. Martin stood up immediately and I followed his lead.

'Gentleman, this is Superintendent Vidamour.'

The Inspector introduced Martin and me to the super' and gave him a very brief résumé of the contents of the binder before he sat down and went through it himself.

'And you came up with this all on your own, Richard?' Fuck me, I was in the Alps.

'How many people know about this?'

Superintendent Vidamour looked at me from across the table. Despite his high rank he was young, maybe early thirties, which put me on edge a little bit. In my experience, young high fliers are either inky fingered, shiny arsed, sycophantic wankers or they're very good at their job. He also had a very pronounced scouse twang to his voice – 'Dey do do dat, don't dey, la'. I getting a bit pissed off with the repetitive questions and needed to know where I stood. Would he take this case seriously or would he see it as a box ticking exercise and a competency filler for his staff report?

'Which side of Stanley Park are you from, Superintendent?'

364

'I beg your pardon?'

He had a quizzical look on his face and, more encouragingly, a slight smile.

'I'd just like to know if you're a Red or a Blue.'

Martin and the Inspector both took a double take. This wasn't the forum to discuss the Merseyside footballing divide and seemed to be completely out of context, but I had my reasons.

Vidamour smiled and thought for a few seconds. He too, was wondering why I'd raised such an off-the-wall question.

'If you must know, Richard, I'm a true Blue. Season ticket holder as it happens, only I don't get to many games these days. Why do you want to know?'

My question had been answered and I felt a lot happier.

'I needed to know if you would take this case seriously and give it one hundred percent. After all the work I've put into it, I didn't want it turning into a botched investigation with the Sharples' getting away scot-free.'

Martin and Inspector Lindsay were open mouthed. You obviously didn't talk so openly to the higher ranks. Well, the Crown wasn't paying my wages, but I could do with a stab-vest.

'And now that I've told you I'm an Everton supporter, do you think we'll botch up the investigation or will we give it our all? Quite frankly, I'm intrigued to know.'

'Liverpool or Everton, it doesn't matter to me. The main thing is that you're a football supporter.'

'What relevance does my Blue affiliation have to the case?'

'In my experience, it proves to me that you're a normal bloke and will take the case seriously. A Scouser who's not a football supporter would make you an inky fingered...'

I stopped short. I didn't think that my description of 'promotion at all costs' coppers was relevant and it wouldn't be appreciated.

'Right Richard, time is ticking and I haven't got all day to chat about amateur psychology. As one 'normal bloke' to another, tell me about your findings.'

I went through it all again. The Super' and Inspector then began chatting between themselves. I glanced out of the office window. All eyes were on us. The appearance of the Superintendent was setting tongues wagging. We'd been in there a long time. The Inspector finally spoke to Martin and me.

'Thank you very much, gentlemen. I can honestly say that I wasn't expecting anything like this to cross my desk today. You can leave this with the two of us now; we'll take it from here.'

He walked forward and shook my hand, closely followed by the Super'.

'Richard, do you mind waiting outside for a moment? I need to talk to Martin about something.'

I was shown the door. I was going to stand while I waited, but fuck it; I sat at a nearby desk. I didn't think the Superintendent would mind.

They chatted with Martin for about five minutes. There were lots of questions from his bosses, it seemed, and lots of talking, shaking and nodding of Martin's head. I was summoned back in.

'Obviously Richard, I can't discuss any specifics with you, but we'll need to contact you at a later date, just to run through a few things with you, that's all. The most important thing is that you don't discuss this with anyone; anyone at all.'

'I understand fully, Inspector. Like they say, 'walls have ears'. That's unless you're in a sound-proofed office like this one.'

The Inspector and Superintendent exchanged uncomfortable glances. They had little mounds of earth on the floors of a lot of their offices.

'Thank you Richard and Constable Bormann, that will be all for the moment.'

They shook Martin's hand as he left. I swear he was six inches taller on the way back through the office.

'Hey Bormann, what's all that about then?'

The Sloane Ranger couldn't keep his curiosity to himself.

'Nothing much, Sloane. We were just discussing a few up-and-coming disciplinary cases with the Superintendent and my friend here from H.R. He's the Diversity and Disciplinary expert. As a matter of fact, your name came up more than once.'

We left Sloane with a worried look on his face.

'What was the private chat about, Mart? Was it me?'

We headed out to the car park before Martin replied.

'Partially; they wanted to know about you and if you could be trusted. I said that you could and that you were just a regular guy. They also asked me why you'd made up the file. I said that you, and me for that matter, had a history with Ena.'

'What else?'

'It's going outside to another force and investigation team. This is big, Richie, fuckin' massive. I'm not sure if you realise just how big I mean. They've been after the Sharples' for a long time and this might be their opportunity, thanks to you. And also thanks to you, this has given a massive boost to my career prospects. Special Branch, here I come. Thanks buddy.'

'Glad to be of assistance. Maybe Ena will finally do us both a favour. Are you up for a beer tomorrow night?'

'Sorry Richie, but I've got a date.'

Martin, on a date? But he hadn't met anyone on our nights out recently and I didn't think he'd go back to Maureen and her epileptic clitoris any time soon.

'Going for an Indian, by any chance?'

Martin smiled sheepishly, 'In a manner of speaking, yes'

'And I thought you were a racist bastard. Have a good time, mate and catch you later.'

I'd been at the nick for a lot longer than I'd anticipated. Going back to the office wasn't an option. I still had a letter to write for Vic and also had to pick up the plans of the council offices, but before that, I had to ring the hospital.

I'd thought about making a visit to the hospital, but it was far too soon after my lucky escape. In fact, that was only yesterday, but it seemed an age ago; a lot had happened since yesterday lunchtime. I settled down on my trusty park bench and dialled the main switchboard number. Amazingly, I'd actually mastered storing numbers in my phone's memory!

'Can you put me through to the Cancer Ward please?'

The forwarded call was picked up within a few rings.

'Good afternoon, Cancer Ward. How can I help you?'

'Good afternoon nurse. My name is Richard Head. I believe you have a patient on the ward by the name of Nicola Williams.'

I waited for a reply, which took a little longer than expected.

'What's the nature of your call, sir?'

There was no confirmation that she was there. I suppose she had to be careful under patient confidentiality or, as with a lot of phone calls I make, the name Richard Head is synonymous with a wind up.

'I was at…' Bloody-hell, I nearly admitted to being in the ward yesterday. Bad move.

'… a friend's of Nicola's yesterday evening. Cynthia Blenkinsopp, Nicola's best friend. We were discussing Nicola's condition and her urgent need for O Negative blood. Well, to cut a long story short, it turns out that I have the same blood group as Nicola and I was wondering if I could be tested for a match. Would that be a possibility?'

There was another pause at the end of the line.

'I'm afraid things have changed over the last twenty-four hours with regard to Nicola's condition. Unfortunately blood transfusions are no longer an option. We've had the results of further tests and things weren't as they initially appeared.'

This was sounding more than a bit worrying.

'But the nurse said yesterday that all she needed was blood and that bone marrow wasn't needed.'

'I'm sorry, but the nurse you spoke to wasn't in possession of the full facts regarding Nicola's condition. When did you say you spoke to the nurse?'

'Sorry, slip-of-the-tongue. It was Cynthia who got the update. But does this mean that she needs bone-marrow?'

'I'm sorry, sir, but I can't discuss specifics regarding Nicola's condition. I can only give information to her immediate family, and as you're not on my list, I'm afraid we can't discuss this matter any further.'

She had a point. It was patient confidentiality. But she'd already given me a lot without being specific. Nicola needs bone marrow and perhaps I could still help.

'I'm sorry nurse, I fully appreciate the confidentiality aspect and apologise for putting you in an awkward position.'

'Thank you for being so understanding. You'd be surprised how feelings can run a bit high, especially when a friend or loved one is in here and you don't know what's going on.'

'Well, I'll cut to the chase, nurse, without being too specific. As I'm her blood group, am I in a position to help?'

She was weighing up her options. I'd given her a way out without going into any detail.

'Yes, you might be, Richard. I'll give you a number to contact and they will be able to give you details of what to do next. I'm afraid I can't be any more specific than that.'

I wrote the name and number down. It was *Anthony Nolan*. She'd explained that they were previously known as the *Anthony Nolan Trust,* a charity that specialises in the treatment of blood cancers and the recruitment of donors.

I thanked the nurse for her help and rang the number she'd given me.

The call took about another fifteen minutes. I explained the situation and how I believed I could help. A lady took me through what I would have to do and said she was sending me out a pack for my GP which should arrive in about two days. It was too late for me to get it in the morning. All I'd have to was to take it to my GP and they would take a sample of blood from me and send it back to them for analysis and registration. That was the initial stage. If my blood tests were OK, then a further sample would be taken for a more in-depth analysis to see if I was a compatible donor. She explained that the likelihood of me being compatible to Nicola was very unlikely though. If I wasn't, then at least I'd tried my best and I could help some other unfortunate soul when I'd registered.

The process sounded simple enough but I hated needles. There was no way I could be a drug addict; I'll stick to beer.

In the space of a couple of hours, I'd got the ball rolling on the two things that had been dominating my every move over the last few weeks. I felt quite pleased with myself, and a little apprehensive. I wasn't sure where either was going and, for the first time, I didn't have any control over them. It was out of my hands now, which was a bit disconcerting. It was time to concentrate on something that I could control.

I went home and started to write. Hopefully, this would scare Ena shitless.

After about an hour of writing and scanning through the phonebook, I'd completed the letter. I'd even had to consult Mum's medical guidebook that she had used every time we coughed or sneezed when we were kids.

I popped downstairs for a bit of tea. Sis was unusually quiet. I got the impression that she was up to something. I'd better not ask, especially at the table.

'Mum, do we have any relatives by the name of Williams?'

I'd been thinking about my blood group. She thought for a moment.

'Not that I know of, Richard, but I never knew a lot about your father's side of the family. In fact, I never got the chance to know much about him either, come to that. Why do you ask?'

'Oh nothing, I just wondered.'

Now she thought I was up to something. We sat around, each giving the other suspicious glances.

'Right, I've got to go. Just popping round to Vic's to borrow his expertise.'

'I don't think you're going to expand on that either, are you?'

'Sorry Mum, work stuff that's all.'

Vic had the information I'd asked for laid out on his kitchen table. It was the complete floor plan of the council offices. Luckily for me, it was an older building, and not open-plan, like most modern builds. When this was built, people still valued their privacy over office space. There was also the headed notepaper from the hospital.

'Are you going to tell me what you want with all this stuff, Richie, or am I going to find out when I'm charged with aiding and abetting?'

'Well, I'm not planning a bit of breaking and entering, if that's what you're worried about. I thought I might be able to have a laugh with it on Saturday night, with a little help from Dev.'

'What's Dev got to do with the council offices?'

'Best not to spoil the surprise, Vic. Just wait and see.'

'I just hope that it doesn't end up like the other Saturday night. Fuckin' near gave me a heart-attack, that did.'

I got my letter out of my rucksack and handed it over to Vic.

'Think you can type that up on the NHS header? It's a little present for Ena.'

He took the letter and scanned through it.

'Fuck me; you really are an evil bastard. Yes I can do that. Just give me five minutes.'

He set to work on his laptop and, true to his word; it was coming off his printer five minutes later. I picked up the end result.

'Perfect Vic, great job. This should take Ena's mind off things for a little while.'

The letter looked very professional. It was even signed by an actual doctor who worked in the STD clinic at the hospital whose name I'd got over the phone. I'm afraid it was another bogus doctor ringing up for a bit of advice on a patient. Like Mrs Edgar said, the phone is often mightier than the sword. It's amazing how trusting some people can be; as long as you sound confident and plan what questions to ask, very few people will have the nerve to confront you. I rechecked the wording.

The letter head gave the originating address as the Sexually Transmitted Disease Clinic at the hospital, with the corresponding phone number. It was addressed to Mr Timothy Sharples with a care-of address at his office on the High Street. It read:

'Dear Mr Sharples,

I apologise for sending this request to your place of work, but it is the only definite contact address we could obtain for you.

I have recently treated a young lady at my clinic with whom it is strongly suspected that you have had a sexual relationship. I'm afraid that I cannot disclose her identity to you, as this would breach her Human Rights; namely Article 8, her right to privacy.

We have obtained the results of the examination and it is with these in mind that I am writing to you with some urgency.

The lady in question has proved positive for the following conditions:

HERPES SIMPLEX

CHLAMYDIA

GONORRHOEA

NOBERIA ROTENTEOUS

This fourth condition is particularly worrying. It is a macrobiotic infection which can attack the penis, and in particular, the testes from within. It is a strain of the flesh-eating bug which is unfortunately becoming increasingly hard to treat. Basically, it will take some time to develop.

As you can appreciate, it will be necessary for you to attend this clinic in order for us to carry out the specific tests relating to these diseases. I'm sure that you can understand the urgency of the situation and the effects these conditions may have on your health if they're not detected and cured within a relatively short time-span.

Please do not contact my office by telephone; there is no need at present. Just make regular checks on your genital region over the next ten days. No appointment is necessary after this period. Just turn up at the clinic between the hours of 0900 and 1600 and your condition will be reviewed.

In the meantime, please pay particular attention to your testes in relation to the macrobiotic infection. As I have said, this disease attacks from the inside. To test, it will be necessary for you to tap your testes at least twice a day and listen for a warning sign. If your testes sound in the least bit hollow, then this probably means that the infection has taken hold. This test may be a bit painful, but it is unfortunately necessary.

It is vitally important that you refrain from any sexual activity and contact over the forthcoming ten days.

Yours sincerely,

Dr Umar Gull

Consultant Urologist,

Sexually Transmitted Disease Clinic.'

I was pleased with the results and thought that the letter would take Ena's eye off things for a few days at least, whilst things were hopefully unravelling around him. Nothing focuses the mind more than the impending loss of your manhood.

'Ena's going to be shitting hot conkers when that lands on his desk, Richie. I wish I could be there to see it.'

'With a bit of luck, I might be able to, at a short distance anyway.'

'What's Noberia Rotenteous when it's at home? I never want to catch that. Sounds bloody horrible.'

'I don't think there's much danger of you getting that Vic. Take the first three letters of each word and what do you get?'

'**Nob Rot**. He'll spot it for sure.'

'No he won't. He'll be in such a blind panic from an urgent letter from the STD Clinic that all normal brain function will go out of the window. Let's hope so anyway. Right, thanks for this lot, Vic, I owe you one. Catch you on Saturday.'

375

I signed Doctor Gull's signature and popped the letter into a suitably official-looking envelope that I'd nicked from work. A first class stamp followed. The letter would go into the post on the way back home.

My walk home was brightened up by the vision of Ena, with his bollocks out on the kitchen table, and whacking them with a spoon. Fuck me; that was going to hurt, hopefully.

I was feeling a bit drained and I thought about getting a bottle of Shiraz on the way back. That was probably not a good idea. I settled for a pint in the local and caught up on the football. I didn't mind sitting in a pub on my own. It gave me an opportunity to catch up on my thoughts over a beer and do a spot of people-watching at the same time. It was usually guys trying to chat-up girlfriends and others bigging up their day's work with their mates. I found it fascinating. Perhaps I should retrain as a psychologist but, then again, it might frighten me. I'd find out too much about myself. I was turning into a scheming, evil bastard. Maybe that's true, but needs must at the present moment.

I left the pub after a pint of orange and lemonade. There was something I'd forgotten to do. I needed to make another phone call.

'Cynthia, its Richard.'

'Hi Richard.' She sounded very upset. She must have heard about Nicola.

'I'm sorry, Cynthia.'

'You know? Already?' She was surprised and upset.

'Sort of; I rang the ward this afternoon about the blood. The nurse couldn't say much, but it wasn't difficult to put two-and-two together.'

She burst into tears. I let her cry it out.

'What are we going to do, Richard?'

'All isn't lost, Cyn.'

I felt I could get a bit informal at last. After all, she had grabbed my cock.

'I may still be able to help after all. I'm having tests to see if I may be able to give her my bone marrow.'

I explained the procedure with *Anthony Nolan* and that I should have an answer within a relatively short period of time.

'You'd do that for her? Thank you, Richie. I can't say how much I appreciate it.'

I left it at that, saying that I'd be in touch when I'd heard back after the test. She was crying again.

I contacted my GP's receptionist first thing the following morning. Luckily for me, it was just off the High Street and I made arrangements to visit early on Thursday morning on my way into work, providing the sample kit arrived. It should, because our postman still visited us early in the morning, unlike many.

Thursday morning arrived and I sat at the bottom of the stairs like a kid waiting for Santa on Christmas morning. The kit thumped onto the floor, along with various bits of post advertising solar panels, insurance for over fifty-fives and the local supermarket offers.

I grabbed the kit and took it straight to the GP's. I arrived just before half eight and was the first through the door.

After introducing myself to the receptionist, I was ushered into the practice nurse's room and handed her the kit. She opened it up and got a couple of bottles out. Then she went to her cupboard and pulled out a needle and syringe carrier. Next, she screwed on the needle.

At the sight of this, my bollocks nearly ended up in my throat. I looked away.

'Now if you could roll your sleeve up, please Richard.'

The cool antiseptic swab cleaned the inside of my arm, right in the elbow joint. I still couldn't watch.

'Now, this might sting a bit. But I'm sure a big strong boy like you won't have any problems with a little needle.' Don't speak too soon, nurse.

I gritted my teeth as it went into my arm. It wasn't that bad really.

I glanced down to see what she was doing, despite my phobia. She was inserting one of the trust bottles into the syringe carrier. Once in, she pressed the plunger and the bottle slid down onto the needle. I wasn't expecting the next bit. Blood shot into the bottle; my blood. I thought that it should be OK, as I'd stayed away from alcohol the night before.

'I've just got to do the other one, Richard, and then we're all done.'

She repeated the process and put the second bottle on the table with the first. My arm was swabbed again and she put a small plaster on the sample area.

'There, it's all done, Richard. I'll get these off by courier to the trust and they'll contact you directly. That will either be by phone or letter, depending on the urgency.'

'Do I get a cup of tea and a biscuit now, nurse?'

'If you stop at the café down the road, then yes. I'm afraid we don't run to such extravagancies here, Richard. Goodbye.'

I was first into work, despite my appointment. Tina and a grumpy Carol arrived a few minutes later. I busied myself awaiting the arrival of the post over the road. Ena's letter should be in their sack.

It arrived twenty minutes later. Ten minutes after that, Ena's post was placed on his desk by the office girl. I was pretty sure the letter wouldn't have been opened because I'd used our CONFIDENTIAL stamp on the back.

A minute later he had it in his hand. He looked at it, front and back, then set about opening it. It only took a few seconds to take effect. Firstly, his body lurched forward so his nose was nearly against the letter. Then he held it out in front of him and gazed out of the window, probably trying to think of the appropriate girl. He read on. Next, he shot to his feet, still holding the letter. The girls in the office were looking at him now. I swear that I could see the colour drain from his face as he got to the Nob Rot bit. His hand went down to his bollocks and he began to scratch. Then he took a furtive look down. The poor fucker looked like he was in shock. His eyes were as wide as saucers as he ran out to the back of the office, busily shaking his head either at his own questions or in disbelief at his plight. I bet he was in the crapper examining his tackle with a magnifying glass.

It must be just the same as when someone mentions fleas; you immediately start to itch and scratch subconsciously. The mention of STDs and a bollock munching microbe must have been sending Ena's nervous system into overload. He probably had the wire-brush and antiseptic scrub out already.

It took him a full fifteen minutes before he returned to his desk. He must have been hammering on his bollocks for a long time. He looked ghostly pale as he took a glance over towards me. I found it very hard not to piss myself laughing. The fucker must really be going through it. Well, you've only got another ten days; ten nervous, scratchy, bollock-banging days. They'd be the size of tennis-balls by the end.

'You look happy with yourself, Richard.'

It was the first courteous sentence Carol had chucked my way in days.

'You could say that Carol. Just thinking of a letter I sent to an old friend the other day. He needed to catch up on a few things. You could call it a bit of infectious humour.'

I rang Vic when I got home and told him that he'd missed a treat. I'd sat at my desk and had watched Ena squirm, scratch and sweat all day. By the time he went home, he was looking positively grey. He was also walking a bit funny. I think that he should have used a smaller mallet. Perhaps I was turning into a bit of a sadist as well, because I'd enjoyed every minute of it.

Not long after chatting to Vic, I got a call from Martin.

'Fuck me, Richie; you've really put the cat amongst the pigeons. There are rumours flying around all over the place. Some say there's an internal disciplinary team down here doing a number on us; others say it's an anti-terrorist job in the area. Tongues are sure as hell wagging.'

'Just as long as people don't start to put things together, then the team might have time to do their job.'

'I even had Sloane trying to butter me up in the canteen at lunchtime.'

'Was that a deliberate pun?'

'No, sorry, but he started asking questions about who you were and why the Super' was getting involved. It's surprising the effect that two little single-syllable words can have.'

'But you've got to get them in the right order to have the desired effect, Martin. I know how intellectually challenged you boneheads can be.'

'Fuck off.'

'There you go. You must have been one of the top in your class during training. Congratulations, here's a funny pointed hat, truncheon and handcuffs; now go downtown and beat some poor drunk over the head.'

'Is this a serious conversation or ritual humiliation? I called to do you a favour. What's it to be?'

'Sorry mate. It's been a long day at the office. I'm going a bit stir crazy. What is it?'

'I'm worried about Sloane. I'm sure the fucker's bent. He's just asking too many questions that are way above his pay-grade. I'm just giving you a bit of a warning, that's all.'

'Cheers mate, I'll be careful. I'd already made my mind up about him. Great minds and all that, hey?'

'Yeah, only mine's greater than yours.'

I filled him in on Ena's letter from the Clap Clinic. Martin was another one who wanted to be there. We arranged to meet early on Saturday. We were both looking forward to a bit of a blowout.

'One more thing before I go, Richie. I've been chatting to my mum and dad about the assault. I've also had a chat with Mira and her brother. They're starting to remember a few more bits and pieces and things are starting to come together, especially descriptions. Its early days, but I think we might know who it was. And 'we' includes you.'

'Who do you think it was?'

'The Milibands.'

Chapter Fifteen

I had a bit of a shock on Saturday morning when I received a call from *Anthony Nolan*. After laying in bed, thinking about the coming night's revelries, I suddenly had to get my head together. My blood-tests and registration were OK, so it was on to the next and more crucial, second stage of the tests. Was I a match for Nicola? Another pack was being sent out to me and I would have to arrange another session with my GP for the Practice Nurse to do her thing. That would mean more needles, but the last time wasn't too bad. I'd just have to be a big brave boy again.

I rang Cynthia straight after the call to put her in the picture.

'Hi, Cynthia, it's Richard.'

She sounded as if she was in the bank. I'd naturally assumed that she'd be at home, but I'd forgotten that banks were slowly coming into the twenty-first-century. They might even start lending money to customers again, or was I getting way ahead of myself there?

'Hi Richie, you must have some news for me if you're ringing on a Saturday morning. Is it good news or are you going to ruin my day?'

'It's good news of sorts. I've just had a call to say that I've got through the first stage and can go forward and have another test to see if I'm a match. That's early next week, so fingers crossed, hey?'

There was a long sigh of relief down the line.

'That's brilliant. You're a regular knight in shining armour.'

'I've been known to do a bit of jousting in my time, Cynthia.'

I hoped she'd take the innuendo the right way.

'Clam jousting more like, you randy little sod.'

She was laughing now. Our relationship had completely turned around in such a short space of time.

'I'm known as Sir Richard of Head on the jousting circuit, complete with a shiny purple helmet and a very long luncheon-meat lance. I've even been known to go for a full three jousts before getting out of the saddle.'

'Well, you had your chance the other night, but didn't even get on your horse.'

This was getting a little bit too friendly. I had to try and keep a little bit of perspective.

'You're doing yourself down, Cyn; you're much better-looking than that. Anyway, I'll be in touch as soon as I get more news. Have a good day.'

'Bastard. You too. Maybe see you around town tonight?'

She sounded a lot happier. In some ways, I hoped I didn't meet up with her tonight. After a night out on the town, and with my prescription beer-goggles on, I didn't trust myself with Cynthia. I realised that I'd have to be careful.

I knew my beer-goggles would come out at some stage tonight. I normally get them on after about six pints. I've heard it said that all girls are beautiful; it's just relative to how much alcohol you've had. That is so true. Well, at least I wasn't married and waking up next to the same woman every morning. I just wasn't ready for that at the moment. Not many of us from school were married, but a few weeks ago, I'd met up with an old mate for a coffee in the lunch hour and discovered that he had actually been married for a while. It brought it home to me just what married life could be like. He said he'd gone on a works bender and had woken up alongside this fat, ugly bird the following morning. 'Thank God for that' he'd said, 'at least I'd got home all right!'

I could hear Rodney outside in his back garden. I hadn't seen him all week. He must be trying to get over his wrestling bout with Laura and the admonishment from the Vicar. I guessed he was breaking himself back in favour via the back garden before moving around to the front into the public's, and particularly the Vicar's eyes.

He'd suffered a lot at my hand recently, so I made a conscious decision not to do any 'Rodney baiting' tonight. My luck would surely run out sooner rather than later and I just had too much on my plate at the moment to get involved with Rodney or the police. I put him on the back-burner whilst I thought about my day ahead.

I still had a few hours to go before my night out. It dawned on me that I had nothing to do apart from mundane household jobs. To be brutally honest, my life was pretty boring. Once this Sharples' thing was over, and I'd done what I could for Nicola, I'd have to find an interest or a sport. I sometimes envied the likes of Martin and Dev. They had interests outside of work which didn't include alcohol and women.

Perhaps I'd take up golf. I'd always fancied trying my hand at the game, but it was the age of most of the participants that put me off. I'd visited the local golf club and, to me, it resembled God's waiting room rather than a vibrant participation sport. Maybe I'd have another look because, after all, I was getting on a bit. I was twenty three, for goodness sake.

I busied myself by having another look at the council office plans and marked out the offices that were of interest to me. Next, I got the relevant telephone number I'd need for tonight. With the night's entertainment sorted, I started my domestic chores. I did myself a favour and left off the pinny and yellow marigolds. You never know who's going to come to the front door with their camera-phone and *Facebook* account. Suddenly, your long-cultivated image of a macho, testosterone-fuelled male is shot away in a sixty-fourth of a second's shutter-speed.

I had the house to myself, so I could crack on and do some work for Mum. She was at work and sis was out and about around town with her mates.

Time went quickly and I was pretty pleased with the end results. I'd make someone a good husband, even if I did say so myself.

As I finished, the girls came home and I lapped up the praise. It was time to get ready and hit the town for a bit of R&R. After the week I'd had, I could definitely do with some.

The clans were gathering in a town-centre pub. I'd chosen it because the clientele were very easy on the eye and it also had a clear view of the council building.

After I put on my best clothes, I did my hair. The scar was still noticeable but it was fading. If my hair started to recede, it would be a real bugger. After a quick splash of aftershave, I strutted around in front of the mirror; I'd be fighting them off with a big stick tonight. Let's hope it wouldn't be Ena and his mates; that was the last thing I needed. I hoped that Ena wouldn't be out tonight as he would have had a lot on his mind. My mood went up a couple of notches when I thought of him sat on his bed, listening for an echo in his bollocks.

I set off for town early whilst there was still a lot of light. I examined the council building as I walked towards the centre and imagined what it would look like in about two hours or so. If my plan worked, then it should be a bit of a showstopper.

Martin and Vic were already in the pub. Vic went for the beers as I walked in and I had a couple of minutes to catch up with Martin.

'Any news?'

Martin was careful to talk in guarded terms.

'Shitloads. Everyone knows something's going on but not what. It's rumour control around the building. The word's getting out that some lads have come across from another force. It looks like they're housed in another building; but again, no-one knows a thing.'

'That sounds good then. Are you sure no-one knows the subject of their investigation?'

'As sure as I can be with my very limited access. I'm just a bobby-on-the-beat, mate, and I don't have many ears around the building but, as I said, nothing's coming out.'

'Brilliant. Fingers crossed then. The quicker these lads act, then the better the chance of a result. I'd hate those bastards to get away with it again. It'd be a shame after all our hard work.'

'Don't you mean 'my' hard work or are you referring to someone else?'

'If you want to go fishing, buy some maggots and a fuckin' rod. My lips are sealed.'

Martin still wasn't convinced that I'd done all the work for the file on the Sharples'. He was right not to be, but I wasn't letting on.

'I knew a girl like that once, but after a bottle of white wine and my persuasive charm, she came around in the end. Alright then, have it your way, but be very careful. A lot of people have got some very long rods out and quite a few of them have seen us together. Watch your back very carefully.'

I would. We'd gone too far down the line to blow things now. Martin glanced over my shoulder as Vic came back with the beers.

'Talking of very long rods, here comes Devon. Sorry Vic, but, as you're in the chair, it looks like you're back to the bar for another one.'

Devon caught sight of us and strolled over. We giggled and went through various fishing jokes which included words like codpiece, bloater, pollocks and a one-eyed trouser eel.

'Are you bad boys talking about my cock again? You're going to get a phobia if you're not careful. Next time, I'll sue. It's not easy going through life with a huge knob, you know.'

Martin was rising to the bait. He enjoyed a bit of banter with Dev.

'My heart bleeds purple piss, you lucky bastard. Just don't take up the hundred metres, because you'd get disqualified in every race. With the size of your dick, you'd knock the guys on either side of you out of their lanes once you had got into your stride.'

It was a sight that disturbed me for a second.

'Guys, can we change the subject for a minute? I'm feeling a bit uncomfortable about the conversation and the way it's going. I won't sleep tonight now.'

Our voices went down an octave or two as we talked about manly things like football and girls. That was better.

Dev had played in the afternoon and was quite excited. There'd been a number of scouts there and the word was that a few trials, or even a signing, might be in the offing. I had my fingers crossed for Dev. He deserved it after all his bad luck with injuries over the last couple of years.

I needed a word with Dev about the exercise in the morning at the council building. I got a pen and paper out of my pocket.

'Dev, got a minute? I'd like to pick your brains about the exercise that you were involved in this morning.'

Dev looked at me a bit quizzically, especially as I had a pen and paper in my hand.

'The council offices? It went as well as could be expected. We carried out the usual check of the building and ran through various scenarios based around the fire and escape-plans. Pretty normal stuff really. Why do you ask?'

I wasn't going to tell him. I'd let it be a surprise for later.

'Nothing really, I've just got a little plan I'd like to try out.'

'Is this little plan going to get me and the others into any trouble, Richie? I couldn't cope with that tonight. I just want a few beers and latch onto a nice young lady who doesn't mind walking like John Wayne for a day or two.'

There were too many images flying around my mind tonight.

'It'll be cool, Dev, trust me. All I need is the name of the big boss at your place or the name of the head guy on tonight.'

He looked at me with more than a hint of suspicion.

'I know I'm going to regret this, but the big boss is Jonathan Smith. The guy on tonight, the Watch Commander is Christopher Churchill. Just what are you planning, Richie?'

'Wait and see. Now, where's the nearest phone-box?'

'Phone-box? Why do you want to use one of them? Use your mobile.'

'Can't Dev. I don't want the call to be traced.'

The worried look came back on his face.

'If you must know, there's one next to the fossilised remains of the T-Rex down the road, right next to the Viking long-ship with the Penny-farthing leaning against it.'

'If I want sarcasm, mate, I'll watch a political debate on television. Where's the nearest phone?'

As it happened, it was just around the corner. I left my beer with the lads and headed off to find it. A quick glance at the surrounding buildings confirmed that there were no CCTV cameras covering the area around the phone-box. You can't be too careful in this day and age, especially when you're about to place a bogus call.

As I fed the money into the phone, I glanced down to try and get some idea of what I was standing in. I couldn't see anything but it smelt like a public toilet in there. There were also various cards by the phone, advertising the services of a number of exotically-named girls. I scanned the cards for any mundane adverts but didn't find any. I wondered if I could dummy one up for a friend of mine.

'Madame Ena offers discreet and intimate book-keeping services in the comfort of your own home. Let my fingers play over your glistening, hard keyboard. Absolute discretion assured. Let me crunch your numbers. It all adds up with Madame Ena.'

I put that out of my mind for another day and rang the number from my scrap of paper. I got straight through to the night security chap for the council building.

'Good evening, my name's Chris Churchill. I'm the Watch Commander down at the fire station. Who am I talking to, please?'

I could hear the guy at the other end of the line sit up in his chair. I'd used the name Churchill as I thought it sounded like it had a bit more authority to it.

'Malcolm, sir, Malcolm Smithers; I-I'm the Night Security Guard.'

'Hi Malcolm, I'm sorry to trouble you, but this is a follow-up to the exercise we had at your offices earlier in the day. I'm sure you know all about it. It went very well by all accounts. Did your lads let you know what we need for tonight's scenario? I'm sure they passed the details on to you.'

There were a few seconds of frantic paper shuffling at his desk.

'Sorry, sir, but I can't find anything on my desk. What is it that you wanted tonight?'

I explained what I wanted him to do. I had the list of rooms and offices that I'd identified and passed them to him down the phone.

'I hope that makes sense, Malcolm. The main problem we have in buildings like yours is light, especially in critical areas. If we need to get people out fast, and we haven't got any light in the area, it can greatly hamper our chances of getting people out. So, if you could go around on your nine o'clock rounds and switch on the lights in those areas, it would be a great help to us. Please start the switch-on at the top. I'll be outside with a couple of officers and we'll monitor the areas from there. We don't need to come inside for this exercise. Now, have you got all that?'

'Yes, sir, it's all written down. I'll get on to that at nine. Glad I can be of assistance, sir.'

'Thank you Malcolm. You've been a great help. I'm sure your superiors will get to know what you've done in due course. I can guarantee that.'

'Thank you, sir.'

I was sure they would know very soon. I had a pang of guilt as to what I'd done. I hoped that Malcolm wouldn't lose his job.

The lads were well into their next pint when I got back. It was getting dark and I glanced over at the council offices. They were all dark except for a couple of ground-floor lights. That would probably be Malcolm.

I glanced at my watch. It was getting on for eight, so there was only an hour to go.

'Where the hell have you been?' complained Vic, 'It's your round; Dev is getting worried about what you're planning and so am I, having given you the plans.'

'Shush, walls have ears, guys. All we have to do is take our beers outside at five-to-nine and wait for the floorshow. It'll spoil the surprise if I tell you now.'

We had a few more beers over the next hour. Everyone was glancing at their watches. Cynthia came in with a couple of Nicola's mates. Their attitude had changed entirely; they were smiley and friendly. I guessed that Cynthia had told them about what I was doing. I hope she hadn't mentioned my clandestine visit to the hospital though. There were too many people knowing too many secrets at the moment.

The guys noticed the girls' sudden change of demeanour towards me. I wasn't saying much.

'You've either got it or you haven't, lads. I've obviously got it.'

'So has Ena by the sound of it,' came back Martin. It was nice laughing at Ena's expense for once.

The girls headed off just before nine, so we filed outside with our beers. It was pitch-black by now, or as pitch-black as a town or city centre ever gets at night. There was still a lot of light pollution but it was dark enough, especially around the upper floors of the council building. It wouldn't be long now.

I imagined Malcolm heading upwards in the lift with his trusty torch in his hand. He would have a little spring in his step as he was taking part in the fire exercise, which was a lot better than his routine patrols around the building. It would give him a sense of importance, which should take his mind off what he was really doing.

I looked at my watch. It was nearly nine o'clock.

'Won't be long now lads.' I tried to sound a bit confident. Dev looked worried.

'You're not a closet arsonist are you? This isn't going to turn out like *Towering Inferno* is it?'

'Trust me, Dev. It's just a bit of modern art.'

At that moment, the first light flickered on in an office on one of the upper floors. Then a couple more came on as Malcolm headed down the building. It was slow going because I guessed he was using the stairs. At last, things started to go faster. Office lights came on one after another along a whole floor. The horizontal line covered about three-quarters of a floor. My design was beginning to take shape.

The lads were getting interested now. Vic had twigged what I was up to.

'I hope this isn't what I think it is, Richie. If it is, then that poor fucker switching on the illuminations is going to get the sack.'

I had a pang of conscience for what I'd done, but it was too late now.

A few more random lights came on then Malcolm set about another horizontal row on a lower floor.

'Oh fuck, Richie, what have you done?'

Devon was getting very scared. The initial stage had been illuminated and the outline of a giant fluorescent cock shone out across the town. People were starting to come out of various pubs and clubs to see the sight. Cars were beginning to pull up on the side of the road and their occupants were getting out to see if their eyes were deceiving them. All the while, more lights were coming on from the floors below as my design gradually took shape.

'Oh Christ, there aren't more, are there?'

It was Martin's turn to start getting a bit flaky. The outline of a giant ball-sack was gradually appearing below the equally giant cock.

People were clapping and shouting as the image appeared. Poor old Malcolm.

After another ten minutes, the final outline was complete. Flashes from mobile phone cameras were going off all over the place and the Saturday night party-goers were whooping and hollering. It was a pretty impressive sight.

By this time, the whole of the town centre had ground to a halt. Cars were abandoned all over the roads and their drivers and passengers were out on the street to get a better look. A few police cars got through and I thought it would be only a matter of time before the plug was pulled on my masterpiece. Sure enough, they started to go out soon afterwards. In fact they were going out a lot quicker than they'd gone on.

Malcolm was probably running like mad after either a phone call or a visit from the police. By the time he got to the top, he would be absolutely knackered.

We watched as the lights went out and shouts of disapproval echoed around the streets as the cock disappeared. The traffic was back to normal now and we went back inside to replenish our glasses. None of us wanted to go back inside and get the drinks whilst the lights were coming on. Devon was the first to react.

'Please tell me that I'm not going to get involved in this. I do actually like my job.'

'You're going to be fine, mate. I used a phone-box around the corner so the call can't be traced, not to me anyway. I used the name of the Watch Commander, Chris Churchill, and said it was a follow-up from this morning. So, there's no comeback on any of us, unless the local police have voice-recognition software up and running.'

The three of us looked at Martin. He shook his head.

'Still, keep your mouths shut. I'm not getting roped in as an accessory. That was some serious shit, Richie.'

He thought for a second, then burst out laughing.

'But it was bloody funny. Probably your best yet, mate.'

We all laughed our heads off. There was more than a hint of a nervous release, especially from the fireman and the policeman.

We weren't the only ones laughing. People were showing their mates pictures from their mobile phones and sending them to friends. I bet that a few had made their way on to various websites and to the media. What sort of headline would you put to that? 'Cock and Ball Multi-Story.' I'd wait and see.

The rest of the night was great. We wandered off to a club and mingled with old mates and met a few new girls. Cynthia was also there with her mates. I didn't get an offer for any clam jousting but she was unusually tactile. In the end, I decided to leave because my beer goggles were well and truly strapped to my head. I didn't want us to do anything that both of us would regret in the morning.

Having said my goodbyes, I headed for home. The walk would do me good, and hopefully, I wouldn't have anyone trying to part my head from my shoulders this time.

I started to walk home just as the pavements were filling up a bit. A lot of people had the same idea as me. I looked around to see if I could recognise any mates. I didn't see any friends; quite the opposite. Coming towards me, thankfully on the other side of the road, was Ena and one of his hangers-on. This guy was so ugly that I reckoned he'd been rescued off a Turkish beach from the clutches of an unscrupulous photographer. He wasn't eating a banana though.

I kept my head down and shielded myself from their sight by way of a large group walking in my direction. Ena slid by with no problems. As I glanced over, I noticed someone a few yards behind him. There was something familiar about her but I couldn't see her face. She had a big jacket on with the collar up. That was strange, as it wasn't that cold.

Then I recognised her. It was sis. What on earth was she doing? As I slowed down and watched, it became all too apparent. She was following Ena.

Then I noticed another thing. I couldn't see her right hand. It was mostly tucked up her sleeve; it was as if she was holding something. I suddenly got a very cold feeling in the pit of my stomach. I knew she had something on her mind, but not this, please.

I crossed the road and cut in behind her. If I went in too early, Ena would see us and things would kick off. I waited until we got to the shop doorways and closed the gap. As we got to a particularly deep doorway, I moved up behind her; I hoped no one would see what I was about to do.

I came up behind her, got her in a bear-hug and pulled her into the doorway. That's not really the best of things to do to a girl who had recently been the subject of an attempted rape.

She screamed and started to fight immediately. Her right foot went straight down my shin and smashed into the top of my foot. Fuck, that hurt. I nearly lost my grip and if my suspicions were right, it was the last thing I wanted to happen.

'Sis, sis it's me, Richie. It's Richie. Don't make a scene.'

She continued to struggle for a second, until she finally realised it was me. There was a metallic clang on the floor between us. I let her go and we both looked down at one of Mum's kitchen knives, a particularly sharp one as I remember. I looked up at her.

'Sis, are you mad? You'll go to jail, for Christ's sake.'

A couple of handy-looking lads stopped at the doorway. They looked like they were ready to rearrange my dental work. I let sis do the talking, as I didn't think they'd believe a word I said.

'It's OK, boys, it's my brother. We're just having a bit of fun, sorry.'

They took a step towards us to make sure she was OK. She moved towards them too. It seemed to reassure them.

'Are you sure, love?'

She nodded and walked to the edge of the pavement, away from me, showing that she wasn't in any danger. The lads walked off. Thankfully, they didn't see the knife. She turned towards me with a murderous look in her eyes.

'No I'm not fuckin' mad. I'm pretty calm really, considering what I was going to do, before you stopped me.'

'And what were you going to do? Cut the fucker up or actually kill him? You are mad, sis. You'd end up inside for a very, very long time.'

I bent down and picked up the knife.

'I told you, I'm not mad. I've thought about it a lot. I've thought of nothing else every minute of every day since that bastard laid his hands on me. And you stopped me, you bastard.'

I couldn't believe what I was hearing. She wasn't finished though.

'I wasn't going to kill him; just cut off a few bits and pieces. You know, the really important ones, for a bloke at least.'

'You were going to cut his bollocks off?'

She smiled at the thought of it.

'Yes, and his cock too. You have no idea, Richie, no fuckin' idea, what it's like to have some horrible little shit like that try to rape you. You don't feel human afterwards. You just feel dirty and grubby all the time. It's the sort of dirt you can't get rid of with a shower. It feels ingrained, right down to the bone, like a tattoo; no matter how hard you scrub, it's still there.'

I could hear the emotion building up in her voice. She would have done it.

'Sorry, sis. I can't imagine what you've gone through, and what you're going through now. I'm sorry, but to cut him up? Just think of the consequences.'

'You don't get it, do you, Richie? You just don't get it at all. I've thought it through, all of it. There wouldn't be any consequences. Well, not many, anyway. He tried to rape me, for fuck's sake, and in a state of mental imbalance, the victim exacts her revenge on the evil sex monster. There's not a court in the land that wouldn't have sympathy with me.'

She stood there smiling at my disbelief and enjoying every second.

'Of course, I might have a problem getting a boyfriend afterwards, but it's a small price to pay for getting that bastard back after what he tried to do.'

She had balls; I had to give her that. If I'd been a few minutes later, she might have had Ena's as well.

I felt my whole body fill with guilt. After all, it had been Ena trying to get at me through my sister. I'd put her in this situation. I had driven her to do it, in an odd kind of way. The thought of having Ena gelded was not an unattractive proposition, but not by my sister.

'We need to talk, sis. There are a lot of things going on at the moment. He'll get his just-desserts soon, but we need to talk this over before you do anything stupid.'

I took her arm and we started to walk. She didn't put up any resistance. I think that, secretly, she might have been a little relieved that I'd stopped her.

I dropped the knife down a nearby drain.

'That's Mum's best knife. She'll go mad.'

'You'd get five years inside for carrying a blade these days, sis. I'll buy her another one. It's better to be safe than sorry.'

I filled her in on what was going on around Ena at the moment. She particularly liked the letter from Dr Gull and Ena whacking his balls with a hammer. It seemed to take the edge off her quest for retribution. I swore her to secrecy, especially about the criminal investigation surrounding his property deals. She smiled at the thought of him going to jail. I'd also taken her into my confidence, which I think she really appreciated.

It's strange how you think you know someone, and then they go and do something of which you never thought they were capable. If I upset her in the future, I was definitely going to lock my bedroom door.

I slept well that night. Disaster had been averted. I only had to buy a new kitchen knife on Monday and, hopefully, things would be back as they were.

I was awoken the following morning by the squeak of a sponge on the *E-Type's* windows. This was closely followed by complaints of marks on the dash and windscreen. It sounded like Mo had had another wild night polishing the *E-Type's* leather seats with her arse. At least someone was getting some, unlike me.

I decided to give my Botherer-baiting a miss this Sunday. I wasn't even going to go around to visit any of my mates or their parents. They were all probably sick to death of the sight of me. I'd have a lazy day watching DVDs or the telly. I particularly wanted to catch the local news to see what they had on the council office's lighting scandal. It would be an alcohol-free day spent in a relaxed, and somewhat relieved, mood.

The following morning, I sat on the stairs again like an expectant father. Another sample kit dropped through the letterbox and I was off to see the GP as fast as I could. I didn't have an appointment, but they knew that I may be turning up for more tests. After all, you could say it was a matter of life or death and I didn't think they'd make a fuss.

Sure enough, the Practice Nurse fitted me in before the start of her appointment schedule. This was the important one and although the chances were very slim, some hope is better than none. If I wasn't a match for Nicola, I consoled myself that I was now on the register and I might be able to help some poor soul in the future. I was actually starting to feel quite proud of myself; a feeling that I was actually achieving something at long last and not pissing my life up against a wall.

It was a typical Monday morning. Tina was hung over and Carol was still grumpy, probably grumpy and worried.

Ena was in early too. He was probably having as much trouble sleeping as he was walking. I watched him struggle down the pavement and park himself gently in his chair. I'll give Terence a ring and see if he can lend Ena his cushions for the rest of the week.

It was a boring Monday, a boring Tuesday and a boring Wednesday. Nothing happened. I was expecting all sorts of phone calls. I wasn't sure who from, but I'd convinced myself that the phone would ring; but it didn't. Surely, somebody wanted to talk to me? I was feeling a bit disconsolate on my walk home that Wednesday evening.

I let myself in through the front door and heard voices in the kitchen. Mum and sis were having a chat. Perhaps they were talking about sis' chosen career as a butcher. I hoped it was a vet.

As I shut the door and made my way towards the kitchen, I stopped and listened. It was a male voice. Who the fuck was that? Maybe it was Mum's new boyfriend. 'Hello son, this is your new dad.' No way.

She'd heard the door.

'Richard, is that you, son? There's someone here to see you.'

Oh bollocks, I'd been rumbled for the giant council office cock.

As I walked into the kitchen, my worst fears were realised. It was a copper. I recognised the fat, bald, greasy head from behind. He didn't have to turn around for me to know who it was. It was the Sloane Ranger.

He turned to greet me with a smug, self-satisfied smile. Standing up, free surface effect took hold of his gut and it cascaded over his belt. I could smell him from two feet away. A mixture of coffee, ciggies, body odour and chip fat. He stuck out a hand, which I took very reluctantly. It felt like a cold, greasy, bacon sandwich. If he was in the Masons, I couldn't tell.

'Hello Richard, how are you doing?'

He was still smiling.

'I'm fine, Mr Sloane.'

I wasn't going to flatter him by using his title of Detective. He bridled a little at my slight.

'How did you know where I live and why are you here?'

I wasn't going to pass the day with any formalities with this dangerous little fucker; copper or no copper.

'Well, if you put it that way, I'm a detective, sonny. It's what I'm paid to do and I'm good at my job. Why am I here?

401

Well, I was in the area and I wondered if there was anything I could do for you. You know, perhaps I could answer any questions about what you were talking to the Inspector and Superintendent the other day. I'm here to help in any way I can.'

Firstly, I hated being called 'sonny', especially by a fat, condescending twat like Sloane. He wasn't here about the council office and he sure as hell wasn't here to lighten the burden off my shoulders. He'd found out where I lived and had come around on a fishing exercise. But, for whose benefit?

'Why, thank you, Mr Sloane. That's very kind of you but I'm not the person you need to talk to. I don't know enough about what's going on.'

He looked a bit deflated.

'But I know someone who'd be more than glad to have a chat to you. He'll be able to put you in the picture. You know, to give you an idea of what's going to happen in the near future.'

His eyes opened wide and he looked at me expectantly.

'I'll give him a ring and you can have a chat with him, OK?'

He was nodding like a little puppy. I got my phone out and tapped in the letter, 'G'. 'Graeme' came up with a mobile number. I pressed *call* and it was answered within two rings.

'Hi Graeme, it's Richard, Richard Head. Listen, I'm sorry to trouble you, but I've got someone with me at my house at the moment who'd like a chat with you.'

I passed my mobile over to Sloane. The smug grin was back on his face.

'Hi, this is Detective Constable Sloane. Who do I have the pleasure of talking to?'

The phone snapped away from his ear. I could hear the shouts from a few feet away.

'Detective Inspector Lindsay. Graeme Lindsay, you fuckin' buffoon. What the fuck do you think you're doing?'

The Inspector didn't wait for an answer. Sloane turned away from me. All I heard after that was 'arse in front of my desk tomorrow morning' and 'what the fuck do you think you're playing at?'

He turned back to me with a face like thunder. He was so red that I thought his nose was going to explode. He didn't say anything; he didn't have to. He was totally fucked. My phone was slapped into my hand with some considerable force and he met my gaze with a furious look in his eyes. I'd just made another enemy. The door slammed behind him.

'Sorry, Inspector, but it was the only thing I could think of. Can you give me five or ten minutes and I'll call you back to give you the damage?'

'As quick as you can, Richard, and sorry.'

Mum sat at the table in tears. I'd just had a run in with a detective in her kitchen. It wasn't an everyday occurrence and certainly not something a mother wants to see. Mummy's special soldier was in trouble with the police.

I tried to allay her fears whilst picking her brains about what she'd said to Sloane. Luckily, he'd only been there a few minutes and hadn't got much at all. But Mum did say that I was an estate agent in the town. Bollocks, I needed to make another call.

'Martin, can you talk?'

'No.'

'Well, get to somewhere where you can. This is important.'

He was back on the line a few seconds later.

'This'd better be good mate; I was in the middle of a collar, some shoplifting druggie. What is it?'

'Sloane; I've just come home to find him in my kitchen having a cosy chat with Mum. How did he know where I live?'

'Fuck. I'll brain that fat bastard. Fuck. I don't know, Richie. Everything is as tight as a drum down at the station. I'm pretty sure that no one knows what's going on.'

'Well, he knows that I'm an estate agent.'

'Fuck. I'll get on to Inspector Lindsay and fill him in.'

'No need Mart. I rang him while Sloane was here and he blew him out. It wasn't a pretty sight.'

'Hang on a minute. I saw Sloane chatting to young Carter in the canteen today. You know him; he's the lad who came with me for the tortoise investigation.'

How could I forget?

'He must have told him about our visit to you and got your address. You're going to be the only Richie he knows who's a mate of mine.'

'OK, thanks Mart. I'll ring Lindsay back and will fill him in.'

'Before you go, Richie, I've got a bit of news. The Milibands were lifted this afternoon for the assault on Mum and Dad. They're down at the nick now. I thought you'd like to know.'

I thought quickly. The Milibands were in a very tight spot. Maybe their tongues could be made to wag a bit?

404

'Martin, can I run something by you?'

I took a minute to explain and, although Martin wasn't too happy, he agreed with what I had proposed. I rang Inspector Lindsay again.

It only took a minute to run through what Sloane had picked up whilst chatting to my mum. He wasn't happy either. I didn't let on that it was probably the young P.C. who'd given Sloane my address.

'I'm sorry, Richard. Sloane had no authority to do what he did. His arse is well and truly out of the window. But the fact remains that he knows what you do.'

'And it won't take a fuckwit like him very long to put two-and-two together and make a phone call, will it?'

There was an uncomfortable silence at the end of the phone. I'd basically said that Sloane was bent. The truth hurts.

'Is this a secure line, Richard?'

'How the fuck should I know? I'm talking in private, but if the Sharples' have got someone in at GCHQ, as well as your office, then I guess we're all in big trouble, aren't we?'

Ouch.

'Sorry, but please don't be so candid with your assumptions. I can't possibly agree with what you've alluded to. Now, back to the job at hand. If Sloane knows what you do, then I agree that we have to move fast. Just keep your head down and I'll see what I can do at this end. I'm sorry, Richard.'

'One other thing before you go, Inspector. I've got a bit of information that might just help in getting some more dirt on the Sharples'.'

'Do we need any more?'

'That's up to you. You have two brothers by the name of Miliband locked up in your nick for assault and robbery. That's pretty common knowledge, but what isn't, is that they were hired by the Sharples to give me a bit of a beating a few weeks ago. I spent a night in hospital as a result. In light of their current predicament, they might be willing to spill their guts and give you something on the Sharples'. It's just a thought.'

'How the hell did you come up with all of that? Who told you?'

'You should know better than to ask a question like that, Inspector. An informant handler never reveals his sources. I've a duty of care to protect my sources at all times. And, unlike you, I can guarantee anonymity and they won't have to appear in court.'

He laughed, despite the obvious pressure he was under.

'OK, Richard, I'll bear it in mind, but it might be too late to go down that line. Listen, I've got to get on; I've got lots of calls to make and I think it's going to be a long night.'

Chapter Sixteen

I didn't sleep well that night; all the work and effort that Mrs Edgar and I had put in could all go for a ball of chalk, thanks to one bent copper. There was nothing I could do about Sloane at the moment, but if this didn't work out, and the Sharples' got off lightly, then he was going to be top of my list for a bit of payback.

The main problem for me was that if the Sharples' got off, then I was going to be at the top of their retribution list. Mr Sharples in particular wouldn't be too happy about me trying to bring down his financial empire and see him, his son and a few associates sent down for a few years. It wouldn't be some bungling druggies like the Milibands that come after me next time. A monastic life in the Italian hills was starting to sound very appealing.

I got up early and jumped in the shower. There was no point in lying in bed worrying about things over which I had absolutely no control. It was best to get up, look the world in the eye, and face up to whatever was going to come my way. I wasn't happy though, as I kept thinking about Sloane, and the image of his smug smile was on my mind all the way into work.

I was the first to arrive at the office and quickly brewed up a coffee. It tasted bitter as I sat at my desk gazing across the road towards Ena's office. The banana and apple I ate between slurps tasted just as bad.

Outside, the roads and pavements were starting to get busy as the day began to build up. Tina was early for a change and she was bright and breezy as well, for once.

'You're in early, Richie. Shit the bed, did we?'

She wasn't far off the mark. My chocolate starfish was going from a sixpence to a half-crown; decimalisation had ruined a lot of the old English language phrases. I was feeling like shit and probably looked like it.

'Couldn't sleep Tina, so I decided that I might as well contribute to the firm's output, rather than lay in bed trying to look up a female news-presenter's skirt.'

Despite the sarcasm in my voice, she looked over and knew something was wrong.

'Are you OK, Richie? Do you want to talk about anything, you know, while Carol's not here?'

'I'm alright thanks, Tina. Things will work themselves out, hopefully.'

To give Tina her due, she'd kept quiet after my chat with Carol. The office had been a bit tense since then, but Tina had kept her head down and had not been nosey.

'Well, if you need to talk then I'm here, or there's always Clint, if he can help with anything.'

She was a lot cleverer than we gave her credit for. Carol came in soon afterwards. She gave me her usual grunt then looked me up and down for longer than usual. The strain must have been showing on me, but she didn't ask any questions.

Ena wasn't in yet and it was ten past nine. Perhaps he had a viewing. All sorts of things started to flash through my mind. It was difficult concentrating on work; maybe it'd be best if I went off sick.

At that moment, things started to get interesting. Ena's old Audi screeched to a halt across the street. I looked over to see him career into the curb right outside his office and dash in through the front door. He was closely followed by his passenger, Fido. This wasn't looking good.

I could see through the windows of his office that the two of them were dashing about all over the place. Ena was pulling papers out of filing cabinets and Fido had eventually settled down in front of a computer, his fingers dancing over the keyboard. Papers were being stuffed into bags and a briefcase. They were in a hurry. Obviously, Sloane wasn't as thick as I thought he was; I had to do something.

I rang Inspector Lindsay as quick as I could but my fingers weren't working well amidst my panic. The call went to answer-phone. I weighed up my options, which were basically none. A citizen's arrest wasn't an option. What could I arrest them on? Unless they bashed their quizzical secretary in the office over the head, I was powerless. I'd have to sit and watch them clear the office of evidence, load up the car and then drive away into the sunset. Bollocks, my goose had been cooked way before Christmas.

A car horn sounded further up the street, closely followed by the sound of high-revving engines. Then the cavalry finally arrived. A marked police car, closely followed by two unmarked cars, roared up and stopped in the street outside Ena's office.

Ena was at the door with an armful of papers and a briefcase heading for his car. A look of panic spread across his face. It was fight or flight time. He opted for flight and took off down the street.

A plain-clothed copper flew out of the back door of one of the cars and shouted at Ena, who ignored him and just kept on running. It was easy pickings for the copper who just cut down his angle to Ena and took him down with a straight-arm clothesline across his neck. Ena's legs kept going, but the rest of his body went backwards as he ran in mid-air, pivoting against a muscular arm. He went down like a sack of shit, landing on his back on the pavement. Papers flew everywhere from his bags as he was turned over by the officer and cuffed where he lay.

Both uniformed and plain-clothed police rushed into the office and arrested Fido as he sat in front of the computer. He was swiftly led out and pushed into the back of one of the cars. His seat in front of the computer was taken by a studious looking policeman who began tapping at the keys. Amongst the mayhem, I recognised Inspector Lindsay. This was too good to miss.

Tina and Carol had by this time come to the front window to get a better look.

'Is that young Sharples they've handcuffed? What the hell's going on?' Carol was looking at me as she finished her questions.

'I'm afraid Timothy Sharples has been a very naughty boy. I'll be back in a minute.'

I wanted a chat with the Inspector to try and find out what was going on. It was no wonder he hadn't answered his phone.

A smile broke out on my face as I saw Ena being dragged up from the pavement in handcuffs. This was turning out to be a good day, for me anyway. Lindsay was in the doorway.

'You had me worried for a moment there, Inspector; better late than never.'

'Perfect timing, Richard, perfect timing.'

Ena was shouting as he was led away towards a car.

'Do you know who my father is? I want my lawyer, now! You can't do this to me.'

I turned to watch the show. His eyes were on me now, as I was standing next to the Inspector.

'You're fuckin' dead; you little shit, fuckin' dead.'

The spittle was spraying from his mouth, projected by the force and venom in his threats. A hand went to the back of his head and he was pushed forcibly down into the back seat. His head bashed into the top of the door frame as he went into the car. It shut Ena up and a wry smile appeared on the policeman's face as he uttered a very sarcastic 'Sorry'. The door slammed and Ena was sped away.

The Inspector's gaze followed the car down the street.

'Nasty little fucker, that one.'

'And then some. I know you're a bit busy, Inspector, but have you got a minute?'

Another police car pulled up and four guys got out and went inside.

'Yeah, OK, but only one. What can I do for you?'

We moved down from the doorway, away from earshot of anyone.

'You had me worried there, Graeme. I thought Ena was going to get away with it.'

'Who's Ena? Oh, I get it. You're not the only one. After your visit from Mr Sloane, we had to bring everything forward a few days. It's been bloody manic. We had to get all the warrants in place for a knock this morning. There's some very tired and pissed off Magistrates around at the moment. As you can see, we only just managed it in time, or at least, I hope we did.'

'So, are there more warrants being served?'

'Yes there are, as we speak, Richard, at various offices and houses. The only problem we might have is tracking down young Sharples' dad. We didn't have enough troops around last night to jack up any surveillance. Hopefully, he should be rounded up with the others this morning.'

He didn't sound very confident, but I didn't challenge him on it. He had enough on his plate.

'And what happens now?'

'The case is being run by a Detective Chief Inspector Paul Binge. He's from the neighbouring force that is carrying out the investigation. He'll be in touch with you when he needs you. I can't be more specific than that. And before you ask, he doesn't drink. He's a teetotal. We all have our crosses to bear, hey, Mr Head?'

He shook my hand as a bundle of documents in evidence bags were being carried out from Ena's office and dumped into the boot of one of the cars. They certainly weren't hanging about.

'Thank you, Richard, for everything you've done. We couldn't have done this without you. Oh, and one other thing, watch your back very carefully. You've upset some very powerful people with this, and their influence won't stop at the prison gates.'

He'd said nothing that I hadn't already realised. Once the full details of my involvement were out in the open, it would redouble the Sharples' thirst for a bit of payback.

I wandered back to the office. Carol and Tina were still at the window and Carol looked particularly excited. They must have seen me shake hands with the Inspector.

'Is this what you've been up to these last few weeks, with all this cloak and dagger stuff?'

I couldn't deny it. They'd know soon enough anyway.

'I'm afraid so. You can see now why I couldn't say a word. It was all a bit too close to home.'

Tina made three coffees and I filled them in on Ena's scam. They were very impressed. I left out a lot of the details and just gave them the hard facts about the undervaluing scam and subsequent developments.

'And you did all this off your own back, Richie?'

I'd have to lie, again.

'I did, Carol, all on my own. It took me a while, but in the end, I hope it's all worth it.'

Many more questions flew at me from the two girls.

'I've got to ring head office and tell them what's going on. This is going to hit the Sharples' company hard and we may pick up a lot more business as a result. No one's going to use them now, not after this goes public.'

She picked up the phone and explained everything to one of the bosses. By this time, a couple of photographers had appeared outside the office over the road and had started taking pictures of the police while they were removing pile after pile of bags of evidence.

When Carol had finished her call, I asked her a favour.

'Can you spare me for an hour or so, Carol? There are a couple of things I've got to do. They won't take long.'

She was like a dog with two dicks. Her smile was ear to ear.

'The Directors are mounting an immediate advertising campaign to scoop up the extra business. They're over the moon, and they want to see you as soon as possible, Richard, as soon as possible.'

I wondered if I'd have to put a large magazine down the back of my trousers for the meeting. I might get a right spanking for doing most of the investigation in the firm's time.

413

'And can I have the hour off?'

'Yes, yes, take it. Make it two, but there are a lot of people who'll want to talk to you later.'

I picked up the firm's car keys without asking. I didn't think Carol would mind. She was probably working out how to spend her bonus already.

As I drove down the street to Mrs Edgar's, the police were still busy. Mrs Edgar would be dying to know what had happened.

She greeted me with tea and cake as usual. I wasn't allowed to say anything until we were sat comfortably in the front room.

'Now, why are you so excited, Richard?'

It didn't take me long to tell her the events of the last twenty-four hours, and particularly the last two. Her brow furrowed when I told her about Sloane. In her day, and in her job, he'd probably have disappeared by now.

'It sounds like the police managed to get their act together just in time, Richard. If it hadn't have been for your phone call, I don't believe they would have been able to arrest everyone.'

There was a creak in the doorway behind us. We both turned around at the noise to see Sharples senior and a particularly nasty-looking bloke stood alongside him. He almost filled the doorway.

'Not everyone, Grandma.'

Sharples walked into the middle of the room with his minder. There was a vicious sneer across their faces. It wasn't difficult to guess what was coming next. I didn't imagine they'd let me text my will to my mum.

'It was a stroke of luck, seeing you in your firm's car park around here. It gives me, or to be precise, Mr Muscle here, a chance to tie up a few loose ends.'

They were in front of us now as we sat on the settee, with the tea and cakes on the table separating us.

'You've caused me a lot of trouble, Mr Head, but now it looks like you've given me the opportunity to put an end to your meddling. I was on my way to a private airstrip, but seeing you was too good an opportunity to miss. It also saves me a few grand in fees down the line as well. This way will give me and my friend here a lot more pleasure, as it's going to be a bit more hands on.'

Mrs Edgar started to get up.

'What the fuck do you think you're doing, Grandma?'

The minder stepped forward, but she waved him away.

'Mind your language, young man. Now why don't we have a nice cup of tea and discuss things, before they get a bit out of hand?'

She poured a brim-full cup of tea. I noticed she hadn't put milk in it. She turned to the minder and walked towards him.

'Here, have a nice cup of tea, young man. You'll feel all the better for it.'

As she stepped forward, her feet seemed to get entangled and she fell forward. As she toppled towards the minder, the tea flew from her hand straight into his crotch.

I winced as it hit him, blanching his bollocks good and proper.

He screamed immediately and his hands shot down to his steaming hot crotch. To my amazement, Mrs Edgar then deftly delivered a short, sharp chop to the side of the minder's neck.

He didn't make a sound as he collapsed in a motionless heap on the tea-stained carpet.

Sharples and I looked on for a second. I was the first to react, but I had a few feet to get to him. Before I'd stood up, Sharples had pulled a gun from his pocket. It was a nasty-looking snub-nosed revolver.

'Stay exactly where you are, especially you, Granny.'

He looked down at his minder. It was hard to tell if he was alive. Sharples was thinking on his feet.

'This was going to look like a bungled robbery but, as usual, you've fucked up my plans again'

He thought for another couple of seconds.

'You're coming with me, both of you. We're going for a little trip over the Channel and then you can have a closer look at it; a much closer look.' Mrs Edgar looked at me.

'Oh dear Richard, this doesn't look good, does it?'

She turned to Sharples.

'Have I got time to change and take my cake out of the oven? It seems such a waste to leave it to burn.'

Sharples just laughed and shoved us towards the front door. He wasn't going to hang about. His car was by the side of the house; he hadn't driven on the gravel, which would have alerted us. We marched down the front steps, leaving Sharples at the top. From the corner of my eye, I saw a figure in a dark suit spring from the side of the porch on Sharples' right; his gun hand.

The gun was deftly and expertly twisted from his grip whilst the other hand smashed into Sharples ribs, just under his armpit. The air exploded from his lungs in a loud

416

'whoosh'. The attacker then drove the gun butt down onto the top of Sharples' right shoulder and he collapsed to his knees at the top of the steps. A foot was placed into the middle of his back and he was launched down the steps, landing with a sickening crunch on the drive. He was out cold.

'Oh dear, Mr Sharples seems to have fallen down the steps, the silly man.'

She turned to the well-dressed young man stood at the top of her steps.

'What took you, Mr Smith? I had to take matters into my own hands and may have ruined one of my best carpets. We brought it all the way back from Istanbul, if I remember correctly.'

She casually walked over to examine the prostrate Sharples. The tip of her shoe lifted his head slightly and she gave a satisfied grin. Rather than let his head down gently, she gave it a bit of a flick so it thudded back down with a crunch on the gravel.

'Granny, indeed; no manners or breeding at all.'

She addressed our saviour.

'I see they are training you well these days. That was very efficient.'

She turned back to me.

'You've already met Mr Smith, haven't you, Richard, in the park the other evening, I believe?'

I looked up at the man at the top of the steps and recognised him as my saviour from Miliband's knife. It was becoming clearer now. I glanced back to Mrs Edgar, but she beat me to the punch, again.

'He's my guardian angel, Richard. He keeps an eye on me from time to time; just in case, you know. I asked him to keep an eye on you as well. We couldn't be too careful, could we?'

He stepped forward, urging us inside.

'It's time to go, Mrs Edgar. We don't want any awkward questions, do we?'

We walked past the prostrate Sharples and Mrs Edgar turned to me as she reached the front door.

'I'm off to bed, Richard. You did a very good job in disabling the gentleman inside and disarming Mr Sharples. I wish I'd been awake to see it. Now remember, don't mention myself or Mr Smith to anybody. That's not his real name, obviously. Call your Inspector friend and get him here as quickly as possible. We don't want these two waking up before they arrive.'

I looked back at Sharples through the door. He wasn't waking up any time soon. Mrs Edgar disappeared inside and I rang Inspector Lindsay. I told him to come over and pick up Sharples and his minder.

'Oh and Inspector, you'd better send an ambulance as well. They're in a bad way.'

A few minutes later, he roared onto Mrs Edgar's drive, accompanied by a couple of cars and an ambulance. The ambulance crew put both the bodies onto stretchers and they were accompanied to the hospital by the police. They'd both be arrested as soon as they came round.

'Are you saying you did all this all by yourself; flattening Goliath inside, then disarming Sharples and braining him as well?'

'The answer's the same as before Inspector: yes.'

'And as before, Richard, I don't believe you.' He was a detective after all.

I'd told him that I was on my way home and popped in to see if Mrs Edgar wanted any shopping doing. I was followed in by Sharples and his minder, who were intent on a bit of damage before they flew out of the country. I'd chucked tea over the minder and disabled him, then caught Sharples on the steps. We tussled, he dropped his gun, and then he fell down the steps. The old lady was asleep upstairs the whole time, and probably still is.

'You know Richard, when I was a kid I used to watch a lot of television. My favourite of them all was *Jackanory*. Did you ever watch it yourself?'

'No, Inspector; I was at a martial arts class.'

'Well, good job son. We'd have had egg all over our faces if Sharples had got away. Now he's been nicked, that's all of them in custody.'

The ambulance pulled away, followed by a couple of cars.

'I'd better be off to meet Mr Sharples when he wakes up. Thanks again. If you ever need another job, just give me a call and I'll put a word in for you. Speaking of which, I think the Chief Constable will be contacting your bosses shortly with a sort of commendation.'

'Do I get a medal?'

'No, we rip up your parking tickets, or Mr Sloane might. That's where he'll be working if he gets to keep his job.'

He followed the cars out of the drive and I said my farewells to Mrs Edgar. Mr Smith was nowhere to be seen.

The next few days were absolutely manic. Everybody wanted a piece of me: the local paper, television, my Board of Directors and all my friends.

It was fun, to be honest, and I was revelling in the attention I was getting. I had a copy of the local newspaper's front page for the day after the arrests. It was tacked onto my bedroom wall. The headlines were about the Sharples' fraud but just as interesting to me was the story and picture of the local council building, which had second billing, with the scandal of the obscene picture emblazoned across the skyline. Only a handful of people knew the full story. I was happy to read that Malcolm, the security guard, was to keep his job. Apparently, he'd been given an almighty bollocking, but the recording of the official-sounding request from the local Fire Brigade had saved his job.

I appeared on the local news channel and got a pay rise from the firm. I didn't need the thick magazine down my trousers when I met the Board and I was even taken out for lunch with them. As my stock was quite high, I asked for Carol and Tina to be invited along as well. They couldn't turn me down.

I spoke well of them both over lunch, which went down well. I gave Carol a lot of credit for being such an understanding boss during my secretive investigation; she certainly liked that. I did take one liberty though. I floated out the possibility of getting Tina trained up to give me a hand. After all, we would be getting a lot busier in the near future. She gave me a big kiss afterwards, although there were no tongues involved.

It was a wonderful, but quite stressful few days and I enjoyed basking in my new-found celebrity status. I was brought back to reality very quickly by a phone call on the following Monday. It was *Anthony Nolan*. They had the results of my second test. I'd resigned myself to what they were going to tell me.

I went through a short preamble with the chap on the other end of the phone. How was I? Did I have any ailments or colds at the moment? I thought this was a bit odd but then I was hit with the result. I *was* a match and I was asked if I could go into a local private hospital on Saturday to have some bone marrow extracted. I was gobsmacked. I wasn't exactly going to say 'no' and if I could help Nicola, then of course I would.

We went through the arrangements for the weekend and I rang Cynthia straight afterwards. She cried again, which wasn't surprising in the circumstances.

'It's the same as before Cynthia; Nicola's not to know.'

She agreed and cried again.

I laid off the drink for the rest of the week and rested up a bit. I'd been told that the procedure can be a bit painful and would knock me out for a day or two. I still had a few interviews to do, but these were pretty easy really.

There was also a visit to the police station to go through a few things. The Sharples' had apparently applied for bail but, in the circumstances, this was rejected. Trying to skip the country, carrying a gun and a possible attempted murder charge, weren't exactly likely to fulfil bail conditions in the eyes of the Judge.

Saturday soon came around. I had to relent a bit about not telling anyone about the procedure. I couldn't just disappear off the face of the earth for a few days, so I told Carol and my family.

Carol was shocked. She was in awe of me anyway, but when I went to her and said I was going into hospital over the weekend to donate bone marrow for an urgent patient, the tears welled up in her eyes and she gave me a big hug. All she could say was how you could totally underestimate someone you thought you knew well. I made the same comment about Tina.

Mum and sis were shocked and worried. Mum went into a tizzy, walking around wringing her hands, asking if I would be alright. Despite my assurances, she was still worried sick.

Sis did ask a few awkward questions, but I just said I had no idea who the recipient was and that it was a chance in a million that I was a match, but my marrow could save their life. What option did I have?

I told the lads that I was going away for a couple of days with work. There were all sorts of jokes about film tests for the new James Bond film or flying down to Cannes for the weekend to meet some of my new-found celebrity friends. If only they knew.

With my bag packed, I headed off to the private hospital in my trusty little banger. I'd wondered what to take; would I need pyjamas or not? I hadn't worn jimjams for years and when I found them they were hopelessly too small; in fact, they were Oompa Loompa size. I invested in a new pair, a deep purple with a Paisley pattern. All I needed was a cravat, and with my hair slicked-back, I could join the local Gentlemen's Club.

The hospital wasn't exactly what I'd expected. For starters, there was no chance of contracting lung cancer as you fought your way past the throng of smokers outside the front door. It was all clean and tidy and had an air of quiet efficiency; this definitely wasn't the NHS.

From thereon in everything went off without a hitch; I was taken to a private room and given the once over. After that, the doctor who was carrying out the procedure gave me all the details and I felt quite reassured. I wasn't looking forward to the needles, but I wouldn't see them as I would be out for the very long count.

The food was brilliant as well. I spent Saturday night watching television which was the usual rubbish, unfortunately.

I was wheeled down to the theatre on Sunday morning, to be greeted by a gaggle of doctors and nurses. Before I knew it, I was waking up in the recovery room with a funny taste in my mouth and a few aches and pains in my nether regions. It was all over and done with.

I was allowed to leave on the Monday morning after a check-up by the doctor. I bid my farewells to the staff and went home to bed. The anaesthetic was still making me feel woozy and the drive back was a bit uncomfortable. They'd taken the marrow from my pelvis and it was quite sore but I had taken a bundle of painkillers and the pain would soon go after a bit of R&R.

I took the following day off work as well. One reason was that I still felt a bit groggy from the procedure, but the main reason was that I was getting a bit pissed off with all the attention; especially the people who suddenly came out of the woodwork and greeted you like a long-lost pal, trying to bask in your moment of glory and notoriety. I found that my bosses were the worst. A few days earlier, none of them knew who I was. Now, I was everyone's protégée and I'm told that they'd seen the promise in me a long time before the Sharples' case, but just hadn't had the time to take me under their wing. I could sense a career change in the offing.

But the fame and glory soon wore off and, before very long, I was history. I'd enjoyed it at first; there were the free drinks, people recognising you in the street and wanting to chat, but it soon faded. All that was left were a few meetings with Chief Inspector Binge and his colleagues, but even that ground to a halt after a while.

At least, while I was still involved with the police, it gave me an excuse to visit Mrs Edgar. She would brief me on the details of specific information so I could sound credible to the police and on the witness statement. After all, I might have to appear in court and talk about some of the evidence that was collected by her, not me. If I couldn't, and didn't sound credible, then I'd look a bit stupid. Even worse, it would be picked-up on by the Defence and I would probably be torn up for arse-paper.

It was on one of my visits a few weeks after the arrests that she announced she had decided to go ahead with her move to Devon. It seemed so long ago when I'd first pulled up on her drive to value her house. That day was the catalyst for the chain of events which now saw Ena, his father and a few associates in custody, and now she was leaving. I'd miss Mrs Edgar, but I reckoned I still had a few weeks of tea and cakes before she left.

All in all, life went back to its usual cycle of boring work through the week with a piss-up and recovery over the weekend. To be honest, I was getting fed up of it. After the excitement of the previous weeks, I needed something more in my life other than very predictable work and a very predictable social life. I was still looking over my shoulder all the time, but my paranoia was wearing off a bit. Everyone walking behind me was no longer the possessor of a wickedly sharp knife or a silenced pistol.

We weren't seeing as much of Martin these days either. He was loved-up with Mira and was spending an increasing amount of time with her. Vic had also found a soul-mate, but we weren't allowed to meet him. He was kept very firmly in the background and Vic wouldn't give us any details about him at all. Of course, this made us all the more intrigued. I say us, but now, that meant just Devon and me.

Apart from the two lads' relationships, nothing much happened in the months up to Christmas and New Year. I hadn't heard anything from Nicola but, then again, why should I? Cynthia gave me the odd update on her condition which was always the same; that she was doing fine, improving every day and looking a lot better. There were never any real specifics.

The only noteworthy event didn't involve any of my immediate friends. It involved Mo from next door and Rodney's precious *E-Type Jag*.

I was at home one evening, channel-hopping on the television, trying to find something to watch, when my mobile rang. It was Martin. I was a bit surprised because I knew he was working on this particular night; I'd tried to drag him out for a beer earlier in the week, but he'd explained he was working the late shift.

'Hi Martin, what can I do for you?'

He sounded excited and slightly out of breath.

'Get up to Shaggers' Woods and bring a camera if you've got one. Be as quick as you can. You don't want to miss this for the world.'

He hung up the phone. I didn't have a clue what he was on about but it sounded good. I jumped in the old banger and rushed up to the local arboretum of fornication.

As I got near the woods, I could see something was happening. It all looked a bit surreal, like something from a sci-fi film. The trees, naked without their leaves, were highlighted against numerous blue flashing lights, vehicle lights and a few powerful arc lights. People's shadows were thrown up against the trees and the dark of the night, making them look about twenty feet tall. I parked up and headed towards the scene.

Martin was stood next to his police car. There were two fire engines and an ambulance on the scene as well. I soon noticed the unmistakable figure of Devon wandering over towards us.

'What brings you out at this ungodly hour, Richie? You city boys are usually home at five and tucked up in bed by now.'

'I called him, Dev. She's his next door neighbour. I thought he'd like to see her, before they cut her out.'

I hadn't seen the slight smile on Martin's face. I suddenly went into a bit of a panic. Something had happened to Maureen.

'Maureen, what's happened to her? Is she dead?'

They played their part very well. There was no sense of a wind-up at all. Martin sounded very professional.

'It's not a pretty sight, mate. She's been stripped naked. We found her in the front seat; she's still there now, poor girl. There's evidence of blunt force trauma. It looks like she's been attacked with a short heavy weapon, maybe over a long period of time. The weapon is still in her but we're extracting the bodies now for further examination.'

I was shocked and felt sorry for poor Mo.

'What do you mean by bodies?'

Dev sounded grave.

'I'm afraid there's more than one, Richie. You'll have to prepare yourself for what you're about to see.'

I didn't question anything as I was too shocked. They walked me through the cordon to the red E-Type. It was only when we got closer that I began to hear her voice. She wasn't dead.

The *E-Type* was surrounded by uniforms; Police, Ambulance and Fire Brigade. The rev of big diesel engines masked most of the conversation, but not Mo's shouts of protests.

'No, you can't do that. It's my husband's car', was quickly followed by 'get this fat knacker off me.'

The uniforms parted for a second and I got a full view of the car. The *E-Type* was bathed in light. The driver's seat was empty, but on the passenger side, all you could see was one giant white arse. It completely filled the windscreen. As I looked on, the naked rump was quickly covered over by a heavy-duty blanket. The next thing that arrived on the scene resembled a giant lobster claw carried by two of Devon's colleagues. Mo screamed even louder.

'No, he'll kill me! It's his pride and joy.' For a moment I thought they were going to chop the bloke's cock off.

'She's not dead, you gits. What the hell is going on?'

Dev explained.

'Well it looks like your neighbour was getting her rocks off in her old man's car when the guy's back gave out, completely paralysing him in-situ. Poor bugger is locked solid with your neighbour trapped underneath him. He managed to make a call on his mobile and here we are.'

'So what happens now, guys?'

'As for the car, that one's easy. We're about to cut the roof off and extract the male and cart him off by ambulance to the hospital. The car will be taken by a low-loader and chucked-off on Maureen's drive.'

Martin cut in and dealt with Mo.

'As for the lady, that's another story. I'm afraid she's probably in a whole world of shit with her husband. This will be all over the papers by tomorrow with various pictures of

427

their predicament splashed over the front pages, not to mention the damage to the car.'

At that moment, there was a wrenching sound as the first door column was sliced through by the huge hydraulic pincers. Mo was wailing uncontrollably. I was pretty sure she wasn't having an orgasm. I hoped her insurance, or Rodney's, covered back-spasm orgasms.

The roof soon came off, revealing Mo's partner. His modesty was covered but he was soon exposed as the paramedics started to prise him off the hysterical Mo.

'There by the grace of God.'

Devon and I both turned to look at Martin as he uttered his rather prophetic words. We knew that Mo was in trouble but, for the first time, we began to think about the bloke. Was he married as well, and so on? If he was, then he knew the chances he was taking. Kings have lost kingdoms for as much. Tonight's loss was just modesty, marriage and an E-Type Jag.

Maureen was out of the car, frantically putting her clothes back on. Devon's boss was explaining to her that they had no choice other than to remove the roof to get her paralysed lover out of the car. His health was more important than a fifty year old lump of classic metal.

She was crying and screaming whilst trying to put on her shoes and she was hopping on one leg; eventually falling over onto her arse in the mud. I felt really sorry for her as she sobbed helplessly.

'How's she getting home?'

It was aimed at both of them.

'That's one of the reasons why we invited you up here mate, as well as to catch the show. Any chance you can give her a lift?'

'Do I have a choice, Mart? I could get into a little bit of trouble if I get involved.'

'Just take her home please, Richie! Drop her off near home if necessary. She needs to talk to someone who's not in uniform at the moment and I'm sorry, but you sprung to mind. Please help her, mate.'

I didn't have any choice. She was distraught and in a mess, in more ways than one. Tears rolled down her cheeks on to the shiny wing of the Jag as she stood alongside it, surveying the damage.

Her partner was now in the back of the ambulance and on his way to the hospital. I wandered over to see what I could do.

'Maureen, this is Richard from next door. I've got my car here; can I give you a lift home?'

She turned and blinked away the tears, trying to work out why I was there, in that place at that time.

A question never came. I think she was in a bit of shock.

'My friend Martin, he's a policeman and knew I lived next door to you. He thought I might be able to help.'

She still didn't talk but just nodded her head up and down, whilst looking at the mangled remains of her husband's pride and joy.

I put my jacket around her shoulders and led her gently away to my car. She climbed inside and completely lost it. She cried and cried for a few minutes.

'What am I going to say, Richard? He's going to find out, everything. And his car, it's ruined.'

'To be honest, Mo, you haven't any choice. You've got to tell him the truth. As far as I can see, you haven't got an option. He's going to find out very soon and it's much better if it comes from you. I'm sorry to be blunt, but this moment was coming, sooner or later. To be brutally honest, you deserve better than Rodney. You're a lovely lady and you've got the rest of your life in front of you. It's up to you what you do now.' That was blunt, but it was from the heart. She did deserve better than Rodney and I did have a very soft spot for her. By all accounts, a lot of blokes had something a bit harder.

I dropped her around the corner from their house and carried on home on my own. I heard her front door close about five minutes later. There was no shouting, smashing of cups or windows from next door. It was unnervingly quiet.

I was awoken in the early hours of the morning by amber flashing lights whirling around my room. The low-loader was delivering Rodney's car back into his possession. The roof was probably there too. He always wanted a soft-top; well, now he had one. He should have looked after his wife as well as he looked after his car. It served him right and it was Mo I felt sorry for.

That was the only exciting thing that happened in the lead up to New Year. By the end of the next day, the Pratt's house was on the market. I caught glimpses of Rodney over the next few weeks, but Mo just disappeared. I would have liked to say goodbye.

I remember sneaking the odd glance at his patio over the following days to see if there'd been any disturbance. Obviously there wasn't, but I had to check. The only cynical act Rodney was capable of was squeezing the toothpaste tube from the middle or not replacing the shit-ticket roll, the bastard.

Christmas and New Year were as much of a let-down as the preceding couple of months. No matter how hard I tried, I just couldn't get excited or worked up.

The best thing that happened to me over the festive period was that I met up with Cynthia in an effort to get her drunk, so she would spill the beans on Nicola. Boy, can that girl drink. It cost me an awful lot of money to find out that her capacity for fine wines and spirits far exceeded my own. At the end of the night, I still hadn't got any more information about Nicola, other than the usual nebulous bollocks that I'd been spun before.

Despite that, I'd had a wonderful evening. We'd even had a meal at a trendy new eatery which was surprisingly good. All in all, we were both in very good spirits when I dropped Cynthia off outside her apartment. This contrasted with our feelings the next morning, when we woke up in each other's arms.

It was a bit embarrassing for both of us at first, but we actually talked it over like adults. Why shouldn't we have a night together if we felt like it? Neither of us was seeing anyone and nobody got hurt. That's not entirely true, as I walked with a bit of a limp for a day or two. I'm sure Cynthia could suck a golf ball through a twenty metre hosepipe in about five seconds flat. At one point, I thought the double glazing might implode. She was certainly quite a girl.

We came to an understanding. Nicola would never know about our liaison. She didn't need to know. We also decided that if either of us was desperate for a shag in the foreseeable, then the respective fuck-buddy would come to the rescue. It couldn't take place at my house though; my mum had gone through enough over the last few months. I didn't think she'd appreciate a chorus of high-pitched screams in the early hours.

I didn't make any New Year resolutions. My drinking had reduced dramatically, mainly because I wasn't going out. I didn't smoke and the only gamble I had was the occasional ticket on the Lottery. I did win ten pounds on one occasion and it did indeed change my life. I went out and bought a Lamb Bhuna from the local take-away and got the worst bout of food poisoning ever. I nearly had to have reconstructive surgery on my corn beef eye, after two days Super-glued to the crapper.

I was becoming more and more disillusioned with my job. I'd even contemplated joining the Police. Both Inspector Lindsay and Chief Inspector Binge had urged me to do so, but in the end, I decided against it. I just couldn't see myself in uniform, dealing with lads who were just doing the same as I'd done over the last six or seven years. Sure, you can diversify after a while on the force, but I couldn't do the training and the first few years of banging heads together.

My behaviour over the next few weeks made Howard Hughes look like an attention-seeking boy-band wannabe. I became more and more reclusive until no one bothered contacting me. Even my mates gave up on me because I always had an excuse as to why I wasn't coming out. My joie-de-vivre had disappeared as completely as Maureen next door, or wherever she was now.

The only people I ever saw were the God Botherers. I'd met them on one of their, and increasingly my, frequent visits to Mrs Edgar. We began a chat over tea once and I actually found the conversation stimulating. Of course, they were wrong, and I was right, but I began to enjoy the intellectual jousting and arguments, so much so that I started to plan my visits to coincide with theirs. They weren't winning any arguments or converts with me or Lyn, but it was enjoyable.

I went to work, did what I had to and went home to my bedroom and lost myself in the telly or a DVD. This was no way to live. In the end, I knew that I had to do something about it. I needed to talk to somebody; an amateur trick cyclist would do, and the only person I could think of was Mrs

Edgar. She still hadn't moved yet, although I knew it was imminent.

I didn't ring her beforehand; I just turned up on her doorstep begging for help. I really didn't like what I was turning into. I'd had my Andy Warhol fifteen minutes of fame, but I was becoming disillusioned with life, and more importantly, with myself.

We sat down with the usual and I poured out all my woes in the hope that she could help me. A bit of sound advice as to what I could do to drag myself back into the land of the living.

'It's very common what you're going through, Richard. It happens all the time, but most people don't recognise it. Up until a few months ago, you had a fairly humdrum life. Sorry for being blunt, but the only excitement you ever had had been getting into trouble on a Saturday night. Before you knew it, you were involved in a large-scale criminal investigation and you had suddenly got people trying to cause you no end of harm. It's exciting, the adrenalin gets pumped around the body and you feel alive. Then, as quick as it came, it all disappears and you're back to what you were: Richard Head, the local estate agent. You've experienced danger, the thrill of the chase and you've seen a side of life very few people see. As you've probably gathered, from my work and actions over the last few weeks, and my continuing liaison with Mr Smith, I've seen people in your predicament many times before.'

I absorbed her words for a long time before my reply. These were wise words from a little old lady, who had seen more life than I ever would.

'So, how do I get back to normal?'

'That's entirely up to you, Richard. You are normal, by the way. You're just craving what you had, in that brief

433

moment; that moment of excitement, fear and exhilaration. You could mope around, feeling sorry for yourself, much as you're doing now. You could turn to crime or drugs to try and fill your void - I've seen that many a time - or, you can get up off your backside and make the most of life. Life doesn't owe you any favours, Richard. You've got to go out there and grasp it with both hands and make of it what you can.'

That was blunt, but true. We talked for another hour about all sorts of things. I left her with a promise that I'd visit her when she was settled deep in the South Hams of Devon. I was looking forward to her scones, clotted cream and home-made jam already. I bet she'd already bought her National Trust card.

When I phoned around the lads that evening, trying to ingratiate myself back into their favours, I got what I was expecting - a wall of derision and sarcasm. To be honest, I couldn't blame them. Once I'd done the rounds, we'd all agreed to meet up on Saturday night for another fun night in town. I couldn't believe that it had been a few months since the chase through town with the latex lovelies on our backs.

We decided to go as the Blues Brothers this time. It wasn't a novel choice, but it was last-minute and didn't need much, if any, planning. Most people had a dark suit, a white shirt, a black tie and sunglasses. The only difficult thing was the hat.

We all turned up at Vic's uncle's pub and caught up on the last few weeks. I felt a right twat about my behaviour and was a bit uneasy at first, but after a couple of pints, it was as if I hadn't been away. I didn't have any party tricks planned for tonight though; I'd just see how the night went.

As it turned out, we all looked pretty similar in our hastily created get-ups. We'd raided our party clothes bin bags and all looked reasonably similar. That is, all of us apart from Dev who, dressed in black with black shades on, almost

434

disappeared when he walked into a shadow. Just smile a lot, Dev.

Before long, the pub resembled a Mafia gathering at a 1950's Las Vegas casino. We weren't the only crew who'd hit upon the Blues Brothers for the theme of the night.

After a few minutes of embarrassment between the various groups, everyone got into the swing of it and it soon developed into a huge competition. Each group was vying to be the best and the only songs that came out of the juke box were Blues Brothers' tunes. We all tried to out-dance each other for the next hour. It was a real hoot, and this was before we ended up at the fun night.

As there were so many of us, we all decided to join forces and descend upon the club en masse. We were one huge group of incestuous, Mafia lookalikes, all apart from Dev that is, and he was feeling a bit self-conscious.

Clint wasn't on the door tonight, but we got in all the same. There were so many of us and it would have been hard to turn away any one of us.

We regrouped inside and the beer started to flow, despite the very high club prices. It was so good that we were all together again and enjoying each other's company. I hadn't realised how much I'd missed the camaraderie.

The more guys have to drink, the more emotional they can get. I don't mean fighting and posturing. Between really close friends, if the bond has been broken, even for a short time, the re-establishing of that relationship, that bond of friendship, can be quite emotional.

It must have looked strange for any onlookers to see four Blues Brothers hugging each other.

'Love you man. Missed you.'

There was even the odd tear running down a cheek. We soon got over it and concentrated on getting drunk and getting laid. It was the order of the day. If we got any more drunk, then a Rhino Hunt would be called. We busied ourselves in an effort to pick up a partner before the last rites were administered on the evening.

I hadn't drunk like this for a while and the copious amount of beer was taking its toll. The other three were well away.

I saw Vic dancing with a very exotic young lady. She looked bloody gorgeous and they were up close and dirty. The more I looked on, I realised something wasn't right. Then I clocked the Adam's apple. It was a bloke. Maybe this was Vic's secret he was hiding from us? I was too pissed to bother, but it was definitely 'tache as opposed to gash.

Devon and Martin had copped off with two lady Blues Brothers. I suppose you could call them Blues Sisters. It wasn't in the spirit of the Rhino Hunt, because they looked gorgeous. I suddenly felt like Billy-No-Mates, stood around with a beer in my hand and no one to talk to; it was just like the last few weeks.

Two leather-gloved hands (I suppose three would have been a bit freaky) came from around the back of my head and covered my eyes. Please don't let this be a seventy-five-year old car driver in a trilby hat, scarf and overcoat. The one thing I remember my granddad saying was never trust a driver wearing a hat; it's either a copper or an old fart. The gloves felt cool on my face and I could smell perfume and alcohol, as well as the leather. It must have been a hell of an abattoir.

What felt like a cool, leather-clad body nestled against my back, and then a head rested upon my right shoulder. Things were getting interesting. *'Driving Miss Daisy'* was never like this.

I wasn't expecting the blow of air into my ear and I turned slightly at the tickle. Fuck me, it was Cat Woman.

A girl stood before me; she was wearing a black leather cat-suit, black leather boots and gloves, with a black leather mask that covered her eyes. All I could see were cat's eyes - cat's-eye contact lenses. She looked stunning. Her hair was very short, blonde and was spiked up by a bit of gel. And what a body. I couldn't believe my luck.

She licked her lips very sensuously and reached down for my hand. With my hand grasped in hers, she walked towards the dance floor with me in tow. She looked even better from the back. I suppose a black leather cat-suit would always do the trick but she had a perfect arse; two boiled eggs in a handkerchief.

I got glances from a lot of blokes as I walked to the floor. I couldn't help but smile. Look at me, guys, you losers. Ha, ha.

We hit the dance floor and she turned towards me. Her hands went around my waist, pulled me close and she nestled into my chest. Her gloved hands worked up my back and neck whilst she slowly rubbed her cat-suited body all over my front. It was all starting to have an effect on my testosterone levels. If I dropped dead now, there was no way they'd be able to get the lid on the coffin. I eased myself away from her embrace a bit and I think she could sense my embarrassment. Well, if it wasn't my embarrassment, then it was something else.

She gave me a light kiss on the lips and smiled.

'Shall we go and sit down somewhere? I'd like to get to know you a lot better.'

That was fine by me. I didn't have a goldfish swimming around my scrotum. No, it felt like a bloody dolphin and he was doing back-flips. If I had to fumble for some change in my pocket for a drink, then it would be all over - over everywhere. I didn't even have my pack of handy tissues that my mum used to try and put in my pocket every day for the last ten years. 'Just in case you get a runny nose', she'd say.

I followed her over to the seated area. As she walked ahead, I was struck by a vague recollection that I'd seen her before, but I just couldn't place her. She was familiar though. She sat on a small sofa. I tried to take the initiative, despite being a medium for a bubbling testosterone ferment.

'Can I get you a drink? Sorry, but this has all been a bit sudden. I'm lost for words. Sort of premature enunciation.' She smiled the most sensuous smile I've ever seen, and licked her lips at the same time. Premature enunciation my arse! I had more little swimmers lining up in my love spuds than Christmas morning on the Serpentine.

'A mineral water, please, with ice and lemon. Thank you, and hurry back.'

Bloody hell, my luck was in tonight. I hurried back with the drinks.

'And what's your name, handsome?'

She sipped her drink and smoothed my hair with her free hand.

'Richard, its Richard. Do I know you from somewhere?'

I was looking at her eyes. They looked very odd with the contacts in.

'I'm not sure Richard. Have we met before?'

I was starting to sound a bit lame and decided to change the subject.

'Are you here on your own or are you with anyone?'

'I'm with you now, Richard, but I've got some friends around somewhere.' She smiled and sipped a bit more of her drink.

'They're around somewhere, playing a little game.'

'Playing a game, in here? What's that then? It's not bloody hide-and-seek is it?'

I was intrigued. What on earth could they be doing?

'Oh, just a little game us girls like to play every now and again. And tonight, I think that I'm the winner.'

She laughed and smiled and waved to someone in the crowd.

'What do you mean, you're the winner?'

'That's easy, Richard. It's a little game called Rhino Hunt. Whoever picks up the ugliest minger of a bloke in here tonight is the winner, and I've won hands down. I've picked a right munter. Surely, you've played it before?'

I was getting confused. Me, ugly? She couldn't be serious. She must be winding me up. Then I saw the group walking towards me. Cynthia was in the lead with a bottle of bubbly, closely followed by her friends and my three mates. Something was wrong here.

I thought for a second. The only person missing was Nicola. Then it clicked. I turned to Cat Woman. She'd taken her mask off and removed her lenses. I looked into those big eyes I'd first seen some months ago. God, she looked gorgeous and, I'm glad to say, very well. I really liked her hair too.

She didn't say anything as she leaned forward and took my face in her gloved hands. She then kissed me on the lips for what seemed an age.

'Thank you Richard. Thank you for everything you've done. I might not be here if it wasn't for you.'

I looked around at Cynthia and she just shrugged her shoulders and smiled.

'Cynthia told you? I asked her not to. It was supposed to be a secret.'

She kissed me again.

'She's my best friend and crap at keeping secrets. Besides, I made it my mission when I came out of hospital to find my donor, to thank them. When I found out it was you, I was shocked, truly shocked. Then I cornered Cynthia and got the truth out of her, and here I am, to say thank you.'

A couple of bottles popped their corks, followed by a chorus of cheers. Glasses of bubbly were passed around and they raised their glasses to us. Cynthia had obviously been busy filling the lads in with all the details.

Nicola toasted me with her glass.

'You and I have a lot of catching up to do, Richard.'

'Only if you can convince me that you didn't win the Rhino Hunt tonight. My self-esteem is low enough as it is. Anyway, I've got a question for you, how the hell do you get that leather suit off?'

I got an even bigger kiss this time.

'Wouldn't you like to know?'

I held her in my arms and she held me in her gaze. For the second time, I was swimming in the pools of her gorgeous eyes, only this time, there was a mischievous glint in them. She was the feline, but at that moment, I felt like I was the cat who was going to get the cream. All the planning, all the risk, time and effort of the previous months, all came together in that one embrace, plus the promise of what I hoped would come later; both of us, hopefully!

I didn't answer her question. I just gave her a beaming smile and a Roger Moore eyebrow. We left hand-in-hand, closely followed by a raucous tirade of hoots and claps from the crowd of friends behind us.

Would she be the future Mrs Head? Only time would tell and I hoped we'd spend a lot of it together.

THE END?

N.B. No tortoises were harmed in the writing of this novel.

'The best thing he's ever written.' Nick's mum

'The only thing he's ever written.' Nick's dad

'Utter filth, perversion and profanity. I loved every word of it.' Next door neighbour

'The ideal beach book. Throw it at the Germans when they try to steal your sun bed.' Local Vicar

'This book's got everything: danger, love, betrayal, intrigue, a tortoise and blow-up dolls.' Nick's Probation Officer

'The product of a warped and disturbed mind. See me next Thursday.' Nick's psychiatrist

'You need an apostrophe after 'fuckin', Roy, the proofreader.

Sorry, Roy; I usually have a cigarette!

About the author

Lonely male writer. 56 but YAH, VGSOH with soft, bloodshot, hazel eyes. Enjoys travel (to and from the pub), good food and nights in front of roaring fire.

Desperately seeking readers aged 18 to 80. Looks unimportant, but sense of humour appreciated.

Could you be the one for me?

If you have any comments regarding the book or if you want to catch up on what's happening then you can visit my Facebook page @ *nickhiggins-rhinohunt@facebook.com*

Acknowledgements

I would like to thank all of my family for the faith, encouragement and support in actually persuading me to sit down and write this novel. Without them, this story would never have been written. I hope it's lived up to your expectations.

To Roy Allen of A-Presto Proofreading Services, Bristol, thank you so much for your hard work in transforming this novel into something resembling the English language.

Also, a big thank you to *Anthony Nolan.* I hope I've shown due deference to the sensitive subject of leukaemia within what is, essentially, a comedy novel. I have taken a liberty with regard to the timescale between initial test and second test. It is, in fact, a bit longer than portrayed in the book. This is purely to fit in with the timelines of the other plots.

The good news for needle-haters is that the initial test has changed from one of a blood sample to a saliva sample. Blood and needles make for better reading as opposed to spitting in a dish though.

Although this novel is a work of fiction, the work and commitment by *Anthony Nolan* is not. If this novel has raised your awareness about blood cancer, then why not register with them and become a donor? You never know, you could save someone's life!

Call *Anthony Nolan* on *0303 303 0303* or visit their website at anthonynolan.org

Printed in Great Britain
by Amazon